Competition and Liberalization
in European Gas Markets

During the financial year 1998/9 the Energy and Environmental Programme is supported by generous contributions of finance and technical advice from the following organizations:

Amerada Hess ● Ashland Oil ● British Gas
British Nuclear Fuels ● British Petroleum ● Department of Trade
and Industry, UK ● Eastern Electricity ● Enron
ENI ● Enterprise Oil ● Esso/Exxon ● LASMO
Mitsubishi Fuels ● Mobil ● National Grid ● Nuclear Electric
Osaka Gas ● Powergen ● Ruhrgas ● Saudi Aramco ● Shell
Statoil ● TEPCO ● Texaco ● Veba Oel

Competition and Liberalization
in European Gas Markets
A Diversity of Models

Jonathan P. Stern

THE ROYAL INSTITUTE OF
INTERNATIONAL AFFAIRS
Energy and Environmental Programme

First published in Great Britain in 1998 by
Royal Institute of International Affairs, 10 St James's Square, London SW1Y 4LE
(Charity Registration No. 208 223)

Distributed worldwide by
The Brookings Institution, 1775 Massachusetts Avenue NW,
Washington DC 20036-2188

Paperback: ISBN 1 86203 017 0

The Royal Institute of International Affairs is an independent body which promotes the rigorous study of international questions and does not express opinions of its own. The opinions expressed in this publication are the responsibility of the author.

Typeset by Koinonia Ltd.
Printed and bound by The Chameleon Press Ltd.
Cover illustration by Andy Lovell.

HD
9581
.E82
S72
1998

To the memory of my father
Walter Marcel Stern

Contents

Figures

Maps

Boxes

Acknowledgments

Many people have contributed to this study over the two-year period of its preparation. I would particularly like to thank those who attended the study group at Chatham House. As far as individuals are concerned, colleagues at *Gas Strategies* have shaped my thinking during debates on these issues. Gay Wenban Smith and James Ball (who is the inventor of the term 'unravelling' as it is used in this study) were important contributors to the early work which started me down this road. Oliver Quast helped me with the material on Germany, and Anita Gardiner prepared the maps and figures with her usual expertise and good humour. Others to whom thanks are due are: Ian Wybrew-Bond, Tore Holm, Alan Phillips, Mike Parker, Keith Westhead and Peter Odell, whose work in this area I hope I have (finally) understood and done some justice to.

At the Energy and Environmental Programme, Michael Grubb was patient in the face of (seemingly interminable) delays to the manuscript. Ben Coles and his team coped admirably with my last-minute panics over statistical preparation. Margaret May's editorial team brought the manuscript swiftly and efficiently through its final stages.

Needless to say, I take full responsibility for the opinions and errors in the final text.

April 1998   Jonathan Stern

About the Author

Jonathan Stern is an independent researcher and consultant specializing in natural gas issues. Over the past decade he has become an internationally known author and consultant on natural gas issues in Europe, the former Soviet Union and a very wide range of countries around the world. This is his fourth study on European gas markets to be published in the past 15 years.

He works as a consultant on international energy and natural gas issues on both sides of the Atlantic and in Japan, including assignments with the European Union, the World Bank, the International Energy Agency and the Energy Charter Secretariat.

He is Senior Vice President at the Consulting Firm *Gas Strategies* and a partner in the *Alphatania Group* – which gives management training course in the gas industry. From 1985 to 1992, he was Head of the Energy and Environmental Programme of the Royal Institute of International Affairs in London. From October 1990 to September 1991, he was Director of Studies at the Institute. He remains an Associate Fellow of the Institute's Energy and Environmental Programme.

Abbreviations

bbl	billion barrels
btu	British thermal units
BCM	billion cubic metres
CIS	Commonwealth of Independent States
ECT	Energy Charter Treaty
EFTA	European Free Trade Association
FCO	Federal Cartel Office (Germany)
FSR	former Soviet republics
GATT	General Agreement on Tariffs and Trade
GME	Gazoduc Maghreb-Europe
HCV	high calorific value
LCV	low calorific value
LDC	local distribution company
LNG	liquefied natural gas
MMC	Monopolies and Mergers Commission
Mtoe	million tons of oil equivalent
OECD	Organization for Economic Cooperation and Development
OPEC	Organization of Petroleum Exporting Countries
TPA	third party access
UKCS	UK Continental Shelf

Summary and Conclusions

Gas markets: west and east

For most of their 40-year history, west European gas markets have been managed by a consensus between governments and merchant transmission companies, supported by the European Union and the OECD. That consensus was based on the perception of limited, high-cost resources within Europe, which would need to be supplemented by imports of distant, high-cost, insecure non-European supplies. This perception legitimized both the dominant 'gatekeeper' status of transmission companies and the concentration of gas sales into 'high-value' end-use markets which, for long periods of time in a majority of countries, specifically excluded the development of baseload gas-fired power generation.

In the early 1990s this consensus began to break down owing to changing national and international policy agendas, especially:

- increasing attention to national and European industrial competitiveness, which laid significant stress on reducing fuel prices to the industrial sector;
- adapting to the post-Cold War environment, specifically the development of cooperation, trade and investment links with newly independent states in central/eastern Europe and the former Soviet Union;
- a greater stress on local, regional and global environmental aspects of fossil fuel use which enhanced the attractiveness of gas over other fuels.

This consensus was further eroded by a number of gas- and electricity-related developments including:

- the discovery of gas resources substantially greater than previously thought to exist, both within and around Europe, combined with the ability to deliver those resources to markets at much lower costs than was previously believed possible;

• the growing commercial and environmental attractiveness of gas-fired power generation based on combined cycle technology;

• the privatization of gas and electricity utilities in all parts of Europe, including sales of equity to foreign investors;

• the deregulation of North American gas markets, and privatization and liberalization of the British gas and electricity industries, which introduced competition into these sectors by requiring access to networks.

In central and eastern Europe, the breakdown of Soviet control in the former Comecon countries, followed by the collapse of the USSR itself, caused immediate and fundamental changes to gas trade. The desire of governments to demonstrate political and economic independence was reflected in aspirations to diversify away from the overwhelming dominance of Russian (oil and) gas supply. This was greatly helped by many of the changes just listed (particularly resource availability and privatization), but also by Russian insistence that all gas deliveries (with the exception of those under existing government-to-government agreements) should henceforth be paid for in hard currency at prices prevailing in the western part of the continent.

The arrival of competition

Throughout Europe, but particularly in Western markets, competition between suppliers for market share has become increasingly evident. By 2000, with the expansion of pipeline infrastructure, the major suppliers, Gasunie (Netherlands), GFU (Norway), Gazprom (Russia), Sonatrach (Algeria), and sellers through the Interconnector (Britain), will have gas supply and pipeline export capacity additional to their traditional long-term contracts, equivalent to some 50 billion cubic metres (BCM), representing around 10% of total European gas demand. The most important catalyst for change will be the arrival in late 1998 of British exporters, selling through the Interconnector pipeline to Belgium (with onward connections to other European countries). Although more than half the capacity of the Interconnector will be accounted for by long-term contracts, a substantial amount of short-term trading can be expected. This will contribute significantly to the start of serious gas-to-gas competition, and the emergence of a spot (and eventually futures) market, initially in the northwest of Continental Europe. Whether large-scale British gas exports prove to be a long-term phenomenon, or will be replaced (or counterbalanced) by equally large-scale imports, will not alter the importance of the Interconnector in establishing gas-to-gas competition and a short-term trading regime in Continental Europe.

In central/eastern Europe, competition also surfaced as Hungary and the Czech Republic signed long-term import contracts for gas from non-Russian sources. Traditional Western suppliers were clearly becoming increasingly interested in potentially lucrative markets hitherto denied them. Seeing the possibility of a significant loss of sales in markets which had traditionally been captive, Gazprom rapidly revised its strategy and began to reintroduce barter trade as an incentive to remain loyal to Russian gas. In the southeast of the Continent, where supply diversification remained more problematic, the new issue for Gazprom was expansion and control of transit routes to its fastest growing market – Turkey.

From the perspective of consumers, the opportunity to purchase gas on short-term contracts, at (what may be) significantly lower prices than are available from the merchant transmission companies, will become extremely attractive. Power generators, cogenerators and chemical companies will be among the first to take advantage of these opportunities. But the means by which they will be able to gain access to this gas and arrange for it to be delivered to their premises is not yet established.

The development of liberalization and access

The EU process

The issue of access to pipeline networks (and other facilities) – so called third party access (TPA) – has been on the agenda of the European Union since 1988. However, so successfully did Continental European gas industries enlist the support of their governments, that nearly a decade passed before an EU Directive dealing with the opening up of gas industries to competition and liberalized access to networks was agreed. The Directive represents a significant achievement for established gas production and merchant transmission companies in their strategy of opposition to liberalization. Not only are most of the crucial commitments and provisions defined in rather general terms, but the option to adopt 'negotiated access' (rather than 'regulated access') could give many transmission companies an ideal opportunity to indulge in protracted and inconclusive 'negotiations'.

Under the Directive, power generators, and possibly cogenerators if they receive the support of their governments, and those using more than 25 million cubic metres of gas a year, will be eligible to request access to pipelines, and will therefore have considerable market power at their disposal. But in 2008 it will still be possible for an EU member state to prevent customers using under 5 million cubic metres a year from having a choice of supplier as long as 43% of the national market is open to competition. This is a long time to insist that relatively large customers remain captive to merchant transmission and distribution companies. It is also crucial to understand that the Directive *allows* the opening of markets, but does not *require* such opening. If barriers to entry and weak regulation allow dominant players to maintain their dominance, the provisions of the Directive supply no basis for the Commission to intervene. This is important given the failure of competition in the British gas market during the period 1986–91, which gave rise to massive intervention by government and regulatory authorities specifically targeted at destroying the dominance of British Gas.

The value of the Directive, therefore, lies not so much in its specific provisions, which are likely to be rapidly overtaken by events in individual countries, but rather in the fact that it establishes both the principle of access to networks, and the assurance that opponents of competition and liberalization cannot indefinitely procrastinate in the opening up of their gas markets. Those who expect anything more concrete to emerge from the Directive will almost certainly be disappointed. Two of the most important battles – determination of tariff methodologies and regulatory provisions for enforcing competition and access – were lost even before the first attempt at agreeing a Directive failed in 1994. Without these provisions, individual countries will be allowed to proceed at their own pace according to the principle of subsidiarity. EU oversight of these processes will be minimal and may require lengthy court procedures, the prospect of which may well provide a strong disincentive to companies pursuing greater competition.

National initiatives

The relative failure of the EU process means that attention has switched to developments within individual EU and non-EU member countries. In virtually every country, major competition and liberalization developments are taking place, or are within sight. The much-publicized British experiment will complete the process of extending the liberalization process down to the residential level by mid-1998, but this is unlikely to provide many direct and immediate lessons for Continental European gas markets. What is emerging in Continental Europe is a diverse variety of models. Thus far, the most well defined of these are:

- Germany: pipeline-to-pipeline competition is well advanced in the form of Ruhrgas and its partners competing against the Wingas (Wintershall and Gazprom) joint venture. The new German Energy Law – likely to be passed during 1998 – will abolish demarcation and concession agreements, thus removing the basis for local and regional monopoly. However, this law will not involve access provisions other than those contained in the Gas Directive. Despite efforts by some market players, rapid development of access in Germany remains uncertain;
- the Netherlands: the Dutch Energy White Paper of 1995 signalled the government's intention to introduce competition and radical liberalization measures into electricity and gas industries. The merchant transmission company, Gasunie, has already reconciled itself to losing up to 15% of market share as power generation, chemical and gas distribution companies have purchased gas from British producers selling through the Interconnector pipeline;
- Spain: a government-expressed determination to reduce electricity and

gas prices to industrial customers as a result of privatization in both utility industries has led to access provisions being introduced which are most likely to be exploited by three or four large energy and utility conglomerates. The structure of Spanish industrial gas demand is likely to see an accelerated opening of the gas market to competition.

These examples are notable for their diversity. But the Spanish and Dutch examples have three similarities: the speed of the change in policy towards liberalization by new governments entering office; the expressed determination of those governments to move towards opening up markets more quickly than dictated by the EU Directive; the importance of the electricity industry as a catalyst for change.

Even in countries where 'nothing' appears to be happening, such as France and Austria, realignments of forces are clearly visible. The strategic alliance between Total and Gaz de France, allowing both companies to move into different parts of the chain, is a recognition of the need for change. The 'invasion' of the Austrian merchant transmission company OMV's home market by Ruhrgas, even though it does not involve access, is an act of unprecedented hostility between former allies.

Competition and liberalization: stages and scenarios

Fierce gas-to-gas competition will arrive at Continental European borders as early as 1998 and no later than 2000. One scenario would see border prices drift down to lower levels around $2.00–2.25/mmbtu (around 20% below 1997 levels) over a period of 1–2 years and markets *evolve* into the new era of liberalization with the dominant transmission companies remaining in overall control of the process. An alternative scenario would see prices crash down below $1.50/mmbtu (around 40% below 1997 levels) within a period of weeks and markets *unravel* into a new era of liberalization with the dominant transmission companies losing overall control. To the extent that crude oil and oil product prices also fall to lower levels during this period, the effect on gas-to-gas competition could be accelerated since there will be less scope for gas to capture additional markets from oil products.

The second stage of the process will be the introduction of liberalized access for larger customers, which will be completed around 2005. The third stage will be the opening to competition of smaller consumers, which will start around 2005 in some countries. This process will be faster to the extent that markets unravel, rather than evolve. But developments will be specific to each individual country. While no Continental European government has so far adopted the ideological commitment of the British, the Dutch and Spanish governments appear to have become 'convinced proponents' of their own brands of liberalization. Elsewhere, governments appear to fall between the categories of 'willing acceptors' and 'grudging acceptors' of liberalization. However, given the potential for change in policies, and the change in personnel that elections often bring, the potential for a shift in government positions should not be underestimated.

Structural change

Changes in the structure of the industry are also well under way. A strategy of vertical integration has been chosen by many, principally upstream, players. This is based on a fear that upstream margins will be squeezed first in the competitive process, and that integration will allow them to 'lock in' both access to markets and downstream margins. This was the motivation behind Gazprom's creation of joint venture trans-mission and marketing ventures throughout Europe with the major trans-mission companies. The development of pipeline competition in Germany provided a clear demonstration of the potentially adverse consequences of rejecting the Russian company's advances. Subsequent attempts by Statoil and Sonatrach to move downstream are examples of similar thinking on a smaller scale.

Meanwhile, in the marketplace, horizontal integration – with mergers and alliances – will provide the resulting buyers with stronger negotiating positions and a platform for creating new marketing opportunities. Both established and new power generators will be crucial actors, as weak regulation will lead smaller customers to form alliances with those who are commercially powerful. As this process develops, new marketing com-panies will emerge and the arbitrary demand thresholds defining consumer eligibility in the EU Directive will rapidly become irrelevant. Governments, regulators and transmission companies will find it increasingly difficult to resist consumers insisting on their right to a choice of supplier.

The types of markets which are emerging will favour companies which can make quick commercial decisions, reposition themselves and repackage their services to take advantage of emerging opportunities. This will be particularly important for suppliers to prevent a loss of market share. In this respect, the determination of successive Norwegian governments to maintain a centrally planned approach to gas exports – rejecting both unitization and optimization of offshore transmission systems and changes to the Gas Negotiating and Supply Committees' export sales arrangements – appears ill advised in the short term and untenable in the long term.

Regulatory weakness and uncertainty

Throughout Continental Europe there is little sign of any strong commitment to regulation of the gas industry. The German government has stated categorically that regulation will continue to be handled by the Federal Cartel Office. This continues the principle of competition regulation and rules out the creation of a specialist energy authority. The Spanish government created a specialist electricity regulator (CSEN), but arrangements for the gas sector remain uncertain. In the Netherlands, regulation of the industry will remain a ministerial responsibility with the possibility that this may be transferred to a specialist competition authority in the future. Regulatory authorities covering both gas and electricity industries have been set up in both Italy and Hungary. Access to pipelines has been in operation in Romania since the mid-1990s, with no discernible regulation. In some respects, the countries of the former Soviet Union are more advanced in the creation of regulatory regimes: Russia has a Federal Energy Commission (and regional energy commissions) and there is provision for gas to be transported through Gazprom's system within Russia, on payment of a tariff.

But in no one country has there been any clear recognition of the crucial role to be played by regulatory authorities in the implementation and policing of competition and liberalization. This is why, in a European context, the term 'deregulation' should never be used as a synonym for liberalization. Given the lack of regulatory powers contained within the Gas Directive at an EU level, a major part of the unfolding story of competition and liberalization in Continental European gas industries will be the *creation* of national regulatory institutions and regimes.

Anglo-North American versus Continental European models

This is the principal reason why the British and North American models, with their emphasis on complex regulatory systems enforcing the provision of unbundled services provided on a non-discriminatory basis, implemented by non-elected regulatory bodies deemed to be 'independent' from government, have thus far found little resonance in Continental Europe. There remains concern about how such models would work in countries heavily dependent on imported gas supplies, and how problems with take or pay contracts with foreign suppliers would be resolved. In fact, take or pay is unlikely to be a significant problem, unless markets unravel very rapidly. Serious physical or contractual disruptions of supply – arising from political turbulence in Algeria, or a decision by a future Russian government to break up Gazprom – would certainly cause problems for individual countries and companies, but would not force a decisive turning away from competition. Indeed there are circumstances in which such problems could accelerate the competitive process.

The vindication of the British and North American philosophy would see an acceptance by Continental European governments that the lowest possible gas (and electricity) prices to industrial customers, and hence national competitiveness, can only be achieved by rapid and radical liberalization. Once accepted, complex regulation and contractual and institutional upheaval would be seen as a reasonable price to pay for these benefits. The vindication of the Continental European position would be that gas-to-gas competition would produce lower prices, which would be maintained by a slow evolution of liberalization without the contractual and institutional upheavals, and the regulatory complexity, of the Anglo-North American models.

But European gas markets are unlikely to develop in such a way that a clear 'winner' emerges between these positions. The next decade will see both continuity and change in these markets, with the challenge being to identify the speed and content of this process in *individual countries and regions* as a series of diverse models unfolds throughout the European geographical space.

Introduction

Gas industries have moved into the spotlight of European energy and environment debates as a variety of issues ranging from international relations to national industrial competitiveness focuses attention on a sector which, for much of its 35-year history, has been of little interest even within the relatively limited field of energy policy and energy studies. In the late 1990s widely anticipated changes are those in the direction of competition and liberalization. Thus far, the only 'true believer' in competition and the liberalization of gas markets, both of which have been on the agenda of the European Union since the end of the 1980s, has been the United Kingdom or more properly 'Britain' (since it is only the British market which has been liberalized), which has replicated and in some areas overtaken the developments which commenced in North American markets in the early 1980s.

Since the early 1990s there has been a general feeling that the 'old order' in European gas markets is about to give way to fundamentally different type of market organization. There is a degree of consensus in recently published work[1] on likely developments in Continental Europe to the effect that:

- what emerges may not look similar to either Britain or North America;
- the driving forces for change are likely to come from the market rather than from regulation and policy (either national or European Union).

---

[1] For example Javier Estrada, Arild Moe and Kare Dahl Martinsen, *The Development of European Gas Markets: Environmental, Economic and Political Perspectives* (Chichester: John Wiley, 1995); Michael Stoppard, *A New Order for Gas in Europe?* (Oxford: Oxford Institute for Energy Studies, 1996); Oystein Noreng, 'Structural change in the European gas market: implications for industry and the security of supply', in *The IEA Natural Gas Security Study*, IEA/OECD, Paris, 1995, Annex 1, pp. 221–35.

The rationale for writing this study now is twofold:

(1)   a belief that, in early 1998, many of these long-anticipated changes
       are imminent and that market forces and institutional developments
       are combining in ways which are likely to produce fundamental change;
(2)   a desire to explore in more detail how Continental European models
       of competition and liberalization may both differ from what has gone
       before in Britain and North America, and may evolve over time.

This study is not concerned with the theory of liberalization and competition, or detailed descriptions of European gas infrastructure. That has been dealt with in a range of other studies including this author's earlier work.[2] Nor is it principally concerned with the numerical aspects of European gas markets, in terms of supply, demand and trade. Readers can obtain a multitude of forecasts from academic work, consulting studies and the conferences which are held (seemingly every week) on this subject.

No study can pretend to look in great detail at how the liberalization/ competition interface may develop in more than 30 Continental European gas markets extending from Ireland to Ukraine, and Finland to Turkey. The focus here is on how these developments are likely to be different – potentially fundamentally different – in different countries. In seeking to include a wide range of countries, including the countries of central and eastern Europe, it tries to indicate how different institutional traditions, historical and cultural experiences, and political priorities may transcend the drive towards the fashionable 'economic correctness' of competition and liberalization. This is the sense in which this study tries to break out of the British/North American liberalization paradigm to focus on the extent to which different models of liberalization and competition model are discernible.

Because of the speed at which events are moving, it is important for readers to know that the text was substantially completed by the end of 1997.

[2] Jonathan P. Stern, *Third Party Access in European Gas Markets: Regulation-driven or Market-led?* (London: RIIA, 1992).

Chapter 1
The Changing European Political Landscape and Energy and Utility Agendas

Gas arrived late on the energy scene in Europe and, as a consequence, was poorly placed to achieve any kind of prominent position in the region's energy balances.[1] At the outset, the pattern of development followed the pattern of postwar political and security landscape. Thus much of 'western' Europe came to be supplied with indigenous gas and 'eastern' Europe with Soviet gas. Not until the late 1960s did the western (or to be geographically exact the 'central/western') part of the Continent begin to receive Soviet gas – a trade which defied the Cold War and continued to increase throughout the final decade of the USSR's existence. However, as with so much else in Cold War Europe, the gas business was geographically defined in east–west terms.

The traditional west European energy agenda: oil 'supply gaps' and price shocks

In Continental western Europe, the development of the industry was fundamentally linked to the Dutch discovery of the Groningen field and the decision to export gas to neighbouring countries (especially Germany, France and Belgium).[2] This was supplemented with Algerian gas – first as liquefied natural gas (LNG), then as pipeline gas – bringing gas to France, Spain and Italy. Soviet (now Russian and CIS) gas supplemented domestic

---

[1] For the early history of European gas markets, see Javier Estrada, Helge Ole Bergesen, Arild Moe and Anne Kristin Sydnes, *Natural Gas in Europe: Markets, Organisation and Politics* (London: Pinter, 1988); J.D. Davis, *Blue Gold: the Political Economy of Natural Gas* (London: George Allen and Unwin, 1984); Jonathan P. Stern, *International Gas Trade in Europe: the Policies of Exporting and Importing Countries* (London: RIIA/Heinemann Educational, 1984).

[2] In fact, the actual name of the field is Slochteren, but it is generally known as Groningen because this was the nearest large town.

and imported supplies in Austria, Germany, France and Italy and allowed a gas industry to be created in Finland.

In 1973 the first OPEC-inspired major oil price increase caused an upheaval in world energy markets and ushered in a 10–15-year period during which the twin fears of high and rapidly rising energy prices, and insecurity in the supply of imported energy (principally Middle East oil) overwhelmed all other issues. In 1973, aside from the Netherlands and Britain, large-scale natural gas markets had barely been established in Europe. This era of acute concern about a return to high energy prices and oil supply security should logically have drawn to a close around 1986, but wars and foreign military operations in the Gulf kept it alive – at least in the minds of many commentators and policy makers.[3]

During this period the term 'energy' was largely a synonym for oil, while 'electricity' largely denoted the coal and nuclear power industries. Natural gas was a fuel to which few paid attention, except in the context of oil. Gas was found (largely) by companies looking for oil, and (largely) priced against oil products wherever it was sold. During the 1973–86 period, the emphasis of national and international energy policies was on developing indigenous energy sources, and diversifying imported energy sources away from Middle East oil. As such, the steady expansion of gas markets during this period of oil price increases was welcome, but the rationale for increasing the share of gas in energy balances was not entirely clear:

• on the one hand, gas was not oil and imported gas did not come from the Gulf region, the principal source of European oil imports;
• on the other hand, it was believed that an increasing share of gas supplies would need to be imported, principally from the Soviet Union and North Africa, areas which brought with them different, but no less important, security problems.

In the late 1970s Norwegian North Sea gas provided further diversity for the northern European countries (Germany, France and Belgium), while at

---

[3] This process is described in John V. Mitchell (with Peter Beck and Michael Grubb), *The New Geopolitics of Energy* (London: RIIA, 1996).

the same time supplementing Britain's indigenous gas. While countries such as (the former West) Germany, Italy and France had discovered significant indigenous gas, this was not sufficient to meet anticipated demand. Neither were the substantial British gas discoveries considered sufficient to meet that country's need without additional imports. As a result, competition for external supplies between British Gas and Continental west European buyers for imports, especially of Norwegian gas, reached its height in 1980.

In the same year, the newly elected US administration of President Ronald Reagan opposed the expansion of European imports of Soviet gas, causing a major crisis in the Western Alliance (see Chapter 2 for details). In the wake of the second major OPEC oil price increase, the Soviet invasion of Afghanistan and a rekindling of the Cold War, European energy security briefly focused on natural gas supplies, but only in a grand geopolitical and strategic context.

The new agenda: privatization, competitiveness and environment

When international oil prices collapsed in 1986, a corporate crisis was witnessed with energy companies desperately scrambling to reduce their costs in order to remain competitive with low-cost sources of energy, notably Middle East oil. For the European gas market, this focused on British and particularly Norwegian supplies, with the recently signed Troll contracts committing the sellers to a giant and relatively high-cost development.

Alongside the drive for cost reduction, the structure of energy – and specifically energy utility – industries was on the threshold of a major upheaval. The perceived inefficiencies of state-owned industries, and the inability and unwillingness of governments to continue financial support for those which were loss making, led to a wave of privatizations. Energy utilities – gas and electricity – were in the forefront of privatization programmes all over the world, as governments discovered that this was a means both of shedding responsibility for complex commercial and political decisions and of adding substantial revenues to their exchequers.

Privatization raised important issues as to how industries which could be considered 'natural monopolies' should be regulated, and the extent to

which competition could be introduced into their activities.⁴ Having
pocketed the revenues from the sale of assets, government interest shifted
from ensuring the profitability of these companies towards controlling the
prices which they charged to end-users. In North America – where the
utility industries were already in private ownership – natural gas
'deregulation' had already begun the process of separating out the
contestable elements of the industry from the natural monopoly elements.
Spot markets had started to spring up, and the gas industry launched into a
more competitive era with lower prices.

From the mid-1980s, as energy industries adjusted to lower international
oil prices, the traditional energy agenda began to be replaced by issues of
competitiveness, international environment and sustainability. The impending
completion of the 'Single European Market' within the European Union at
the end of 1992 was intended to improve the competitiveness of EU
industry. The Single Market initiative gave rise to an intense debate within
EU gas and electricity on the merits of liberalizing access to networks,
with the dominant market players in Continental Europe fiercely opposing
any change in the status quo (see Chapter 5).

At the same time, growing concern about environmental problems,
particularly those relating to climate change, were focusing increased
attention on fossil fuels as a primary source of carbon emissions. Since the
burning of natural gas produces lower harmful emissions to the local,
regional and global environment than other fossil fuels, the industry
seemed likely to be the beneficiary of these newly espoused environmental concerns (to the extent that switching between fossil fuels might be
seen as part of the solution to the reduction of carbon dioxide emissions).⁵

---

⁴ For a panoramic view of this process see C.D. Foster, *Privatisation, Public Ownership
and the Regulation of Natural Monopoly* (Oxford: Blackwell, 1992).
⁵ For an overview of environmental issues relating to European gas markets see Javier
Estrada, Arild Moe and Kare Dahl Martinsen, *The Development of European Gas Markets:
Environmental, Economic and Political Perspectives* (Chichester: John Wiley, 1995), pp.
69–82.

Central and east European markets in the post-Soviet era

In central/eastern Europe, where Romania was the only country with a substantial indigenous resource base (much of which was associated with oil), it was the development of Soviet gas which created the industry throughout the region. Deliveries of gas, starting in the 1960s, within the framework of the Council for Mutual Economic Assistance (Comecon) opened up the industry in (former) Czechoslovakia, Hungary (with the help of some indigenous gas), Poland, Bulgaria and (the former) Yugoslavia. Joint cooperation projects such as the Orenburg and Yamburg agreements – essentially bartering central/east European finance, labour and equipment for Soviet gas within a government to government framework – expanded the trade significantly in the 1970s and 1980s. By the time that political independence and the breakdown of postwar political and security arrangements arrived at the end of the 1980s, the region was completely dependent on the USSR for external gas supplies.

The collapse of Soviet control over central and east European countries, followed by the collapse of the USSR itself, presented European countries with a series of considerable challenges and opportunities, the ramifications of which continue to unfold. For 'east' European gas markets, the twin issues of developing new relationships through interconnection and equity investments with the 'West' became an immediate preoccupation. For the newly elected governments, the assertion of sovereignty through political and economic independence and diversification of fuel imports were issues of paramount and immediate importance. So were the issues of privatization and foreign investment, both to raise much-needed revenues, and to demonstrate to electorates and international funding agencies that capitalism and the market economy had been seriously embraced.

In gas markets, as in so much else, the postwar legacy of geographical classifications of 'western', meaning the European Union and/or the OECD, and 'eastern', meaning former Comecon, rapidly declined in relevance. Nor are the pre-Cold War usages of OECD, NATO and EU any longer acceptable surrogates for western Europe since Hungary, the Czech Republic and Poland joined the OECD in 1996. Poland, Hungary and the Czech Republic were accepted for NATO membership in 1997. Those three countries plus Estonia, Lithuania and Slovenia were invited to commence negotiations for accession to membership of the European Union in the year 2000.

Moreover, these countries are also beginning to import gas from traditional 'Western' sources (such as Norway). If pre-1990 work on European gas markets could largely disregard central/eastern Europe, studies on gas developments for the next century certainly cannot. It has become increasingly difficult and meaningless to generalize events in an increasing diversity of countries by adding the prefix 'former' to nation-states which have long since disappeared: USSR, Czechoslovakia and Yugoslavia. From a broader geographical perspective it is clearly no longer possible to hide behind the phrase 'the European gas market' as a generalization of the situation in 33 countries.

The place of competition and liberalization in the new agenda

This chapter has sought to emphasize that the changing national and international energy agenda and European political landscape will continue to have significant implications for the place and importance of gas in energy balances. These changes altered government priorities and attitudes towards energy industries: as national and international industrial competitiveness rose, national and international security – both energy and non-energy – declined, on political agendas. Not only did oil and gas seem to have become plentiful, but they were also cheap in comparison to the post-1973 period. It was therefore increasingly important for governments to ensure that consumers – and because of competitiveness particularly industrial consumers – saw the benefits of these price reductions. The question was how best to implement such reductions within the existing institutional energy and utility framework. The United States and Canada had started this process in the early 1980s, as contractual crises within their gas industries, and shortages caused by excessive regulation, gave rise to 'decontrol' of prices and 'deregulation' of gas transmission systems.[6] In

---

[6] The development of gas deregulation in North America has been extensively documented. One of the best histories of origins and the early period of deregulation is Arlon R. Tussing and Connie C. Barlow, *The Natural Gas Industry: Evolution, Structure and Economics* (Ballinger: 1984). A useful publication with annual updates of the situation in the United

Britain, the privatization of British Gas and subsequent attempts at introducing competition (Chapter 5), were also aimed at lowering prices. Thus competition and liberalization in gas industries (as elsewhere) should be regarded not as aims in themselves, but as means to achieve the aim of lower prices. The intellectual underpinning of the North American and British positions is that *only* through competition and liberalization can the full benefits of increased efficiency be realized, and consumers continue to be guaranteed the lowest possible prices. Following this reasoning, all means can be justified towards these ends, and this is the main justification for tolerating the ensuing institutional and contractual upheavals. Not only is it uncertain that this reasoning is shared by Continental European governments, but their tolerance of institutional and contractual upheaval may also be less than that of their Anglo-Saxon counterparts. An important thread which runs through this study is the extent to which Continental European governments will follow the competition and liberalization agenda set by North America and Britain. Even if their agenda is similar, it is possible that they will implement it by means of models which are different from those in the Anglo-Saxon world.

States is *Natural Gas: Issues and Trends*, published annually by the US Energy Information Administration: Washington, DC. For Canada, a good summary can be found in *Natural Gas Market Assessment: Ten Years after Deregulation* (National Energy Board: Calgary, 1996).

Chapter 2
European Gas Markets 1960–90: Consensus Management by Gatekeepers and Governments

The first three decades of European natural gas markets have been amply chronicled in terms of resource discoveries, supplies and the development of markets.[1] Less well appreciated, and more important for this study, is the way in which the development of gas markets has been managed by transmission companies which coordinated their actions with each other and with governments.

In the 1990s it has become fashionable to refer to these companies, or groups of companies, as 'monopolists'. In the context of the European gas market every one of these companies would – with varying degrees of plausibility – refute the contention that their position and behaviour could be characterized as monopolistic. It is more accurate (if less analytical) to describe them as the 'gatekeepers' of Europe's gas industries, divided into the gatekeepers of:

- the border or national boundary: transmission companies;
- the city or local area: distribution companies or municipalities.

In addition to the gatekeepers, there were also the suppliers – producers and exporters – whose role is less easy to generalize and to which we return later.

Of the gatekeeping companies, the transmission companies have been by far the most important. In almost every case, the actions of the

---

[1] For early history see Javier Estrada, Helge Ole Bergesen, Arild Moe and Anne Kristin Sydnes, *Natural Gas in Europe: Markets, Organisation and Politics* (London: Pinter, 1988); J.D. Davis, *Blue Gold: the Political Economy of Natural Gas* (London: George Allen and Unwin, 1984); Jonathan P. Stern, *International Gas Trade in Europe: the Policies of Importing and Exporting Countries* (London: RIIA/Heinemann Educational, 1984).

gatekeepers have been to control and constrain the development of gas markets in Continental Europe. This action was carried out with the approval of national governments and in some cases on the orders of international organizations such as the European Union and the OECD.

The gatekeeper concept best describes the large markets in western and central Europe which were established in the 1960s and 1970s, in particular Britain, France, Germany, Austria, Italy, the Netherlands and Belgium. But virtually everywhere on the Continent the model of the single (or dominant) transmission company is in evidence, with variations in the organization of distribution.

In central eastern Europe, the countries of Comecon[2] were economically and politically dominated by the USSR or (in the case of the Baltic states) were part of the USSR. Gas became an important part of the energy integration of the communist bloc. Dependence of the Comecon countries on the USSR, and of the other Soviet republics on Russia, was generally construed as a useful means by which the dominant political entity could exert economic pressure on those states. It was only after the collapse of Comecon and the Soviet empire that the complexity of the issues raised, in terms of the favourable commercial terms enjoyed by Comecon gas buyers and the role of countries through which Soviet gas moved in transit to western Europe, began to be appreciated. But even in communist Europe the model of industrial organization was similar, with single production and transmission companies, in some countries (Poland and Romania) combined with distribution. In Romania – the only substantial gas producer – production was divided between two companies, Petrom and Romgaz, with the former producing (principally) gas associated with oil, and the latter (principally) non-associated gas.

This chapter looks at how markets have been managed by a commercial/political consensus whereby gas was viewed as a scarce resource. It also examines how attitudes towards security and diversity of imported gas supplies changed in different parts of Europe as the political landscape changed.

---

[2] Comecon, or CMEA, the Council for Mutual Economic Assistance, comprised Hungary, Czechoslovakia, Bulgaria, Romania, Poland and the German Democratic Republic (East Germany).

National gatekeepers – the transmission companies

As the natural gas era began in Europe, monopoly regional or local distribution (low pressure pipeline companies) began to switch from 'town gas' production to natural gas. The principal wholesalers of this natural gas became dominant transmission (high-pressure pipeline) companies: British Gas Corporation (known after its 1986 privatization simply as British Gas), Gaz de France, Ruhrgas, Gasunie and Distrigaz. With the exception of Ruhrgas in Germany, these companies were created either as extensions of existing state-owned gas companies, or from a mixture of (private) gas producers and state-owned companies and also (in the case of the Netherlands) a direct government shareholding. Although these companies encompassed a number of different models of ownership, there were considerable similarities, particularly in terms of their *de facto* position as monopsony buyers, monopoly transmission companies and monopoly (wholesale) sellers. (In the case of Gaz de France the import and transmission functions are legal monopolies.)

Only Germany displayed a radically different pattern of organization and ownership with 18 high-pressure pipeline companies operating in 'demarcated' areas, governed by private law agreements guaranteeing that signatories would build and operate pipelines only in their designated areas. The transmission companies signed concession agreements with distribution companies which prohibited the latter from purchasing gas from any source other than the transmission company. A combination of these demarcation and concession agreements came very close to conferring a *de facto* monopoly on the transmission companies in their regions and a convenient way of dividing up the market between them, although, as we shall see (Chapter 5), it would be possible to mount a challenge to this system. Individual German transmission companies are dominant in their demarcation areas, but from an international perspective in the 1970s, Ruhrgas became the leader of the German purchasing consortium which operated in respect of Norwegian and Soviet gas.[3]

---

[3] Ruhrgas negotiated for Soviet gas on behalf of the German companies BEB, Thyssengas and Salzgitter Ferngas. It also headed the Continental consortium which included Gaz de France, Distrigaz and Gasunie, in the purchase of Norwegian gas.

Controllers of the supply/demand balance

One of the most important functions performed by the transmission companies was to keep supply and demand in balance. Because of their contractual position – locked together with producers and exporters in long-term take or pay contracts – it was essential that they managed gas markets within relatively narrow limits. If they overbought gas relative to the demand in the sectors into which they had chosen to sell, they would either have to pay their contractual bills without taking (and receiving revenues for sales of) the gas, or they would need to sell gas into lower value sectors at lower prices, with the risk that such prices might 'infect' their traditional high-value markets. If they underbought relative to demand, they might not have sufficient gas for their traditional markets and earn a reputation as 'insecure' suppliers.

The concentration of gas sales on 'high-value markets' was partly the choice of the gatekeepers and partly imposed upon them by government and international (OECD and European Union) consensus. There was little dissent from the view that gas was too valuable a fuel to be sold into 'low-value' end-uses (e.g. power generation and industrial steam raising) and should be restricted to use in the residential sector and industrial processes where it had specific value and could not easily be substituted by other fuels.

Targeting the sale of gas on these high-value markets allowed gas companies to extract maximum value from their markets. This was particularly well illustrated in Germany by the *Anlegbarkeitsprinzip*, whereby gas was priced a fraction below its value to individual industrial customers. This was just sufficient to prevent the customer from switching to an alternative fuel. In their purchase prices, gatekeepers adopted the principle of 'netback market pricing', whereby gas prices would be based on, and indexed to, a basket of competing fuels in the markets into which they were selling. By this means, the transmission company's margin was 'locked in' at the border.

These companies managed the national supply portfolios of their countries, carefully balancing diversification with the price and availability of gas on offer at the time when they needed to purchase. In general, Continental European purchasers gave clear preference to any indigenous gas which was available, followed by Dutch gas (although for the latter the only available option was to extend existing contracts). The issue of choice between Norwegian, Soviet and Algerian gas tended to be managed mainly as an exercise in diversification. For much of the 1980s, however, the price demands of Algerian sellers led to greater than anticipated sales of Norwegian and Soviet gas into France and Italy. Thus the concept of gas-to-gas competition between suppliers has existed in Continental Europe since the 1970s, but only at specific moments every few years, when transmission companies needed – individually or collectively – to make a choice between long-term contracts with one of two (or at most one of three) different suppliers. Competition between buyers for the same gas supply was virtually eliminated by collective purchase arrangements and it is notable that on one of the few occasions when it did occur – for gas from the Statfjord and Heimdal fields – the Continental consortium committed a major commercial error (see below).

In Britain, despite the predominance of indigenous gas, a similar system operated known to United Kingdom Continental Shelf (UKCS) producers as 'the queue'. By virtue of its monopsony buying and monopoly sales rights, British Gas (known in the pre-privatization era as the British Gas Corporation and before that as the Gas Council) controlled the pace at which gas was brought to the market and the order of fields to be purchased. Norwegian gas was brought into the British market not only to give access to a much larger source of supply, but also to add extra leverage to the British Gas Corporation's commercial position *vis-à-vis* indigenous producers. However, because the British 'depletion' contracts did not contain any mechanism to reopen significant aspects of price and volume for the duration of the agreement, parties incurred a significantly greater exposure to sharp changes in market conditions.[4]

While this account may seem to suggest that the border gatekeepers were in total commercial control, this was not always so. In a small number of cases, transmission companies signed unwise long-term contracts.

---

[4] Depletion contracts are those in which the purchaser contracts for the totality of the reserves in a particular field. British contracts were notable for being largely of this type, in contrast to the Continental European 'supply contracts' which were for a fixed quantity of gas, not necessarily field-specific, and contained 'reopeners'.

This happened because of panic induced by a fear of supply shortage and the very unusual occurrence of competition between the Continental consortium and British Gas. The Continental European purchase of gas from the Norwegian Statfjord and Heimdal fields was signed at too high a price and the buyers were forced to engineer an almost immediate renegotiation. Second, transmission companies always needed the informal (and sometimes formal) agreement of the government prior to the signature of an import contract. Some contracts were imposed by governments for foreign trade and foreign policy reasons, for example the French purchase of Algerian gas in 1980. But within a few years both contracts had been adjusted to take account of prevailing market conditions.[5]

In a different political context, the Orenburg and Yamburg government-to-government agreements signed within the framework of Comecon cooperation in the 1980s – to be paid in soft currency and barter goods – appeared at the time to be a forced investment in Soviet gas resources on the part of central/east European countries. However, with expiry dates in the mid- to late 1990s, countries subsequently found these agreements immensely useful in smoothing the path to hard currency trade in gas with Russia in the 1990s.[6]

Getting the infrastructure in place

The other main task which the transmission companies performed was to build the major domestic and international infrastructure necessary to make the industry a major force in European energy balances. This process dominated the first quarter century (1970–95) of the modern industry's existence.

The building of the individual national transmission systems is a story in itself, with the different rates of progress chronicled in Table 2.1.[7] Large-

---

[5] For details of the Statfjord/Heimdal and Algeria/France contracts see Estrada et al., op. cit., pp. 219–20; Stern, op. cit., pp. 82–8.

[6] For the Orenburg and Yamburg agreements see J.B. Hannigan, *The Orenburg Natural Gas Pipeline Project and Fuels-Energy Balances in Eastern Europe*, Research Report No. 16, Carleton University, 1981; *Eastern Bloc Energy*, January 1990, p. 2.

[7] Details of all major international pipelines built in Europe up to 1993 can be found in Marie Françoise Chabrelie, *European Natural Gas Trade by Pipelines* (Cedigaz, 1993) and *Planned Pipelines around the World* (Cedigaz, 1995).

Table 2.1: Gas pipeline development in Europe 1965–93[a] (thousand km)

	1965	1970	1975	1980	1985	1990	1993
Western Europe	47.6	72.2	98.0	121.1	145.3	164.6	178.4
Austria	1.2	1.4	2.1	2.8	3.1	3.6	3.9
Belgium	1.1	2.1	3.1	3.3	3.4	3.3	3.5
France	13.5	15.8	19.2	23.6	26.6	30.1	31.1
Germany[b]	20.7	32.3	43.6	51.7	66.9	77.2	81.6
Italy	5.4	8.5	13.2	15.1	19.0	23.1	25.8
Netherlands	4.4	8.4	10.1	10.3	10.7	10.8	11.2
Switzerland	0.8	1.2	1.9	2.2	2.6	3.0	3.3
UK	0.5	2.5	4.8	12.1	13.0	13.5	18.0
Eastern Europe	13.8	18.5	26.2	31.7	41.2	46.7	51.8
Czech/Slovak	4.2	6.2	8.4	9.9	12.6	14.0	14.9
Ex-Yugoslavia	0.5	0.7	1.3	2.0	3.4	3.9	4.0
Hungary	0.3	0.6	1.3	1.6	4.2	4.3	4.5
Poland	3.8	5.0	8.0	10.5	12.5	14.5	16.4
Romania	5.0	6.0	7.2	7.7	8.5	10.0	12.0
Total Europe	61.4	90.7	124.2	152.8	186.5	211.3	230.2

[a] National and international transmission (high pressure) pipelines.
[b] Unified Germany.
Source: Marie Françoise Chabrelie, *Planned Gas Pipelines around the World*, Cedigaz, 1995, Table 7, p. 20.

scale international pipeline construction started with the Dutch low-calorific value (LCV) systems which carried Groningen-quality gas to northwest Europe starting from the mid-1960s, around the same time as the first major line bringing Soviet gas to eastern Europe was completed.

The early 1970s was a period of strong growth for pipelines bringing Soviet gas into Europe. During this period the first major systems were completed carrying Soviet gas to Western Europe (Northern Lights, Transgas, TAG and the Finnish link) as well as the first link to southeastern Europe (Shebelinka–Ismail) allowing supply to Romania and Bulgaria. At the same time the TENP line was completed carrying high-calorific value (HCV) Dutch gas to Italy and Switzerland. The distinction between the Dutch LCV and HCV systems is an important issue to which we return in Chapter 3.

The late 1970s saw the first international movements of North Sea gas from Norway through the Norpipe and Frigg systems. In 1980 the Soviet system was boosted by another major pipeline (Orenburg/Soyuz), to central and east European countries. At the same time the Megal line through Germany, France and Austria (WAG) was being completed which would substantially boost Soviet deliveries to western Europe. In 1983 the Trans-Mediterranean pipeline system from Algeria to Italy commenced operation.

Throughout the 1980s and into the 1990s the existing systems were further expanded and new lines were built for:

- Soviet gas to western and eastern Europe through the Urengoy (1984) and Yamburg/Progress (1988) lines;
- Norwegian gas through the Statpipe (1986) Zeepipe (1993) and Europipe (1995) lines. These lines are to be supplemented by NorFra pipe (in 1998) and Europipe II (around 2000);
- Algerian gas through the Gazoduc Maghreb-Europe (GME) line (1996) through Morocco to Spain.

On a smaller scale, but extremely important regionally, were the building of the Danish (Deudan) system in 1984 supplying Germany and Sweden. Also of importance were the Balkan systems linking Bulgaria to Macedonia (1995), then to Greece (1996).

The mid-1990s also saw a rush to build pipeline interconnectors between Britain and both parts of Ireland, and between Britain and Continental Europe. The British/Continental Interconnector forms part of a different story which will be told in Chapters 3 and 5. The two Irish interconnectors, which were completed in 1996, were designed to bring natural gas to the province of Northern Ireland (where the industry had failed to get off the ground a decade previously), and to provide additional supply and security for the Irish Republic where indigenous supply will not be able to meet anticipated demand.

Since 1990 a number of new German pipelines systems have been built, including Midal, Stegal, NETRA, EVW, and more are under construction (Jagal). These are part of the story of gas-to-gas competition which has been emerging in Germany (see Chapter 5).

Alongside this growth in pipelines there was a steady growth in international trade in liquefied natural gas by marine tanker. Volumes were and remain relatively small in comparison with pipeline gas, and in comparison with the Asia-Pacific market where LNG (rather than pipeline) trade is dominant. Nevertheless, LNG provided a useful addition to pipeline gas particularly in southern Europe – especially France, Spain and, in the 1990s, Greece and Turkey – where it was, and in some cases remains, difficult and expensive for pipelines to reach geographically remote markets.

By 1996 European gas demand had reached some 471 BCM. Of this total, around 254 BCM was delivered across international borders: 233 BCM through pipelines and 21 BCM in LNG tankers.[8] These are very significant amounts of energy in any context. However, the aspect of infrastructure development is such that, by the end of the 1990s, much of the European gas network could be considered mature from a physical point of view: the main corridors had been established and the future will be largely about expanding those corridors and creating interconnections between them. From an economic and commercial point of view, the network can also be considered largely mature: most of the infrastructure has been amortized and as related costs fall, profits have increased. Such generalizations clearly do not extend to countries which have introduced gas into their energy balances only in the 1990s (Turkey, Greece, Portugal and to some extent Spain). Nor do they apply to newly completed networks, such as some in the Norwegian North Sea. But in the mature markets, additional pipeline systems were being built for reasons which went beyond the initial imperative of meeting demand. It is this maturity of the high-pressure transmission infrastructure which has formed a large part of the foundation of competition, an issue to which we turn in Chapter 3.

---

[8] *Natural Gas in the World, 1997 Survey* (Rueil Malmaison: Cedigaz, 1997), Tables 39, 40 and 51, pp. 100, 101 and 117.

Local gatekeepers – the distribution companies

In most European countries, gas is distributed by some combination of city and municipal companies. Britain and France are significant exceptions with British Gas (in the pre-1996 era) and Gaz de France (with the exception of 15 *régies*) controlling all distribution.[9] In some countries such as (the western part of) Germany and Italy, hundreds of such companies exist; in others, such as Denmark and Hungary, only a handful.

Local distribution companies are, almost by definition, monopolies which grew up during the era of town gas – derived from gas manufactured from coal and naphtha. When natural gas arrived, this was supplied by the transmission company. Lacking alternative options, distribution companies tend to be 'captive' to their national or regional transmission company. There has traditionally been strong cooperation between these actors to maintain the status quo in terms of monopoly or dominant supplier relationships. Contracts between transmission and distribution companies tend to be of long duration (5–15 years) with 'evergreen' clauses.[10]

However, as with much else in the European gas business, distribution structures are changing.[11] Very few companies are now 'pure' gas distributors – in Germany only 16%, in the Netherlands fewer than a third. The majority of companies are now involved in other businesses – usually electricity and water, but also telecoms, cable TV and a variety of other businesses. Distribution companies are therefore becoming more horizontally integrated, moving towards becoming 'one-stop energy shops' and also into the 'comfort business'.

---

[9] In Britain's liberalized market the physical transmission and distribution function is carried out by BG Transco (part of BG plc) while sales of gas to residential customers are carried out by a variety of marketing companies of which Centrica (one of the successor companies of British Gas) remains dominant until the introduction of full competition in 1998.

[10] In the Netherlands for example, Gasunie has 15-year 'rolling' contracts with the distribution companies, i.e. 15 years' notice has to be given of termination of these contracts.

[11] For a summary of IEA Gas Distribution study see Bjorn P. Saga, 'European Gas Distribution on the Threshold to Competition: status and prospects', European Autumn Gas Conference, Barcelona, 4–5 November 1997.

The commercial arrangements and pricing of gas to different classes of customer are very often shrouded in mystery. 'Public service obligations' generally involve major cross-subsidies between different groups. Moreover, the scope of cross-subsidies may range far beyond the gas or energy industries. Indeed municipalities with wide-ranging responsibilities may use high energy prices to fund other services such as leisure and transport. In these circumstances it is extremely difficult to define the role of gas distribution within the greater whole. This is subsumed into general issues of local and municipal government.

In central and east European countries, significant restructuring and privatization activity is under way, or has been completed in the post-communist era. In Poland and Romania, where a single entity controlled all phases of the industry, production, transmission and distribution companies are in the process of restructuring and privatizing. In Hungary, privatized distribution companies have emerged with significant foreign shareholdings. However, in virtually all countries the question of subsidized pricing – particularly to residential customers – has been and remains a huge problem. Despite visiting delegations of international lending organizations preaching the virtues of the market economy, it remains extremely difficult politically for governments with fragile electoral support to eliminate subsidies and cross-subsidies by raising prices rapidly to 'economic levels'.

Producers and exporters: prisoners of governments and gatekeepers?

A common feature of the history of international exploration and production is that most companies discovered gas reserves while drilling for, and hoping to discover, oil. Not for nothing do the international exploration and production majors describe themselves as 'oil companies'. By the 1990s many companies had recognized that gas comprised an increasing share of their reserve portfolio, and also their profitability. Companies such as Shell and Exxon arrived at this realization earlier than most, because of their ownership in the Dutch Groningen field and consequent equity positions in northwest European transmission companies.

Concentration of production

Table 2.2 shows the concentration of production, in terms of the relatively small number of companies producing the majority of the Continent's gas.

The Netherlands Control over Dutch gas production and exports is evenly divided between private companies and the Dutch government. The principal private companies are Shell and Exxon, the partners in NAM, the company which developed the Groningen gas field. Table 2.2 shows that NAM and EBN, which holds the government's interest in gas fields,

Table 2.2: Natural gas production by company in major European gas markets (% of total production)

UK	Norway	Netherlands	Denmark	Germany
British Gas[a] 17	SDFI[b] 38	Shell 24[d]	Shell 44	Birgitta 31[f]
BP 12	Statoil 14	Esso 24[d]	Maersk 37	Elwerath 20[f]
Shell 8	Norsk Hydro 8	EBN 37	Texaco 14	Mobil 24
Esso 8	Elf 6	Elf 3		RWE 7
Mobil 7	Esso 6			Preussag 6
Arco 5	Phillips 5			Wintershall 6
Conoco 5	Shell 4			Erdöl-Erdgas Gommern 6
Elf 4	Fina 4			
Amerada 3	Saga 3			
Amoco 3				
Total 3				
Top 10 = 75%	Top 9 = 88	Top 4 = 78	Top 3 = 95[e]	Top 2 = 75%
Total 65[c]	Total 26[c]	Total 39[c]	Total = 8[c]	Total = 10[c]

[a] Total for former British Gas, now demerged into Centrica and BG plc.
[b] State's direct financial interest.
[c] Total number of companies producing gas.
[d] NAM joint venture.
[e] DUC consortium.
[f] Birgitta and Elwerath have combined into a single company BEB. The company is owned 50% by Shell and 50% by Esso.

Source: Data are based on average actual and expected production levels for the years 1996–99, obtained from *NatWest/Wood Mackenzie*. German data are based on an average of 1995 and 1996 production levels taken from *Erdgasforderung in Deutschland nach konsortialer Beteiligung 1995 und 1996*.

account for 85% of Dutch production. Ownership of the Dutch transmission and export company Gasunie which has a *de facto* monopoly of these functions is also evenly divided between Shell and Exxon, and the Dutch government through EBN, and directly by the Ministry of Economy.[12]

Norway Despite being firmly in the camp of OECD market economies and considered as a European country (but one which has twice rejected full European Union membership), the Norwegian (oil and) gas sector is characterized by state ownership and centralized planning. It is dominated by the state-owned oil and gas company Statoil which operates not only its own interests in the gas sector, but also the state's direct financial interest. The second largest company Norsk Hydro is 51% owned by the Norwegian government. Despite the presence of a large number of foreign companies exploring for and producing gas in the Norwegian sector, the government exerts tight control over both production levels and exports. As Table 2.2 shows, it is able to do this principally by controlling half of Norwegian gas production either directly or indirectly through Statoil and Norsk Hydro.

Russia In many respects, Gazprom is the only true 'gas company' operating in the European market. A direct descendant of the Soviet Ministry of the Gas Industry, the company accounts for virtually all the natural gas produced in Russia.[13] (About 5% of total Russian gas output is associated gas produced by 'oil companies'.) Three production associations, Urengoygazprom, Yamburggazodobycha and Nadymgazprom – each based on a supergiant (or 'unique') field – comprise 80% of total output. All high-pressure transmission lines within Russia are owned and operated by Gazprom. Gazprom's wholly owned subsidiary Gazexport handles all exports to European countries.

---

[12] In the early years of Dutch gas exports, Gasunie did in fact carry gas for producers selling direct to power companies in Germany. It is not therefore strictly correct to say that the company has always had a *de facto* monopoly.
[13] For a detailed history of the origins of Gazprom see Valery Krylov and Arild Moe, *Gazprom: Internal Structure, Management Principles and Financial Flows* (London: RIIA, 1996).

Algeria   Sonatrach's role as dominant producer and exporter of oil and gas looks to be the most secure of all the major suppliers. However, joint ventures with foreign companies for production and marketing of new gas in the south of the country have somewhat altered Sonatrach's role. The country's resource base is extremely large and new discoveries are likely to extend it further into the future.

Britain   Sixty-five companies produce gas on the United Kingdom Continental Shelf of which the largest are BP, Shell, Esso (Exxon), and Centrica and BG plc (the companies which comprised the former British Gas). Ten companies produce around 75% of the country's gas (Table 2.2) and hold around two-thirds of gas reserves.[14] The demerger of British Gas in early 1997 into Centrica and BG plc has produced some confusion in these figures but they are unlikely to change fundamentally.

Other Continental European producers   Elsewhere in Continental Europe, a relatively small number of companies have dominated gas production within their countries:

- Germany: BEB and Mobil (see Table 2.2);
- Italy: AGIP;
- France: ELF;
- Denmark: Dansk Undergrunds Consortium (Shell, Texaco and Maersk, which is owned by AP Moeller, see Table 2.2);
- Ireland: Marathon.

Producers and exporters as prisoners?

One interesting aspect of the managed market era is the extent to which producers and exporters can be considered to have been part of this management. In countries such as the Netherlands and Norway governments placed limits on the amount of gas which could be produced and where it

---

[14] WoodMac estimates from 'BP remains leader in North Sea asset league as US companies increase share', *Financial Times, UK Gas Report*, 28 March 1997, pp. 6–7.

could be sold. In some respects therefore, producers and exporters were 'prisoners' of both governments and gatekeepers. They could not sell to anybody other than the transmission companies and in many cases were forced to 'wait their turn' to be allowed to negotiate a sale. By the same token, none of the producers appeared sufficiently discontented with this system to make serious attempts to offer lower priced gas to other market players. In general, producers appeared to share the gatekeepers' concern with keeping prices high, by not oversupplying the market with gas.

The British experience shows just how important the gatekeeper function is to maintaining supply and demand at the required balance. Prior to 1990, legal and non-legal barriers prevented British producers from selling gas to any party other than British Gas. Producers which did not believe there was any chance of a sale to British Gas had little incentive to explore for gas on the UKCS. As the British Gas monopsony buying position disappeared, supply surpluses rapidly developed and prices crashed (see Chapter 5).

In general, although producers and exporters did not have the same degree of market power as transmission companies, neither did they have incentives to disturb the status quo. When their turn came to sell gas, it was on long-term contracts, with guaranteed cashflow (via the take or pay conditions of the contract) and – barring major oil price falls – a more than comfortable margin. To the extent that they could be considered prisoners of governments and transmission companies, they were at least in comfortable surroundings.

Security and diversity of gas supply in Europe

The effect of the immediate post-1973 oil crisis period was mostly focused on oil supply, but also had consequences for natural gas. European governments and gas industries vigorously prosecuted the notion of gas as a commodity in short supply for which prices were destined to rise inexorably. Security of gas supply was a treated as a subset of energy (and particularly oil) security. Not until the beginning of the 1980s did European gas security experience a crisis event which made it front page news.

Western Europe in a Cold War environment[15]

At the beginning of 1980 the west European utilities announced negotiations for a major new tranche of Soviet gas exports through a new pipeline system from the Urengoy field. The announcement could not have been more unfortunately timed. The Reagan administration in the United States, newly elected in the wake of the Soviet invasion of Afghanistan, ushered in a dramatic worsening of East–West relations. The administration subsequently made strenuous efforts to dissuade European governments and utilities from importing Soviet gas on grounds of national security. In the wake of the December 1981 declaration of martial law in Poland, the administration imposed sanctions against the Soviet Union and suspended the licenses of US companies exporting equipment linked with the gas pipeline effort. In June 1992 the administration extended its measures extraterritorially to include European licensees of US firms, backdating the measures to cover the period when the contracts had been concluded.

In the event, the pipeline was built with a larger proportion of Soviet equipment than had been intended, and Soviet exports to Europe expanded marginally more slowly than might otherwise have been the case. However, the lasting feature of the 'pipeline episode' (as it became known in Europe) was an agreement on a political/strategic limitation of the Soviet share of the gas market in individual west European countries. After lengthy discussions and studies within the International Energy Agency, governments agreed to 'avoid undue dependence on any single source of supply', which was construed as meaning that Soviet gas should constitute no more than 30–35% of total gas supplies in any west European country (but especially West Germany, Italy and France).

Whether this edict – and indeed the whole episode – had any real effect on the behaviour of utilities or governments is uncertain. Most countries and companies would have considered it imprudent to increase dependence beyond one-third of supplies. The episode did have the effect of bringing the issue of diversity and dependence on foreign sources of gas into the policy arena. However, it did so in the context of Soviet gas, whereas the most acute security problems of the 1980s centred on Algerian gas.[16]

---

[15] For the whole story of the Urengoy pipeline episode see: Bruce Jentleson, *Pipeline Politics* (Ithaca, NY: Cornell, 1986), Chapter 6.

[16] For Algerian gas security problems in the early 1980s see Stern, op. cit., Chapter 3.

Central and eastern Europe in a post-Cold War environment

The Urengoy episode highlighted diversity as an issue in western Europe, but, with the emergence of independent states in central and eastern Europe, this issue was cast in an entirely different context. In the aftermath of independence from the Soviet Union and the break-up of the Comecon economic area, the former member countries of that organization were placed in an extremely difficult financial situation. The Soviet Union demanded that energy deliveries should be paid for in hard currency and at 'world prices'. The only saving grace for the former Comecon members was that they had all participated in development cooperation projects connected with the Orenburg and Yamburg gas fields. These included government-to-government cooperation agreements which guaranteed deliveries of gas under soft currency and/or barter arrangements until the late 1990s. These agreements proved immensely useful for central and east European countries in partly smoothing the path to full commercial relations with Russia's Gazprom.

A similar situation arose in relations between the gas exporting and importing countries within the former Soviet republics after the break-up of the USSR in 1991. The attempts by Russia and Turkmenistan to obtain payment in hard currency at prices akin to European levels plunged interrepublic gas trade into periodic crises resulting from non-payment of bills – a situation which, in 1998, still lacks any kind of long-term resolution. Alone among the former republics, the Baltic countries (Estonia, Latvia and Lithuania) have made the transition to a hard currency payment system at European price levels.

However, to return to the former Comecon member countries, although less than a decade has elapsed since independence, international perceptions of their gas trade relation with Russia have passed through a number of different stages. Immediately following independence, in the transition to hard currency payments at European price levels, it was difficult to believe that these countries would be able to afford the 'inevitably higher prices' that would need to be paid to bring non-Russian gas through new pipelines to this region. Within five years of independence, the economies of central Europe – principally the Czech Republic, Hungary and Poland – began to recover, and energy and gas demand began to rise. At that time, the perception was that Russia's economic and political hold over these countries would be too strong and that Gazprom would seek to punish those intent on diversification away from Russian supplies.

Meanwhile, the Czech Republic, Hungary and Poland began active consideration of projects which would bring non-Russian supplies to the region. When the Hungarian company MOL signed a 10-year contract in 1995 with the German company Ruhrgas for the delivery of 0.5 BCM annually (starting in 1996), it was viewed more as a security measure than as real diversification. The major breakthrough for diversification arrived in April 1997 with the agreement between the Czech company Transgas and Norway's GFU. The agreement provided for the almost immediate start of deliveries (May 1997) and the eventual increase in deliveries to 3 BCM/year by 2000. However, indicative of the prevailing market conditions, the Czechs had no fewer than five offers of gas from different suppliers, of which two were non-Russian and three were Russian gas either directly or by displacement.[17] Decisive factors in the Czechs' eventual choice were a political threat made by the Russian ambassador to Prague regarding the Czech application for NATO membership, and a desire for a source of gas physically separate from Russian production and delivery systems. This long struggle between Gazprom and the Czech authorities had been notable for the steadfastness with which the Czechs had resisted the formation of a joint marketing company with Gazprom in the country, the only major buyer of Russian gas to have taken this stand.

Following the decisive diversification move by Czech Transgas, there are strong indications that both MOL (Hungary) and the Polish Oil and Gas Company (PGNiG) will also opt to incorporate a significant quantity of non-Russian gas within their import portfolios. Given the strong Gazprom opposition to diversification, there must be a question as to whether better commercial deals can be struck with Gazprom by excluding other sources of supply and agreeing to sell jointly with part marketing companies which are part-owned by Gazprom. By 1998 there were indications that both Slovakia and Poland had managed to negotiate new sales contracts which included a significant degree of barter trade.

---

[17] 'Norway's Czech-Mate for Russian gas', *Gas Matters*, April 1997, pp. 1–7.

In the mid- to late 1990s, diversification of gas supplies in central and east European countries appeared to be as much connected with security of gas supplies as with an assertion of economic independence, national sovereignty and a demonstrative break with the economic ties forged during the communist era. It is uncertain whether all of the former CMEA countries – especially those in southeastern Europe – will have the same diversity of supply options, and the same motivations as their northern neighbours, to make the first tentative moves towards a more diversified import portfolio. Ultimately, however, the dependence of former Comecon countries on Russian gas is so great that, for the foreseeable future – even for the Czech Republic and Hungary as the two countries with the greatest level of diversified supply – the issue will be less that of achieving 'independence', and more about restructuring relationships in order to achieve a more acceptable framework of 'interdependence'.

Managed markets and the Odell thesis

Returning to the question of managed gas markets, it is worth spending some time reviewing the work of Professor Peter Odell who achieved notoriety in the 1970s for his claim that gas reserves were far more plentiful than companies and governments believed. As we shall see in Chapter 3, this claim proved to be correct in virtually every European country with the exception of France. Not only have finding rates proved Odell substantially correct, but the advances in technology in the post-1986 period which have drastically lowered the costs of production, particularly in the Norwegian and British sectors, have made a spectacular difference to the availability of reserves.

In the 1990s the looming presence of huge Soviet (now Russian and CIS) and Algerian resources has become an increasingly important element in destroying the 'resource constraint' argument. But that takes nothing away from the general thrust and correctness of Odell's original argument.

However, more interesting for this study than the issue of reserves, for which Odell tends to be best known, has been his continued insistence that the cost base of the industry is low, and that the industry has been managed to maintain relatively high profits of a comparatively small number of players. Nearly 30 years ago, in an appraisal of the development of Groningen gas, Odell wrote that the 'optimal' rate of production:

> represents ... in present value terms ... maximum profits for the companies concerned after taking into account ... the need to avoid frontier price discrimination ... and the desirability of earning sufficient foreign exchange by sales abroad to satisfy the Dutch Government that the country's new resource was to play an effective role in strengthening the economy.[18]

Moreover, given that gas would be taking over Shell and Esso's oil product market in northwest Europe:

> ... another constraint (was) the need for these companies to maintain their previously anticipated rates of return made in their oil refining and distribution systems.[19]

As early as 1988 Odell was able to write that:

> ... if North America can be described as having a 'gas bubble' of supply potential then Western Europe might be said to have a proverbial 'barrage balloon' of the same phenomenon.... Restrained demand, coupled with the increasing availability of gas from new suppliers ... has become the essential determinant of recent and current – as well as expected – levels of demand. This is in sharp contrast with the widely propagated view of the 1970s and 1980s that physical limits on production would determine the size of the industry in Western Europe. ...

The Sleipner/Troll deal can most satisfactorily be interpreted as the means by which the status quo in the European gas market is to be maintained. Indeed the comprehensive – and the exclusive – involvement of all of the parties with a vested interest in a basic 'no-change' gas market situation (in terms, that is, of allocating relatively high-price gas to a limited range of customers with

---

[18] Peter R. Odell, *Natural Gas in Western Europe: a Case Study in the Economic Geography of Energy Markets* (Haarlem: de Erven F. Bohn N.V., 1969).
[19] Ibid.

high-value end-users) ... the development is oriented essentially to the maintenance of the strait-jacket within the confines of which the European gas industry has been moulded and curtailed for almost 30 years.[20]

With nearly 10 years' hindsight, it is difficult to disagree with a single word of that assessment. The difference would be whether, when Troll gas began to arrive onshore in 1996, it could still be described as 'relatively high-price' (as opposed to relatively high-cost) gas.

Managed markets: a convenient consensus

During the first three decades of their existence, major European gas markets were characterized by the imposition of strict limits on the growth of gas, both regionally and sectorally. These restrictions on gas growth were not usually directed at penalizing gas as such, but were the product of a government/gas industry consensus which existed (and to some extent still exists) in most countries, either stated overtly as policy or implicitly in terms of actions. In the western part of the Continent there has been, without doubt, a coincidence of objectives between governments and energy companies (gas producers and gas/electricity utilities):

• Governments wanted gas kept out of certain markets to protect the markets for coal- and nuclear-generated electricity (and in a few cases oil), for reasons of maintaining employment and preventing adverse balance of payments consequences. In the post-1973 oil crisis frenzy, governments were happy to fall in with the conventional wisdom that gas was scarce and expensive and that it required special considerations in terms of security of supply. In this they were supported by both the OECD and the European Community which in 1975–91 had in place a Directive making it very difficult for member states to build new gas-fired power stations;[21]

---

[20] 'The West European gas market: the current position and alternative prospects', *Energy Policy*, October 1998, pp. 480–93.
[21] The original Directive can be found in the *Official Journal*, L178/24, 9 July 1975; it was repealed by the Council in March 1991, ibid., L75/52, 21 March 1991.

- Electricity companies, despite brief flirtations with gas during this period, were culturally more aligned to exclude gas (at least from base-load power generation) so that they could pursue their desire to build large coal and nuclear stations.

The justification for this position was based on two perceptions:

(1) that domestically produced coal and nuclear power were 'secure' and, in the long run, therefore 'low cost';
(2) that imported gas supplies were 'scarce, insecure and expensive', and therefore too valuable for 'low-value' end-uses such as power generation.

The emergence of a national and international environmental policy agenda added another dimension to the price/security spectrum, which was difficult to include in the traditional picture.

Even had they objected to these arrangements, gas production and transmission companies would have had difficulty in resisting either their governments (which in many cases owned or controlled them), or the power companies which were more politically and financially powerful. But in fact this status quo suited them perfectly both in terms of profitability and in the expectation that prices would rise in the future.

It is possible to argue that the restriction of natural gas markets in western Europe should be regarded as a conspiracy between governments – happy to find reasons to protect domestic coal and electricity industries, and gas production and transmission companies, and happy to present a picture of resource scarcity and insecurity as it guaranteed high returns from gas sales. Odell has argued that producers realized all along that the west European resource base was much larger than had been admitted, but needed to foster a culture of scarcity in order to maintain the high-price/high-value end-user status quo that the transmission and distribution companies also favoured.

This author remains equivocal about such judgments when applied to the early development of the European gas business. While, in the 1990s, it is fashionable to attack the high-pressure pipeline companies as 'monopolies'

– or at the least as holders of an overwhelmingly dominant position – it is easy to forget that 30 years previously the circumstances of introducing natural gas into European energy balances seemed rather less straightforward and obviously profitable than they subsequently became. Multibillion dollar investments were required for both transmission pipelines and the conversion of distribution systems from town gas to natural gas. Little was known about how rapidly a market for gas would be created or how much of the customer base would switch to the fuel. Very significant finance needed to be raised in the context of a significant amount of uncertainty and the risks were potentially great. The reason for the cataloguing of some of the detail of international pipeline networks construction is to recall this essential stage of the industry's development without which it would have been impossible for current market conditions to have evolved.

However, as the industry evolved and matured, the habitual arguments about risks and the need to maintain traditional commercial frameworks became less and less valid. Gatekeepers could calculate, with reasonable accuracy, the costs of building infrastructure and the likely markets which gas could penetrate. But as the business became more predictable, so it had become convenient – and significantly profitable – for the industry to maintain the original rationale for the organization of the business. This convenient consensus between companies and governments has been disturbed by the changing political and energy agendas that we noted in Chapter 1.

While the traditional arguments about the need for a certain type of industrial organization and a certain type of contractual framework *may* once have been valid, particularly for the early part of the period 1960–90, they no longer are. Main pipeline corridors have been largely established. In the 1990s and increasingly in the next century, pipeline construction will be a question of expansion and interconnection of existing lines. Furthermore, in the 1990s the building of pipelines in countries such as Germany is increasingly targeted at competitive gas marketing rather than a straightforward imperative of providing a secure supply to satisfy growing demand. European gas markets are moving out of the managed era into an era of greater competition. That process is what the remainder of this study is about.

Chapter 3

Market Developments in the 1990s: The Start of Competition

Supply push

An essential part of the 'managed' market era was that all development of gas infrastructure – pipeline and LNG – was undertaken by the commercial parties only after long-term contracts had been concluded which covered the totality (or near-totality) of the capacity of the facilities. These contracts included 'take or pay' conditions which provided the guarantees for the multibillion dollar financing of the facilities. When the contracts and the financing were in place, construction commenced. Thus under the traditional system it was held to be impossible to build any significant infrastructure in the absence of long-term contracts which guaranteed adequate revenues to the producer and those investing in the facilities (principally the major transmission companies). In addition, the contracts provided a long-term guarantee that the facilities would only be used to transport gas from a specified source (usually, but not always, a particular field) such that the producer could not sell to any other buyer, and the buyer could not buy from any other source. If questioned about this system, the reply from all players was that this was the only way in which major developments could be financed. The corollary of this was also held to be true – if a system of long-term take or pay contracts were to break down, major new gas developments could not be financed.

Another part of the managed market was that the major merchant transmission companies only embarked on one new major international pipeline system at a time. This careful sequencing of major new infrastructure meant that supplies could be moved into the market in line with the natural growth of high-value markets, without disturbing its equilibrium by threatening to oversupply the market.

In the 1990s European gas markets have witnessed a phenomenon not seen in their history hitherto: the building of major pipeline systems on a (partly) speculative basis. As we approach the end of the decade, four major international pipelines will be completed within a period of two years. Some of these pipelines will have uncontracted capacity immediately available, or available with minor additional investment. Some purchasers of gas through these pipelines appear to have contracted gas to supply to the same consumers.

This change is due to a variety of factors but the principal driver is what might be termed 'supply push'. At least two producers (or sets of producers) have a considerable surplus of relatively low cost gas which they appear keen to move into European markets. Established buyers seen unwilling or unable to purchase this gas on traditional terms (i.e. long-term take or pay contracts), in quantities sufficient to take up the totality of the supply and transmission capacity which is being built. Undaunted by the lack of a traditional framework, these producers are in an advanced stage of building the pipelines.

In addition to indigenous Continental European gas production, there are four major sources of supply to European gas markets: the Netherlands, Norway, Russia and Algeria. By the end of 1998 these four sources are to be joined by a fifth – exports from Britain.

The Netherlands: managed flexibility and greater trading

In most respects, the position of Dutch producers is stronger than any other supplier. The delivered costs of Dutch gas to European gas markets are significantly lower than their major international competitors. The resource base has proved remarkably robust with proven reserves identical to those of the mid-1980s and less than 10% below the level of the late 1960s. Successive governments have operated a strict depletion policy for gas since its initial discovery. This has entailed not only a restriction on exports but also some counterbalancing imports, conducted by Gasunie – the sole single export/import organization.

The publication of the 1995 White Paper on Energy Policy revealed both a change in orientation towards greater liberalization, and a desire to continue elements of the present policy.[1] Specifically, the Dutch government will continue 'to guide the rate at which fields are developed'. The basic premises are that current annual production levels (of around 80 BCM) – split roughly between Groningen and smaller fields – will continue, as will the average level of exports (around 40 BCM/year). The existing policy requiring a '25-year coverage' of Dutch gas demand will continue, but this will be operated more flexibly to allow a larger role for traded gas. The position of Gasunie will remain central, but the company will be required to provide access to its pipeline networks to other parties. Under current gas contracts export volumes continue at the present levels until 2005, after which volumes decline sharply to zero by 2017. The extension of current contracts has traditionally been dependent on future reserve discoveries, although there seems to be greater flexibility about future exports than previously.

The principal change in terms of international trade is that Dutch gas sellers (principally Gasunie but potentially also individual producers) and buyers (Gasunie and large customers) can become more active on international markets. While the government appears to have in mind maintaining a balance of trade between exports and imports, these could be at significantly higher levels than previously, taking advantage of commercial opportunities as they present themselves. The White Paper explicitly foreshadowed the signing of a contract to import Russian gas, as well as Gasunie's attempts to export gas to central/east European countries (thus far not successfully).[2] A commercial interpretation of these statements might be that Dutch players are to be given the freedom to purchase cheap gas when it is available, and sell into high-price niche markets where possible.

The White Paper suggested a significant increase in trade, that is an expansion of both exports and imports over the next decade. This was confirmed in late 1996 by the Ministry of Economic Affairs' acceptance of Gasunie's request to expand export contracts by an additional 240 BCM of gas. However, the Ministry allowed this on condition that the company

---

[1] Ministry of Economic Affairs, *Third White Paper on Energy Policy* (The Hague: 1996). For more details on the White Paper, see Chapter 5.
[2] 'Gasunie opens new markets to Gazprom', *Gas Matters,* June 1996, pp. 1–2.

counterbalance these additional exports with 120 BCM of imports.[3] There may be no necessity for those exports and imports to be conducted on traditional long-term contracts as long as they can be presented as 'balancing' operations which do not threaten longer-term domestic supply security (defined by reserve coverage of anticipated Dutch demand). Since the White Paper, a more proactive attitude towards potential exports has been adopted – by a combination of liberalization pressures and market developments. This is leading to an expansion (rather than simply a long-term extension) of gas exports to traditional customers, and gas imports from Britain and Russia. Along with an expansion of trade has come an expansion of gas services: blending, swing, storage, transit and transportation – in short, the metamorphosis of Gasunie from a gas exporter to a fully fledged gas trader.

Domestically, Gasunie made an early acknowledgement that it would be likely to lose 20% of its market share when gas becomes available from the Interconnector in 1999 (although it subsequently reduced this figure to 10–15%). The company's managing director has publicly made the connection between the reduction of domestic sales and increases in exports.[4] Dutch distribution companies have already begun to contract for supplies from Britain and again Gasunie seems reconciled to providing transportation through its network.

An additional dimension of Dutch exports is the distinction between low-calorific value Groningen gas and high-calorific value gas from 'small fields'. LCV gas is a separate product moving through dedicated transmission systems. No competition can develop through these networks because there is no large-scale alternative source of LCV gas. Similarly, if customers of LCV were to express the desire to switch to HCV gas on a large scale, it would be very difficult for Gasunie to find other outlets. Dutch LCV markets could be threatened by customers being offered attractively priced HCV gas from other suppliers. Alternatively, Gasunie might perceive that customers will not wish to continue importing LCV gas for the next 25 years (the present expected lifetime of Groningen

---

[3] 'Gasunie gets export approval with import twist', and 'How Gasunie is adapting to the changes sweeping Europe', *Gas Matters*, October 1996, p. v, and January 1997, pp. 9–10.
[4] See the interview with George Verberg in *Gas Matters*, February 1997, pp. 22–26.

reserves at current levels of production) because this could leave them disadvantaged in respect of gas-to-gas competition as it develops. Either of these developments might motivate Groningen producers to sell LCV gas reserves on an accelerated timetable in an attempt to commercialize them as soon as possible. This might add significantly to annual Dutch export volumes.

As competition and liberalization develop, an important uncertainty will be the extent to which the government and Gasunie will be able to maintain control over the fundamentals of the industry: levels of gas production, export levels and pace of reserve depletion, gas prices and conditions of sale. If there is to be genuine freedom to import and export, and free choice between different sources of gas supply, this may cause tensions if supplies of gas are called forward faster than the government would wish. If government insists on maintaining these policy limitations on production and trade, this could stifle the extent and speed of liberalization.

Norway: optimizing the pipeline network

Norwegian fields have traditionally been considered relatively high cost, especially new fields being developed in deep water requiring long offshore pipelines to export markets. Present knowledge of Norwegian resources suggests exports of gas will be significantly more important than oil in the longer term. Signed contracts require gas production roughly to double from their 1996 levels reaching a plateau of 75–80 BCM by 2005, which will be maintained for around 10 years before gently declining.[5] While production has been synonymous with gas exports up to the present, the future may see small gas-fired power generation (and other) projects being developed within Norway. These projects might account for 2–4 BCM of gas per year after 2000. However, the key question for the future will be whether exports could be significantly increased above anticipated levels during the period up to 2005.

---

[5] The figure of 75 BCM is arrived at by adding the volumes committed to the Czech Republic to the existing commitments of 72 BCM/year. Bjorn Jacobsen, 'Potential for Norwegian Gas Supplies to the Central and East European Region', a paper to the 1996 Central/East European Gas Conference, Warsaw, 29–30 May 1996.

Some part of the answer may be determined by the organization of the industry and the extent to which the Norwegian government chooses to retain present institutional structure for export negotiations (see Chapter 5). Another part of the answer will depend on the opportunities for Norwegian gas in the British market, where unused pipeline export capacity is rapidly opening up in the late 1990s, and how the opportunities in the British market will compare with opportunities in new markets particularly in central and eastern Europe. The agreement to sell 3 BCM/year of Norwegian gas to the Czech company Transgas, signed in 1997, may be a significant pointer to the future in this regard.[6] With the British government's ban on new gas import contracts during the period 1984–97 finally lifted, Norwegian sellers will be free to carry through the contracts which had been signed some years previously.[7] Significant additional volumes of gas could be delivered to both the British and Irish markets, but this will also depend on available onshore transmission capacity.[8]

In 1996 it was reported that export capacity would reach 82 BCM by the year 2000, of which 10 BCM is to Britain (via the Frigg Line) and 72 BCM to European gas markets (Table 3.1 and Map 3.1). The official Norwegian position is that significant increases in exports will require signature of additional long-term contracts and construction of additional pipelines. However, when additional contracts were signed (principally with the Czech Republic), it appeared that with minor technical modifications, transport capacity to the Continent could be increased to 75–80 BCM per year, which will be needed to carry the additional volumes which have been sold (Figure 3.1). The existing (largely unused) capacity of the Frigg pipeline would allow additional Norwegian gas to be delivered to the British market and/or (either physically or via

---

[6] 'Norway's Czech-Mate for Russian gas', *Gas Matters*, April 1997, pp. 1–7.

[7] The GFU had signed contracts with National Power, Scottish Power and the producer Total. However, with the delay caused by British government opposition some of the buyers had attempted to cancel the agreements. 'Norwegian gas – too hot for Scottish Power', *Gas Matters*, June 1995, p. xii.

[8] The 1997 onshore transmission situation suggested that the landing terminal St Fergus had become a major transmission bottleneck. The question of how quickly that situation might be remedied and which companies might be required to pay for additions to capacity remained to be decided.

Table 3.1: Capacity of gas export pipelines on the Norwegian Continental Shelf

Name of system	Annual delivery capacity of system (BCM)	Date of operation
Norpipe	15	1977
Europipe I	13	1995
Europipe II	16	1999/2000
Total to Germany	**44**	
Zeepipe	12	1993
Norfrapipe	16	1998
Total to France and Belgium	**28**	
Total Continental Europe	**72**	
Frigg (UK)	10	1977
Grand total	**82**	

Source: Bjorn R. Jacobsen, 'Potential for Norwegian Gas Supplies to the Central and East European Region', a paper to the 1996 Central/East European Gas Conference, Warsaw, 29–30 May 1996; Fact Sheet, *Norwegian Continental Shelf*, 1997.

Figure 3.1: Norwegian natural gas exports by country – committed volumes

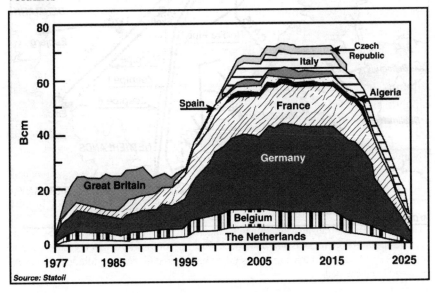

Map 3.1: North Sea gas pipelines

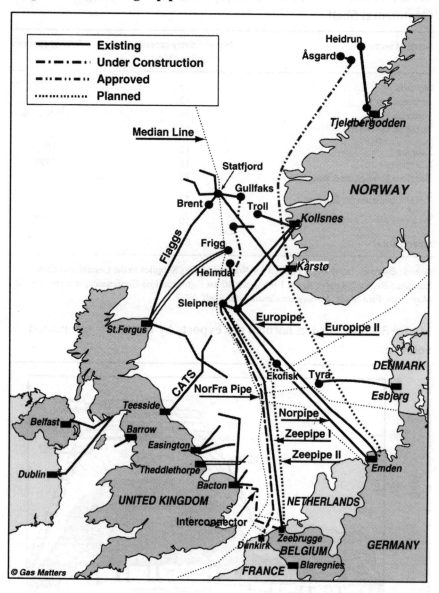

displacement) to Continental European markets via the Interconnector. This would increase Norwegian export capacity to around 90 BCM/year.

Optimizing the network to maximize throughput, however, will depend on the willingness of the owners of the various pipelines, principally Statoil and the Norwegian government. The acceptance of the 'GasLed' concept – by which a large part of the Norwegian offshore network would be unitized into a single network with unified tariffs – would go a considerable distance towards achieving this aim.[9] But this commercial logic presented the Norwegian government with a type of *de facto* open access to Norwegian offshore pipelines which, in 1997, it was struggling determinedly against. Optimizing the pipeline network in this way could further significantly increase the working capacity of the offshore delivery system to Continental Europe, perhaps by as much as another 5–10 BCM/year. This increase in capacity would not be cost free – undoubtedly additional compression and debottlenecking would be required – but it could be achieved relatively quickly and at much lower cost than laying additional pipelines.

From a market perspective, the Norwegian government and Norwegian sellers will need to take decisions between:

- ambitions to expand their market presence in central/east European gas markets to 5–10 BCM/year and
- ambitions to rebuild their presence in the British market – following the lifting of the British government's import ban – and in so doing fully utilize the spare capacity which has already been created in the Frigg system.

There is significant potential to arbitrage between British and Continental European buyers using the existing offshore pipeline systems and the Interconnector (as an actual or displacement transmission system).

Looked at in this way, the capacity of Norwegian export pipelines which will exist by the year 2000 could, with some additional investment,

---

[9] For a description of GasLed see 'Focus on Norway', *European Gas Markets*, January 1996, p. 3; 'Oslo mulls pipe system plans', *International Gas Report*, 24 November 1995, p. 15.

be increased to around 85 BCM/year to Continental Europe, and would therefore be able to accommodate around 15 BCM of additional export sales: 5 to Continental Europe and 10 to the UK. However, realizing this potential in terms of volumes, diversity of routes, and flexibility of customer choice may be restricted by the institutional limitations of the present gas export regime (Chapter 5).

Russia: marketing through diverse export routes and companies

The position of, and outlook for, Russian gas exports in European gas markets is extremely strong. A colossal resource base and a transmission infrastructure delivering to Russia, former Soviet republics and export markets has been established over the past four decades which produced more than 640 BCM at peak in 1991 and 571 BCM in 1997.[10] Russia's Gazprom (a direct descendant of the former Soviet Ministry of the Gas Industry) produced 534 BCM in 1997 (the other 7% of Russia's gas was produced by oil companies and two small producers in eastern Siberia). It owns the high pressure transmission networks, and has complete control of Russian gas exports.

Much industry speculation centres on the likelihood of Russia being a major force for liberalization and gas-to-gas competition in European gas markets. The extent to which Gazprom has any intention to play this type of role is uncertain. However, its strategy since 1989 of developing downstream marketing joint ventures ('joint stock companies' and 'trading houses') in 13 European countries (notable exceptions are the Czech Republic and Britain) provides ample scope for developing additional sales. Some of these companies are involved in pipeline construction as well as gas marketing. There are plans for some to become involved in the construction of power stations and gas storages in European countries. This strategy is based on a determination to capture a larger share of the downstream profits on gas sales, and a desire to create larger market

---

[10] In this section, figures are quoted in Russian cubic metres. These units are measured at 20 degrees centigrade and need to be reduced by 7% to be comparable to other figures in BCMs quoted throughout the study. The reason they are left in the original units here is to avoid confusion with other sources.

opportunities more rapidly than would have been the case had it retained its traditional export role (selling at the border), with its traditional trading partners (the major transmission company in each importing country).

A good example of this strategy was the announcement of the Volta joint venture (with Edison Gas) to move an additional 10 BCM into the Italian market, seemingly an indication of Gazprom's ambitions in terms of expanding exports in one of its largest export markets. While this project will probably not take place in its original conception (it appears to have been renamed the 'South European pipeline') the threat of taking on a new partner may have had the desired effect in persuading Gazprom's long-time Italian partner to sign contracts for additional volumes.[11]

Exports to European markets, after stagnating in the early 1990s, rose rapidly to reach 124 BCM in 1996 (falling back to 117 BCM in 1997). Exports were divided roughly 60:40 between west and central/east European importers. The opportunity to expand Russian gas exports to European markets over the next 20 years is exceptional, mainly because of events within Russia arising from the break-up of the Soviet Union and the move towards a market-based economic system. Huge increases in prices charged to industrial, and to a lesser extent residential, customers – to the point where parity was almost established with export prices – have given rise to widespread non-payment of bills.[12] Unlike the situation in a market economy where non-payment would be grounds for disconnection, a combination of political sensitivity and lack of equipment to carry out physical disconnection of individual customers, has seen Gazprom supply very large volumes of gas – around 190 BCM in 1994 and 1995 – for which no payment was received during those calendar years.[13] Since 1996 estimating non-payment has become less straightforward due to the switch to barter trade and inter-enterprise transfers. Gazprom's first set of

---

[11] For a description of the Volta/South European pipeline project, see 'Yamal slips behind Interconnector', *Gas Matters*, July 1996, pp. 1–6.

[12] For a more general discussion of non-payment see Jonathan P. Stern, *The Russian Natural Gas Bubble: Consequences for European Gas Markets* (London: RIIA, 1995), pp. 37–38.

[13] This does not necessarily mean that payment was not received in a subsequent financial period. Indications in 1997 are that around one-third of Gazprom receivables in a calendar year are late payments from the previous year.

consolidated accounts report that these transactions accounted for 57% of receivables in calendar year 1996.[14]

With a retreat to Soviet-type barter trade, a significant continuing level of non-payment and late payment, and little sign of a government-endorsed and enforceable disconnection policy, there is no way of estimating the real level of 'gas demand', i.e. that volume of gas which consumers are willing and able to pay for, at a specified price. During 1997 some progress seemed possible as for the first time regionally differentiated gas prices were introduced and the government has taken some (very preliminary) steps towards eliminating non-payment. The difficulty is to know to what extent these prices will be meaningful in a market where at least two-thirds of bills are being settled using non-monetary instruments, with less than 10% being settled promptly and in cash.

An entirely new set of market signals is therefore lying in wait to impact on demand levels as and when the economy moves towards cost-based prices paid in money (as opposed to barter trade), and gas companies are able to disconnect customers who fail to pay promptly and in cash. It is hard to escape the conclusion that up to 50 BCM of gas is being consumed by enterprises which are technically bankrupt with little hope of commercial salvation. Also lying in wait is the conservation and efficiency potential – generally estimated at 25–40% of current demand levels – of those enterprises which remain in business, which needs to be factored into a calculation of future demand.[15] The potential for demand reduction – with payment enforcement and low-cost conservation measures – remains truly awesome. Of the 282 BCM gas which was delivered to non-residential/district heating consumers by Gazprom in 1996, some-

---

[14] Recorded in Price Waterhouse's *Consolidated Financial Accounts, 1996.* Gazprom has the power to insist that enterprises unable to pay their bills transfer a part of their production for Gazprom's use. In a number of cases this has extended to Gazprom being awarded equity in these companies.

[15] The figure of 25–40% tends to a general conclusion of the micro-studies of individual plants which have been carried out. These savings are regarded as being achievable with 'no cost or low cost' investments using currently available technology. New plant built with state of the art technology should achieve significantly greater savings.

where between 140 and 180 BCM would have been necessary to support the same level of economic activity.[16] While the future will see increased gas demand resulting from economic growth and increased residential demand, industrial restructuring away from heavy industrial processes and replacement of old plant will work to flatten these increases.

This potential Russian gas 'bubble' is further inflated by exports to former Soviet republics (FSRs) – principally Ukraine, but also Belarus, Moldova and the Baltic states – where non-payment is also a problem. However, the complicating factor in respect of FSRs is the near-total dependence on Ukraine for the transit of Russian gas to Europe. The development of workable interdependence relationships between Russia and FSRs whereby sales of Russian gas are traded off against uninterrupted transit of Russian gas to Europe has been and remains a serious problem in respect of Ukraine, and will become increasingly important in respect of Belarus. During 1997, non-payment of gas bills in the former republics fell significantly, but was still sufficiently serious for Gazprom to cut off supplies by one-third for periods of time.[17] In addition, accusations by the chairman of Gazprom that Ukraine had been 'stealing' Russian gas suggested that relations between the countries remained strained.[18] On a number of occasions since 1991 supplies to European countries have been disrupted because of disputes involving Russian non-delivery of gas to Ukrainian customers arising from non-payment of bills.[19] The credibility of Gazprom as a secure supplier is heavily dependent both on the successful management of the Ukrainian relationship, and on the creation of alternative supply corridors to European markets.

Gazprom's response has been to plan a diversification of routes avoiding Ukraine: further north – through Belarus and Poland; through Nordic countries – Finland and Sweden; and south – across the Black Sea

---

[16] Russian 1996 consumption figures of 337.3 BCM, of which residential consumption was 55.3 BCM. Gazprom Annual Report 1996.

[17] 'Gazprom cuts supplies to Belorus and Ukraine', *Gas Matters*, August 1997, p. 11.

[18] Chairman Vyakhirev at the Press Conference to the 20th World Gas Conference in Copenhagen, 10–13 June 1997.

[19] For interruptions of supply in the period up to 1994, see Stern, op. cit., pp. 60–61.

to Turkey.[20] The routes to Turkey have also been complicated by transit problems with Bulgaria, where Gazprom has been facing a combination of political instability and greatly increased political sensitivity to Russian ownership of transmission pipelines. Gazprom frustration at the difficulty in confirming the rights of companies, in which it has equity, to purchase, sell and transport Russian gas within and through Bulgaria has confirmed its determination to pursue the 'Blue Stream' pipeline across the Black Sea.[21] There is also concern within Gazprom about the long-term security of the pipeline route across the Caucasus (Georgia and Armenia).

While security of transit will remain an important issue for the security of Russian gas supplies, it is hard to construct a realistic scenario whereby supplies are cut off for a protracted period of time. The commercial and political stakes for Russia (Gazprom and the government), the transit countries (Ukraine, Belarus and others) and European countries are too high. The Energy Charter Treaty (see Chapter 4) provides an international legal framework within which these disputes can be arbitrated, subject to binding dispute resolution procedures. From the point of view of physical deliverability, a protracted security crisis would most likely be due to a catastrophic technical failure at one of the major fields, or an explosion in the major Siberian or Ukrainian pipeline corridors (Maps 3.2 and 3.3).

The significance of these developments for European gas markets is that a very large quantity of additional gas can be made available for export at relatively low marginal cost, and huge opportunity cost, to Gazprom. At present there is a lack of transmission capacity to move significant additional quantities of Russian gas to European gas markets. One of Gazprom's most urgent tasks is to ensure that sufficient capacity can be created to take advantage of market opportunities over the next decade, wherever they may present themselves in Europe. In the short term, the principal means by which this will be achieved is the creation of

---

[20] Rem I. Vyakhirev, 'The Perspectives of Russian Natural Gas. Role at the World Gas Market', a paper to the 20th World Gas Conference, Copenhagen, 10–13 June 1997.

[21] For a description of the Blue Stream pipeline see 'Gazprom presents Blue Stream to Botas and the Turkish Government', *Gas Matters*, December 1997, pp. 5–7; for a small part of the contractual difficulties over gas sales and pipeline transit, see 'Bulgaria and Russia settle their differences over Topenergy', ibid., p. ix.

Map 3.2: West Siberian gas fields and pipeline corridors

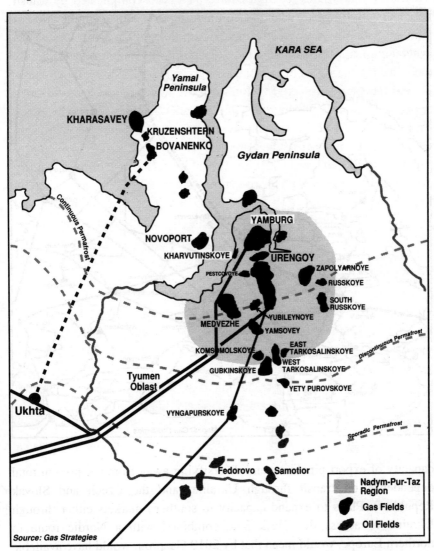

Source: Gas Strategies

a new export corridor through Belarus and Poland (the 'Yamal Pipeline'), comprising two pipelines with the capacity to deliver 55–60 BCM/year to European markets (delivered principally to Germany). The creation of the Belarus–Poland corridor will perform the dual function of increasing the

Map 3.3: Export routes for Russian gas

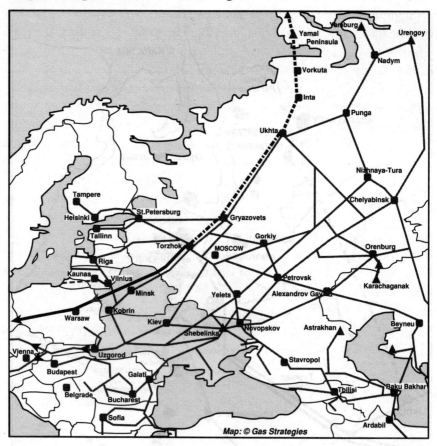

capacity of export pipelines, and diversifying away from the present total dependence on transit through Ukraine (and the Czech and Slovak Republics). Plans to expand capacity to southern markets either through Ukraine or across the Black Sea, combined with a Nordic route to northern Europe, would mean that by 2010 Gazprom would have available some 200 BCM/year of export capacity to European markets.

Whatever the prospects for competitive gas market conditions within Russia (see Chapter 5), the possibility of Russian gas exports creating the conditions for market liberalization in European gas markets is very real.

The building of the first Belarus–Poland line has commenced, in the absence of traditional long-term take or pay contracts to cover anything approaching the total capacity of that pipeline. The reason for this unusual development relates principally to the problems with Ukrainian transit noted earlier. Since the start of construction, contracts have been signed which would, theoretically, account for the entire capacity of the first Belarus–Poland pipeline.[22] However, it is extremely uncertain whether the importing companies will be in a position immediately to take the total annual volume, given the likely market conditions which are unfolding. It seems likely that significant capacity will be available through which gas may be sold outside traditional long-term contracts. While this will not be Gazprom's favoured method of selling gas (it would be much happier to see a continuation of the traditional contractual framework), a combination of availability of gas and capacity is likely to prove irresistible. Assuming spare capacity continues to exist in the first line, a strong indication of Gazprom's future intentions will be the speed with which the company moves to create additional capacity through a second corridor and/or the Ukraine system is reinforced. For the foreseeable future, the availability of gas seems destined far to outstrip the availability of capacity to move that gas to European gas markets.

Whatever the eventual outcome, change is inevitable both for the conduct of the business within Russia and also for the conduct of Russian gas export sales to former republics and export markets. Chronic non-payment problems, and a preponderance of barter trade in the Russian and former Soviet markets, have focused Gazprom even more strongly on European customers in order to raise revenues. But central/eastern Europe – taken for granted as a captive market in communist times – is beginning to look to other suppliers as a combination of purchasing power, and this desire to diversify is meeting increasing keenness to sell on the part of North Sea and other producers. By the end of 1997 there were signs that importers in Slovakia and Poland had used the possibility of supply diversification to extract more favourable terms from Gazprom, with a (partial) return to the barter trade deals of the communist era.

---

[22] The contractual volumes at plateau are Wingas 10 BCM/year, Gasunie 4 BCM/year, SNAM 8 BCM/year. With some gas also being delivered to Poland from the line, these contracts, if delivered at these volumes, would account for the entire capacity of the line.

For Gazprom this is part of the emerging reality of an increasingly competitive European gas market, a development already accepted as inevitable by the top management of Gazprom – including the chairman.[23] This may account for the increasing emphasis on supply to south European markets, particularly Turkey, and the beginnings of interest in developing pipeline connections with markets in East Asia. In both of those regions, competition with other suppliers is (arguably) not well advanced and demand growth is projected to be rapid, providing a strong contrast to Gazprom's traditional markets.[24] However, with Gazprom's supply potential and established marketing companies throughout Europe, the company should be in an excellent position to take advantage of market developments as they unfold. Whether the company chooses to do so using Russian gas only, or a combination of Russian and Central Asian gas, will depend on developments in the Russian gas demand, and the terms on which Central Asian gas may be made available (see below).

Algeria: LNG refurbishment and the expansion of pipeline gas

The position of Algerian supplies in European gas markets is strong and, with the impending expansion of existing and new pipeline capacity together with the refurbishment of LNG capacity, gas exports are set to increase substantially in coming years. In the 1990s agreements with major international companies (principally BP), aimed at developing more reserves in the southern part of the country and exporting gas on a joint venture basis, seem certain to have assured the country's long-term export position. Existing projects, where loans have been paid off, have relatively low costs. The extent to which this can be said about new developments in the south is less certain.

Algerian gas exports are based on its LNG exports from the Arzew and Skikda terminals, and its pipeline gas exports via the Trans-Mediterranean

---

[23] Vyakhirev, loc. cit., note 21.

[24] Competition is less in evidence in southern Europe than in the Far East where a profusion of LNG projects may make it difficult for pipeline gas to compete in some areas of East Asia. See Keun-Wook Paik, *Gas for Power in Northeast Asia* (London: RIIA, forthcoming).

Map 3.4: Algerian gas export pipelines

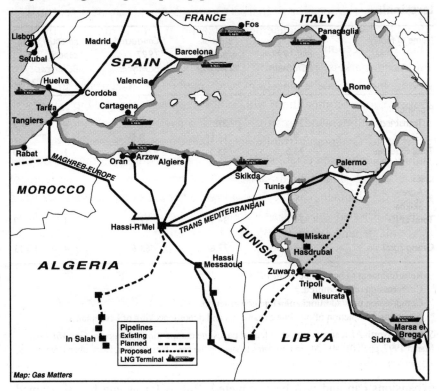

Map: Gas Matters

line through Tunisia (and Sicily) to Italy. With the opening of the Gazoduc Maghreb-Europe (GME) line through Morocco to Spain, Algerian gas gained not only a major increase in capacity, but a significant diversification of routes, and hence markets, for pipeline gas (Map 3.4). With potential security problems – or at least the perception of security problems – arising from a turbulent domestic political situation, diversification is a welcome development.

Table 3.2 attempts to set out current and anticipated pipeline and LNG capacity and contrast this against contracted exports. These figures should not be considered completely accurate since every source gives a different estimate of what the capacity of the newly refurbished plants will be, both in theory and in practice. Sources also differ as to how rapidly the pipeline

Table 3.2: Capacity of Algerian gas export pipelines and LNG terminals

Name of facility	Capacity end-1997 BCM/year	Potential expansion BCM/year	Contracted 1997 BCM/year	Potential spare capacity BCM/year 1997	2000^d
Pipeline:					
TransMed	24	27^b	24	–	0-3
GME	9.5	16.5^c	8.5	1	7
Total Pipeline	33.5	43.5	32.5	1	7-10
LNG:					
Arzew	25.9				
Skikda	8.2^a				
Total LNG	34.1	34.1	31.1	3	3
Grand Total	67.6	77.6	63.6	4	10-13

^{a} Refurbishment to be completed in 1998.
^{b} Compression only required.
^{c} Compression plus additional pipeline construction.
^{d} Assuming completion of pipeline expansions and debottlenecking of LNG plants.

Sources: 'North African gas export potential paces the competition', *European Gas Markets*, March 1997, pp. 8 015–9. 'Algeria prepares to step up the gas', *Gas Matters*, December 1996, p. 26.

expansions can and will be completed. But as far as can be ascertained, Algerian export capacity exceeded 67 BCM in 1997, which suggests capacity in excess of existing contracts of around 4 BCM in 1997 rising to 10–13 BCM by 2000 (assuming the GME pipeline expansion is completed and LNG facilities are fully debottlenecked).

Sonatrach's monopoly over Algerian gas exports has been somewhat diversified with the creation of the Sonatrach/BP joint venture Salah Gas Services (ISG) which will jointly market gas from the In Salah gas development. The announcement that ISG will take over one of Sonatrach's existing export contracts with the Italian power company Enel provides a subtle yet significant shift of both institutional and marketing emphasis.[25] While liberalization initiatives appear to have been rejected in favour of

[25] 'It's *La Dolce Vita* for In Salah Gas', *Gas Matters*, May 1997, pp. 1–3.

traditional contractual approaches, the influence of foreign partners on the thinking of Sonatrach, and the Algerian government in the longer term, remains to be seen.[26] It is possible that, with less immediate gas-to-gas competition potential in the southern part of the Continent, Algerian gas exports may be shielded from the more dramatic developments which can be anticipated further north.

The principal problem for Algerian gas exports is the uncertainty associated with the country's political instability and the legitimacy of the present government. Throughout 1997 violence escalated within the country, with little sign of a reconciliation between the opposition groups and the government. The latter's attempt to 'relegitimize' its rule, following the cancellation of the 1992 elections, has not proved successful. Nor have its attempts to crush what it sees as 'the terrorist opposition' by force. Given the government's resistance to outside mediation in the conflict, it is difficult to see what the way forward might be. One possible outcome would be the eventual rise to power of an Islamic regime, led by the FIS. Possibly the worst security scenario would be a continuation of violence and instability which could escalate to such an extent that the entire fabric of the country could be threatened. The view has been expressed that an alternative (Islamic) government would be required by the country's dependence on export earnings to honour the contractual commitments entered into by their predecessors.[27] Similar predictions proved unreliable following the last major change of government in 1980. Moreover, a new government, possibly with a new management team at Sonatrach, could be ill prepared for dramatic changes in export markets. It seems certain that their attitude towards market liberalization would be as negative as, if not

---

[26] Sonatrach has for example assured the Spanish company Gas Natural that it will not sign contracts with companies such as Endesa and Cepsa, 'which could harm our traditional clients'. 'Prices cut as reform deepens', *International Gas Report*, 11 July 1997, pp. 10–11.

[27] For an up-beat assessment of the potential security impact of the arrival of an Islamic government led by the FIS in Algeria, see Observatoire Mediterranéen de l'Energie, 'Future natural gas supply for Europe, the role of transit countries and security of supply', in International Energy Agency, *Natural Gas Security* (Paris: OECD/IEA, 1995), Annex 2, pp. 241–43.For an account of the disruptions to gas contracts after the change of government in 1980, see Jonathan P. Stern, *International Gas Trade in Europe: the Policies of Exporting and Importing Countries* (London: RIIA/Heinemann Educational, 1984), Chapter 3.

more negative than, that of the present government. If gas-to-gas competition should take hold in European gas markets at the time when a new government had just taken power, resistance and an inability to respond quickly to new market conditions could penalize Algerian exports, and give other suppliers an opportunity to gain market share at their expense.

Britain and the Interconnector

The Interconnector pipeline from Britain has the potential to allow up to 20 BCM of gas a year to be landed at Zeebrugge in Belgium and carried to other European gas markets, starting in late 1998. By the end of 1997 nearly 75 BCM of gas has been committed – approximately 7–10 BCM/year – under contracts with a duration of 7–15 years (Table 3.3). The known British gas resource base appears insufficient to support a major increase in British demand plus a major baseload export for more than a few years into the next century. However, as we shall see, the known resource base at any specific point in time has historically not provided a reliable guide to future availability. Significant additional gas reserves may yet be discovered and developed at competitive prices to support a much higher level of demand. In the absence of such a development, the 1997 conventional wisdom seemed to be a short period of significant net exports followed (within a decade) by equally significant imports; or significant exports, counterbalanced within a relatively short period by imports of Norwegian gas (both through the Frigg pipeline and the Interconnector).

However, this type of analysis is a product of an era where trade has been dominated by long-term rigid contracts. Projections made in late 1997, nearly a year before commissioning, with only around one-half of Interconnector capacity having been contracted, are probably not a reliable guide to the level of short-term trading which will commence once full capacity becomes available. When this potential is added to available capacity in the Frigg line and additional opportunities provided by interconnection of the British and Irish markets, net trade outcomes become unpredictable on an annual basis.

As we shall see in Chapter 5, the Interconnector pipeline was, to a considerable extent, an invention of the British government for the dual

Table 3.3: Contracted sales through the Interconnector as of December 1997

UK seller	Continental buyer	Total contracted volume	Annual delivery and delivery point	Contract duration[a]
Conoco	Wingas (Germany)	10 BCM	1 BCM /Aachen	10 years
BG plc	Wingas (Germany)	20 BCM	2 BCM/Aachen and Zeebrugge	10 years
BP	Ruhrgas (Germany)	15 BCM	1 BCM/Bacton and Zeebrugge	15 years
Centrica (British Gas Trading)	Thyssengas (Germany)	3 BCM	about 0.5 BCM/ NBP[a] and Zeebrugge	7 years
Mobil Europe Gas (Megas)	Norsk Hydro Agri (Netherlands)	12 BCM	0.8 BCM Zeebrugge	15 years
Centrica (British Gas Trading)	Inkoopcombinatie Elsta VOF (Netherlands)	8 BCM	1 BCM/ Zeebrugge	8 years
Cen\ca (British Gas Trading)	Entrade and Delta (Netherlands)	5.6 BCM	0.7 BCM/ Zeebrugge and Zelzate	8 years
Conoco	Gasunie (Netherlands)	b	(approx) 1 BCM	8.5 years starting in 1999
Partners in the Elgin and Franklin fields	Gaz de France	b	b	b
TOTAL		73.6	6.9-9.9	

[a] National balancing point on the British transmission system.
[b] Not known.
Source: Gas Matters, November 1997, p. 9.

purpose of 'exporting liberalization' to Continental European gas markets and improving the country's balance of payments. The succession of Conservative governments which promoted the British liberalization experiment has been extremely keen to encourage similar developments elsewhere in Europe, and the change of government in 1997 does not seem to have affected that position greatly. British producers – to the extent that they are not protecting monopoly and dominant positions in Continental European gas markets – are also keen to promote liberalization. They have nothing to lose and potentially a considerable short-term gain. Without liberalization, their ability to sell their gas in Continental European gas markets will remain limited.

As a surplus of supply emerged in Britain in the mid-1990s as a result of liberalization, producers and marketers, particularly Centrica, the marketing successor of British Gas, have increasingly seen the Interconnector as a useful means of exporting contracted gas which is surplus to its anticipated requirements. In 1997 the surplus appeared as if it would be temporary, peaking in the late 1990s and falling thereafter with Britain moving to a net import position some time before 2010. However, as already mentioned, there is a likelihood that Britain will become a much more significant trader of gas – involving both imports and exports. The critical short-term issue will be, when the Interconnector is commissioned, whether a surge of short-term gas will come forward to fill up the pipeline which, although it may be on short-term contracts – from a few months to two years – could prove immensely destabilizing to the present management of Continental European gas markets.

Other sources of supply

Other internationally traded gas in European markets includes:

- small quantities of pipeline gas from Denmark (to Germany and Sweden);
- LNG suppliers including spot deliveries from Libya, Australia and Abu Dhabi.

None of these supplies is sufficiently large individually to make a significant impact on competition and liberalization of European gas markets. However, continuation and expansion of LNG spot trade could help in the creation of spot gas markets, particularly in southern Europe where competition between pipeline supplies seems less likely in the short term.

New baseload pipeline supplies: Middle East and Central Asia

In terms of reserves, there are a number of countries that could provide sources of pipeline gas for Europe. The most obvious are Libya, Middle East countries (especially Iran and Qatar) and Central Asian countries (especially Turkmenistan and Kazakstan).[28] Libyan, Iranian and Qatari supplies have been considered periodically over the past 30 years (both in piped and liquefied form). Contracts to deliver Iranian gas to Europe, as both LNG and pipeline gas, have been signed in the past, but subsequently cancelled for (primarily) political reasons.[29] Over the past two decades, the political obstacles to major investments in Iran and Libya, particularly in terms of US congressional opposition, have dampened the aspirations of those seeking to push gas projects forward. In terms of Qatari pipeline exports, a combination of political difficulties and high costs has made such a project less attractive at a time when Qatar's LNG trade with southeast Asian countries has taken off spectacularly.

Relatively new have been considerations of exports from Central Asian countries, particularly Kazakstan and Turkmenistan, both of which have sufficient reserves to support a long-distance pipeline project. The general problems with Central Asian projects are the same as in the case of Qatar (although the latter has significantly larger financial resources at its disposal) – political complications with the route, and the construction cost of a pipeline for countries lacking large financial resources. However, the specific complication for Central Asian gas exports is also the only short-term hope for these countries: the position of Gazprom and its willingness to allow Central Asian gas to transit Russia through its pipeline network.

Pipelines exist which have traditionally carried gas from the fields in Turkmenistan through Russia to Ukraine. Less than 200 km from the Karachaganak field in Kazakstan an existing export pipeline carries gas directly to eastern Europe. There is (and will increasingly be) spare

---

[28] There are also possibilities for smaller volumes of gas from Azerbaijan and potentially Georgia; see Ottar Skagen, *Caspian Gas* (London: RIIA, 1997).

[29] For details of the IGAT 2 Pipeline and Kangan LNG projects see Jonathan P. Stern, *International Gas Trade in Europe: the Policies of Exporting and Importing Countries* (London: RIIA/Heinemann Educational, 1984), pp. 46-7 and 135.

capacity in these pipelines. However, as we have already seen, there is a large 'bubble' of gas within Russia to the point where, far from wishing to transport Central Asian gas to Europe – to compete with Russian gas in these markets – Gazprom might have a strong incentive to prevent such gas reaching Europe. The reason that such a judgment may be over-simplistic is because, with established reserves and existing pipelines, it would be extremely cheap for Gazprom to purchase Central Asian gas either for domestic requirements or for export. This could substantially delay the need to open up new fields and build new pipelines from Siberia, in particularly from the Yamal Peninsula.[30] In the short term, the key question may be whether the owners of Central Asian gas fields are willing to accept the statement by the chairman of Gazprom that the likelihood of gaining access to Russian pipeline systems and selling their gas directly to European customers is somewhere between slim and zero in the short to medium term.[31] If they can accept that reality, they may be able to weigh up the option of selling gas to Gazprom at their border, against longer-term options of holding on to the gas until such time as either access through the Russian system becomes a possibility (to which we return in Chapter 5), or alternative pipeline routes to export markets are established. These calculations may be different for Turkmen and Kazak gas.[32] If all of these options prove unattractive or unworkable, Central Asian gas reserves could be a good candidate for the renewed interest being shown in gas to liquids processes in the late 1990s.[33]

---

[30] So runs the argument of one of this author's earlier works, Jonathan P. Stern, *The Russian Natural Gas Bubble* (London: EEP/RIIA, 1995).

[31] At an August 1997 meeting with Turkmenistan's President Niyazov in Moscow, Chairman Vyakhirev and Prime Minister Chernomyrdin made it quite clear that Turkmen gas supplies would be limited to former Soviet republics. At the same time, Chairman Vyakhirev refused to transport Kazak gas through the Gazprom system. 'Gazprom declines Turkmen and Kazakh gas outlets to the West', *Gas Matters*, September 1997, p. ix.

[32] Akira Miyamoto, *Natural Gas in Central Asia: Industries, Markets and Export Options of Kazakstan, Turkmenistan and Uzbekistan* (London: RIIA, 1997).

[33] The owners of Kazakstan's Karachaganak field have already agreed a link with the Caspian Pipeline Consortium to export condensate via the pipeline from the Tenghiz field to Novosibirsk.

New LNG projects: Trinidad, Nigeria, Qatar, Egypt

During the next five years two new LNG projects are planned to deliver contracted supplies to European gas markets. Both Trinidad and Nigeria are using traditional long-term take or pay contracts to underpin the investments which have been made in facilities. As noted earlier, there is a possibility that these projects may contribute small quantities of additional 'spot' gas sales if facilities over-perform and additional gas is available. Moreover, the hiatus in Nigerian LNG trade with the Italian company ENEL, caused by the latter's inability to find a publicly acceptable site for a regasificiation terminal, has been solved by LNG and pipeline gas swaps of a type which will become much more familiar in a competitive and liberalized market.[34]

Neither these projects nor any potential LNG project with Qatar and Egypt, which may start up during the next decade, involve sufficient volumes in themselves to affect general competition and liberalization prospects in European gas markets. However, gas-to-gas competition pressures in individual markets, particularly in southern Europe, could be increased by additional LNG supplies.

Supply and transmission capacity surplus

To summarize this survey of major current and potential suppliers of gas to European gas markets:

- None of the current baseload suppliers has traditionally been in favour of liberalization, or indeed in favour of any significant change to the present industry structure or contractual regime. Most are opposed. In late 1995 the new Dutch government suddenly changed traditional policy and published significant liberalization measures which would affect both domestic supplies and trade;
- By contrast, many British producers have a strong commercial incentive to break up the present monopolistic system and introduce liberalization and competition in Continental Europe. Because of developments in the British gas market, few (if any) British producers would hesitate

---

[34] 'Gas swaps save ENEL's LNG', *Gas Matters*, November 1997, p. 6.

to promote competition by pushing low-price gas into Continental
European gas markets;

- All of the current baseload suppliers are, or will soon be in a position to
sell additional gas through existing export facilities. Liberalized markets
would allow these players to sell significant quantities of short-term gas
to European gas markets. Table 3.4 suggests that these volumes might
amount to 42–58 BCM (pipeline and LNG) by 2000 as a number of
additional pieces of export infrastructure are completed: the (first)
Belarus–Poland pipeline, the British Interconnector, Gazoduc
Maghreb–Europe Phase II, EuroPipe II;

- Even supplies under long-term contracts may have been purchased for
sale to the same set of customers, particularly in Germany.

**Table 3.4: Annual spare capacity in pipeline and LNG facilities:
available or could be created at low cost by 2000 (BCM)**

	2000	
	Pipeline	*LNG*
Netherlands	5–10[a]	
Algeria	7–10[b]	3
Norway	15[c]	
Russia	5–10[d]	
Britain	10[e]	
Total	42–55	3[f]

[a] The higher figure would only be created by a decision to accelerate the development of
Groningen gas.
[b] Assuming construction of phase 2 of GME.
[c] Of which 5 to Continental Europe and 10 to Britain.
[d] Assuming construction of the first Belarus–Poland ('Yamal') line.
[e] Assuming 10 BCM of long-term contract gas by that date (currently 6.3 BCM).
[f] This is conservative as it is limited to Algerian LNG capacity. Additional capacity may be
available from the Nigerian and Trinidadian projects as well a continuation of spot sales from
Libya, Australia and Abu Dhabi.

Demand pull

The gas demand profile of individual European countries varies widely as
can be seen in Table 3.5. For major European countries in the mid-1990s,
the share of gas in primary energy demand varied from a high of 49.3% in

Table 3.5: Gas consumption in major European countries (percentage of gross inland consumption, 1995)

	Europe OECD	UK	Germany	Italy	Netherlands	France	Belgium
Power	18.7	18.1	15.3	21.0	25.7	1.9	18.9
Energy sector[a]	6.6	7.1	11.5	1.5	3.0	1.3	1.0
Industry[b]	26.4	16.7	28.0	33.1	17.7	36.7	32.2
Raw material	4.0	3.7	2.3	2.1	7.6	7.2	6.3
Residential and commercial	44.0	54.5	42.9	42.3	46.0	52.9	41.8
Consumption (BCM)	374.2[c]	89.6	96.0	56.8	48.5	39.2	14.9
% of PED[d]	22.1[c]	31.9	21.9	29.2	49.3	13.8	21.3

[a] Excluding power generation.
[b] Excluding raw material.
[c] Fifteen Member States of the European Union for 1996.
[d] Percentage of primary energy demand.

Source: Cedigaz, *Natural Gas in the World, 1997 Survey*, Tables 4.1 and 4.3, pp. 106 and 121–4.

the Netherlands to 13.8% in France. General gas penetration rates – i.e. customers within reach of a gas supply which could realistically be expected to use the fuel (given price relativities and other factors) – are similarly wide. The huge share of gas in the Netherlands demonstrates the possibilities for increasing demand where there has been a long-term national commitment to develop the market for a domestically produced source of energy. The relatively low share of gas in the French energy balance is also a clear indication of a policy to give other fuels – first coal, then nuclear power – precedence for identical reasons of national commitment to domestically produced energy.

Despite the fact that the figures in Table 3.5 are at a high level of aggregation, it is apparent that there are considerable variations in gas usage, principally in terms of gas used outside the residential and commercial sector. France with its huge nuclear power sector uses almost no gas in power generation, whereas the Dutch power sector accounts for more than a quarter of gas demand. In Britain, barely 20% of gas is used in industrial and raw material (chemical industry) sectors, whereas in France and Belgium the share is around 40%. It is in these two sectors, power generation and industrial demand (particularly the chemical industry), that serious interest has been created in taking advantage of the 'supply push' conditions noted earlier.

Power generation and cogeneration

In the development of national gas markets, one of the most important decisions for the market managers – governments and gatekeepers – was the extent to which gas should be allowed into the power generation sector. In some countries (e.g. Britain and France) no large-scale use of gas was permitted in power generation in order to promote and protect domestic coal and nuclear power. In Britain, market management – specifically government control of the type of generation capacity which would be licensed – was eliminated with the privatization of the electricity industry. This coincided with renewed commercial interest, and major technical advances in combined cycle technology. In the 1990s a frenzy of construction of combined cycle gas-fired power stations – the so-called 'dash for gas' – raised the share of electricity generated by gas from virtually zero to what is expected to be more than one-third (more than 14 GW of capacity) by 2000.

Most of the countries in Table 3.6 (prepared by UNIPEDE) appear to be anticipating a significant increase in gas-fired generation during the period up to 2010, which would amount to a 270% increase over 1994 levels. The International Energy Agency scenarios see gas-fired stations generating between two and five times the amount of power in 2010 compared with 1995.[35] This is significant, because the EU Gas Directive (see Chapter 4) will allow power generators of any size access to networks from the time the Directive comes into force. Of the major markets listed in the table the striking exceptions are Germany, France and the Netherlands. The Netherlands already has by far the highest percentage of power generated by gas; Germany and France, however, require somewhat closer examination.

---

[35] From 196 TWh in 1993 to 380–909 TWh in 2010. International Energy Agency, *World Energy Outlook, 1996 Edition* (Paris: OECD, 1996), Tables A8.1 and A23.1, pp. 242 and 262.

Table 3.6: Electricity generation by natural gas in selected European countries, 1994–2010 (TWh)

| | 1994 | | | 2000 | | | 2010 | | |
	Gas	Total	% gas	Gas	Total	% gas	Gas	Total	% gas
Austria	7.6	50	15	8.9	57	16	17.0	68	25
Belgium	7.9	71	11	20.8	80	26	28.1	92	31
Germany	29.0	490	6	53.0	533	10	59.0	583	10
Denmark	5.1	33	15	12.2	37	33	15.9	41	39
Spain	–	159	0	0.1	188	0	38.1	254	15
Finland	6.0	68	9	9.0	81	11	9.0	99	9
France	3.3	388	1	3.3	440	0	3.3	500	0
Greece	–	37	0	7.0	48	15	7.0	67	10
Ireland	4.2	16	26	9.2	20	46	13.7	29	47
Italy	38.3	254	15	76.9	297	26	106.5	360	30
Luxembourg	0.1	5	2	0.2	6	3	0.2	7	3
Netherlands	43.6	87	50	49.5	95	52	65.7	114	58
Portugal	–	30	0	6.9	40	17	14.5	55	26
Sweden	–	139	0	–	150	0	–	166	0
UK	46.0	323	14	128	356	36	140.0	415	34
Switzerland	–	51	0	–	56	0	–	65	0
Norway	–	112	0	[a]	133		[a]	116	
EUR 17	191.1	2311	8	385.0	2596	15	518.0	3029	17

[a] Gas-fired generation in Norway may be completed by 2000.

Source: UNIPEDE projections cited in *Financial Times, Power in Europe*, 26 February 1997, pp. 4–6.

Power generation in Germany has traditionally been heavily oriented towards plant fired with domestically produced coal which has been heavily subsidized via a combination of high electricity prices and direct subsidies from taxpayers. Although generally expressed in terms of promoting security of energy supply, the principal rationale has been to maintain employment for German coalmining communities. When sulphur emission restrictions threatened the continued existence of coal-fired power stations – and by implication coal mines – the policy response was to retrofit 38 gigawatts of capacity with flue gas desulphurization equipment. In the mid-1990s, subsidies were refocused on taxpayers, at both national and Länder levels. The International Energy Agency estimated that subsidies were running at DM10–12bn per year in the mid-

1990s, with production being sold significantly below cost. From an international trade perspective, questions of unfair competition and 'dumping' have already been raised by British coal producers.[36] However, from a German domestic perspective, the levels of subsidy have become increasingly prohibitive and although these are projected to fall to DM5.5bn by 2005, if prices fall as the electricity industry becomes more competitive in the future, this may prove too slow an adjustment to market conditions.

The traditional German response to this situation has been that if domestic coal production is phased out, the power sector would increasingly rely on imported coal and nuclear power rather than fuels such as gas which would require higher levels of imports from non-European sources. By 1997 there were strong suggestions that the power sector had significantly changed its position and that gas-fired generation was actively under consideration.[37] The major wave of power station reinvestment in Germany is not expected until around 2005, when much of the existing coal-fired capacity reaches the end of its working life. However, the timing of decisions on construction may be strongly affected by the development of a more competitive electricity market.

A combination of the European Union's Electricity Directive and new German energy legislation (see Chapters 4 and 5) seems likely to open up the German electricity market to significant competition in early 1999. Assuming that new entrants, either domestic or foreign, seeking to build new power generation capacity attempt to enter the market at that time, the existing German generators could be faced with uncomfortable decisions as to how to respond. The argument that no significant new capacity is needed prior to 2005, from the point of view of ability to meet demand, may not prove to be decisive in the new competitive conditions of the German market. The British experience, following the privatization of the electricity industry, was that established generators proved unwilling to stand by while new entrants built gas-fired stations because

---

[36] *Energy Policies of IEA Countries*, 1997 Review (OECD, 1997), Table 1, pp. 136–37.

[37] The Chairman of Wintershall referred to the German power industry having made 'a 180 degree turn in its position towards gas'. *FT International Gas Report*, 18 April 1997, pp. 14–15.

of the fear that by the time they needed to replace ageing coal-fired stations, they would be at a severe competitive disadvantage relative to those with new generation capacity. Established generators therefore built new gas-fired stations – in addition to independent power projects – thereby condemning their coal-fired capacity (and much of the British coalmining industry) to early retirement.[38] It is overly simplistic to suggest that the British experience of a 'dash for gas' during the 1990s will be repeated in Germany. But the possibility of a significant construction of gas-fired generation in Germany around the year 2000 should certainly not be ruled out. The British example shows how quickly events can move once policy and commercial attitudes change.

As far as France is concerned the power generation picture has seemed fairly well established with nuclear plants as the overwhelmingly dominant source of electricity and gas very much on the margins. This picture may change only slowly, but the share of gas is likely to rise (unlike the situation shown in Table 3.5) if only because of the need for non-baseload generation. Whether it is conceivable that baseload gas-fired power stations will be built in France, as the nuclear stations reach the end of their working lives, is more contentious. However, if for no reason other than their aspirations as international investors in, and constructors of, power generation projects, French utilities will probably wish to point to some recent experience of gas-fired power generation in their own country.

The trend away from coal-fired and nuclear power generation and towards natural gas is likely to be Europe-wide, but it is not easy to project in individual countries because of the highly political nature of employment consequences from downsizing coal industries, and import dependence arising from increasing the role of gas. A combination of these issues is likely to be strongly relevant in central and east European countries such as Poland, where large coal industries in long-term decline could be pushed faster in that direction by means of increased imports of Russian gas.

---

[38] For background see John Surrey (ed.), *The British Electricity Experiment* (London: Earthscan, 1996).

Cogeneration

The discussion so far has focused on baseload power generation. However, the past decade has seen increasing emphasis on cogeneration – in the form of combined heat and power and district heating – as an increasingly attractive and efficient means of generating power and heat for industrial and residential use. Statistical generalizations are difficult because of different national definitions and data collection.[39] Countries vary from those generating only a few percentage points of their electricity by cogeneration to those with very significant shares (e.g. Austria (23%), Netherlands, (30%), Finland (34%) and Denmark (40%)). In 1997 COGEN Europe summarized the prospects as follows:

> Given policy trends towards energy market liberalisation and environmental concerns, prospects for cogeneration in Europe are very bright. It is difficult to give a European growth forecast since the common feature in all aspects is diversity. However, the achievement of a 30% share of all electricity generation from CHP is available by 2010 [compared with around 10% of EU generation in 1994], amounting to about ECU100bn of new investment. Very generally it can be said that liberalisation will lift important barriers in most countries, but it is also likely to provoke a fall in electricity prices ... New large district heating (DH) networks are not likely to be built in liberalised markets, since they require high capital costs. Gas-fired, decentralised and small-scale DH have brighter prospects, for which the same can be said about cogeneration in the industrial and tertiary sectors. Natural gas will remain the favoured fuel.[40]

The speed with which cogenerators will be able to take advantage of liberalized gas markets is therefore of some importance. As we shall see (Chapter 4), the European Commission was unable to reach agreement with the member states on the issue of access to networks, and the eligibility of combined heat and power producers to request access is left to the discretion of national governments, while all power generators (irrespective of size) are automatically eligible. In some countries, therefore, depending on the policy adopted by government (and the pressure exerted by the

---

[39] *European Cogeneration Review 1997*, Brussels: COGEN Europe, 1997.
[40] Ibid., p. xv.

cogeneration community), a strong increase in gas-fired cogeneration may be more likely than the construction of baseload gas-fired power generation.

Large industrial users, local distribution companies and municipalities

Among large industrial users, the chemical industry has been the most vociferous in pursuit of liberalization of gas networks and lower gas prices. It was not a coincidence that the parent company of Wintershall – the company which (together with Russia's Gazprom) has mounted a major competitive challenge in the German gas market (see Chapter 5) – is BASF, the giant chemical company. Neither is it surprising that two of the first major contracts to be signed through the Interconnector are with chemical companies (see Table 3.3). All large industrial gas users, particularly those which will immediately become eligible for access under the European Gas Directive, will rapidly become more aware of the potential for reducing gas purchase costs and can be expected to take advantage of those opportunities.

A crucial aspect of this process will be the degree of determination of large industrial companies to move their business – in terms of new plant – to countries where they perceive lower cost gas (and electricity) will be available than in their home market. The employment consequences of losing new industrial plants to neighbouring countries will concentrate the minds of governments in respect of energy price levels and how these can be reduced.

The competitive pressures on municipalities and local distribution companies (LDCs) are somewhat less than for large industrial customers, but this may change as the industrial customers within their service areas perceive that lower-cost gas supplies are on offer, to which they are unable to gain access. In extreme cases, industrial customers served by LDCs may opt to 'bypass' the local network by building a direct line from the high-pressure network. But the threat of losing significant numbers of industrial customers should ring warning bells for many LDCs and compel them either to exercise their options for direct purchase, or pressurize their traditional merchant transmission company to offer keener prices. If LDCs find that individually they have insufficient commercial power to reduce prices, they may merge their purchasing efforts to considerable effect. However, there is little pressure from residential customers to lower prices and, with so much of the culture of distribution in Continental Europe reflecting the principles of public service obligations and security of supply – almost at any cost – 'demand pull' tendencies in the residential sector may be a long time arriving.

Demand forecasting: an increasingly difficult task

Many forecasts of European – particularly west European and European Union – natural gas demand are made by commercial and other international gas organizations, and Table 3.7 contains a selection covering the period 2010–15. While the assumptions in these projections are generally not stated, most are dominated by interfuel competition as their guiding principle of the degree of market share that gas can expect to capture. As gas-to-gas competition lowers gas prices, the additional market share that may be captured by gas could be significant.

Table 3.7: European gas demand growth forecasts

Organization	Date of forecast	Region covered	1996 demand BCM	Forecast of demand	
				Year	BCM
Ruhrgas	1997	Western Europe	367	2010	440–464
Eurogas	1997	Western Europe	316	2010	433
IGU	1997	Western/ central Europe	384 (1995)	2010	494–560
IEA	1996	OECD Europe	351 (1995)	2010	364–494
Odell	1996	Western Europe	304 (1995)	2015	497
Odell	1996	Eastern Europe	65 (1995)	2010	113

Note: The EU publication *Eurostat* estimated 1996 gas demand by the EU15 at 334.6 BCM.

Sources: Ruhrgas: Gerhard Enseling, 'Market with growth potential', *Fundamentals of the Natural Gas Industry*, Petroleum Economist, 1997, pp. 22–25; Eurogas: *Cedigaz News Report,* No. 37, 24 October 1997; IGU (International Gas Union): *Gas Matters*, September 1997, p. 11; IEA: International Energy Agency, *World Energy Outlook*, 1996 Edition, Paris: OECD, Tables A8.1 and A23.1, pp. 242 and 262; Odell, 'Europe's gas consumption and imports to increase with adequate low cost supplies', *Energy Exploration and Exploitation*, Vol. 15, No. 1, 1997, pp. 35–54.

Table 3.8: Comparative prices of gas and competing fuels by sector in the six main European gas-using countries, 1996

Sector	Germany	Britain	Netherlands	France	Italy	Belgium
Domestic	5.73	4.03	5.08	5.78	9.50	5.80
Gasoil (Gas=100)	80.3	89.6	117.9	104.3	129.2	65.9
Commercial	3.71	1.65	4.13	3.46	7.18	3.40
Gasoil (Gas=100)	93.3	221.8	110.4	133.2	137.0	84.4
Med. ind. firm	3.30	1.35	2.53	2.35	2.91	2.21
Gasoil (Gas=100)	103.9	221.5	171.1	179.1	–	127.6
LSFO (Gas=100)	57.0	142.9	101.2	94.0	78.4	78.7
Coal (Gas=100)	116.7	120.0	–	114.9	49.1	48.4
Large ind. firm	2.07	1.13	1.89	1.96	2.48	1.83
LSFO (Gas=100)	90.8	170.8	–	112.7	91.9	95.1
Coal (Gas=100)	186.0	93.8	–	79.6	57.7	58.5
Large ind. int.	1.93	0.97	–	1.91	2.27	1.56
LSFO (Gas=100)	97.4	199.0	–	115.7	100.4	111.5
Coal (Gas=100)	199.5	109.3	–	81.7	63.0	68.6
Power stations	2.21	1.48	1.75	1.90	1.75	1.44
LSFO (Gas=100)	85.1	130.4	–	116.3	109.1	120.8
Coal (Gas=100)	53.4	73.6	81.7	82.1	71.4	79.9

Notes: Gas prices in Pfennig/kWh include VAT where applicable and all taxes.
Coal prices in Germany are for indigenous supplies (in power stations for imports/after subsidies; some German industrial users can import at these prices). In France, prices to medium industry are for indigenous coal and for imported supplies in other sectors.
Fuel oil in the UK is about 2% sulphur on average.
Coal use excluding power stations in the Netherlands is negligible, as is gasoil to industry in Italy. LSFO use in Dutch industry and power stations is also negligible.

Source: Peter Odell, 'Europe's gas consumption and imports to increase with adequate low cost supplies', *Energy Exploration and Exploitation*, Vol. 15, No. 1, 1997, pp. 35–54; end-user prices are from *European Energy Pricewatch*, and research by the consultancy Energy Advice.

Table 3.8 contrasts gas prices with those of competing energies used in the different sectors. As Odell points out, the information in this table:

accentuates the position of Britain as the country with the lowest prices. But in as far as this low-tax situation applies generally to energy, other energy sources there are still generally lower priced than gas ... But the price differentials working against gas relative to other fuels are usually even worse in the other countries: expect for the Netherlands. There, only power station coal is significantly lower priced than gas. Significantly, natural gas' 41% share of total energy use in the Netherlands stands at almost twice the West European average of 22% indicating how far gas' substitution for other sources of energy could go in the rest of Europe under gas pricing policies which are more competitive with alternative energy sources.[41]

This creates a major forecasting problem in that it is extremely difficult to devise a methodology which will adequately analyse how gas demand might be affected by a significant fall in end-user prices relative to other fuels. Such an analysis would need to look carefully – country by country, sector by sector – at the substitutability of gas for other fuels. The share of gas in the Dutch energy balance serves as a rough indication of the potential for gas penetration in other European countries. However, the need for micro-analysis – rather than macro-guesswork – cannot be overstressed. Not only is it fraught with difficulty to generalize likely future demand trends across a wide range of countries, but it is even very difficult to generalize future demand in individual sectors across a range of countries. Table 3.8 suggests that analysis should be focused on the residential sector in Germany and Belgium, and on the ability of industrial customers using low-sulphur fuel oil to switch to gas. If gas-to-gas competition does produce gas prices which are significantly lower than competing fuels in major European gas markets, then demand may rise significantly above the current 'conventional wisdom' over the next decade. However, it should not be forgotten that such scenarios are dependent on constant crude oil and oil product prices. If the fall in world crude oil prices anticipated by some in 1998 proves to be correct, then gas prices will need to fall in order to remain competitive with oil products.

Margins and end-user prices: a statistical quagmire

Continental European gas companies – irrespective of their position in the gas chain – have acquired the reputation of being extremely profitable.

---

[41] Peter Odell, 'Europe's gas consumption and imports to increase with adequate low cost supplies', *Energy Exploration and Exploitation*, Vol. 15, No. 1, 1997, pp. 35–54.

Table 3.9: Operating profits of principal European gas transmission companies (nominal)

	British Gas[a] (£m)	Gaz de France (mn Fr)	Distrigaz (mn BEF)	Ruhrgas (mn DM)	SNAM (bn lire)
1984	651	559	n/a	n/a	823
1985	706	3786	2974	431	1132
1986	1001	5136	995	940	1189
1987	1053	4562	1488	726	1286
1988	1120	3267	3403	758	659
1989	1104	2976	3916	961	1173
1990	1652	3424	3411	1004	2129
1991	1668	4602	3755	1339	2838
1992	1103	5710	3239	1222	3083
1993	1340[b]	6817	3395	1019	3107
1994	1092[b]	4846	3694	7643	3132

[a] Current cost accounting.
[b] Operating profit excludes restructuring costs.

Source: Michael Stoppard, *A New Order for Gas in Europe* (Oxford: OIES, 1996), Table 4.8, p. 84.

As Stoppard has pointed out, much of the drive for competition and liberalization is based on:

a common underlying assumption that European gas prices include an economic rent. The rent should be seen as the 'booty' or price around which different political and business interests vie.[42]

Attempting to disentangle the profits being made by gas companies is a task of heroic proportions. Tables 3.9 and 3.10 record the operating profits and return on assets of the major gas transmission companies in Continental Europe. The situation in the Netherlands is unusual with Gasunie being allowed to earn a regulated profit of only 80 million guilders per year. While few would contest that margins have been less than comfortable, comparisons between companies are difficult because of the different structures of industries over the past two decades and

---

[42] Michael Stoppard, *A New Order for Gas in Europe?* (Oxford: Oxford Institute for Energy Studies, 1996), p. 68.

Table 3.10: European gas transmission companies: return on assets[a]

Company	Country	1993	1994
SNAM	Italy	40	33
Ruhrgas	Germany	43	32
Thyssengas	Germany	19	n/a
British Gas[b]	Britain	23[c]	16
Distrigaz	Belgium	13	15
Gas Natural[d]	Spain	16	11
Gaz de France	France	12.5	9
Gasunie	Netherlands	10	9
Enagas	Spain	3	8

[a] Operating profit/tangible assets.
[b] Figures based on gas supply business and historic cost.
[c] Excluding exceptional restructuring charges.
[d] 1994 includes consolidation of Enagas.

Source: Michael Stoppard, *A New Order for Gas in Europe* (Oxford: OIES, 1996), Table 4.10, p. 86.

different maturity of infrastructure. Surveying European and American end-user prices, Stoppard has concluded that European companies have not shown the same efficiency improvements which have taken place in the United States during the 1984–94 period.

Stoppard's general conclusion from his survey of this period is that:

There is no evidence that utilities have felt the pressure of tighter competitive conditions. There has been no serious reduction in their aggregate costs (except in the UK) and ... profit levels have remained strong perhaps with some upward trend. It appears that utilities have managed to defend differentials by re-balancing costs between industrial and residential customers. The more demand inelastic residential customer has borne an increasing share of the downstream costs, while a more vigorous policy towards cutting costs in evident within industry sales ... European costs ... appear to compare unfavourably with trends in the USA and could suggest some degree of cost control lethargy.[43]

This conclusion is strongly supported by Figure 3.2 which shows that during the period 1980–96, downstream (transmission and distribution)

---
[43] Ibid., pp. 90–91.

Figure 3.2: Downstream margins in the German gas industry

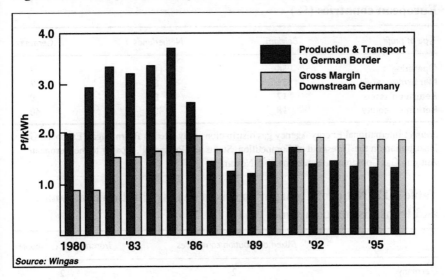

Source: Wingas

margins in the German gas industry have been independent of the border price and have remained constant throughout the period.

While there is an understandable concentration on the rents of transmission companies, the position of the distribution sector is equally interesting and has traditionally attracted less attention. An International Energy Agency study on gas distribution shows (Tables 3.11 and 3.12) no consistent pattern between similar companies in different countries. Not too much should be read into the figure which suggests that the net profit margin of Belgian distribution companies is around 25%. These companies are required to pay most of their dividends to municipalities which use them for subsidizing the other services which they provide.

A major contributor to company margins is the price that the company is able to charge to end-users. Once again, there is considerable difficulty in comparing end-user prices of gas in different European countries. This is not because of lack of data. Many organizations publish 'league tables' of European and/or world gas prices, but these are too often designed to show their particular country, or particular industry, in a good or bad position. Table 3.13 shows pre-tax gas prices in six of the largest

Table 3.11: Profitability of pure gas distribution companies in three European countries (%)

Type of profit	Belgium	Netherlands	Germany
Operating	34	11	7
Net profit margin	25	8	7
Return on assets	17	8	9
Return on equity	18	40	40

Source: International Energy Agency gas distribution study cited in Bjorn Saga, 'European Gas Distribution on the Threshold of Competition: Status and Prospects', a paper to the European Autumn Gas Conference, Barcelona, 4–5 November 1997.

Table 3.12: Net profit margin[a] in mixed gas distribution companies and transmission companies (%)

	Mixed distribution companies	Transmission companies
Germany	2	2
The Netherlands	3	0.5
Italy	7	10
Belgium	25	2

[a] Net profits/sales.

Source: as Table 3.11.

European gas markets based on work by European Energy Pricewatch, an industry price reporting service which therefore removes any innate tendencies towards bias. The starting point is the border price shown in lines a.i. and a.ii. of Table 3.13 where, aside from Belgium, the difference in border prices is within a relatively narrow band (8%). The final two lines in Table 3.13 carry the most interesting message. Line d.i. shows the average price of gas for each country weighted by the percentage use in each sector. The variation is clearly much greater than the variations in border prices. Line d.ii. relates the two different variations and shows that in comparison to Belgium – where end-user prices show the least increase compared with border prices – prices in France, Germany and Italy are 20–30% higher. It is too simple to suggest that these differentials can be

Table 3.13: End-user prices in the six main European gas-using countries, indexed to the border (beach) prices of gas, 1996

		Germany	Britain	Netherlands	France	Italy	Belgium
a.	*Border prices (BP)*						
i.	In $/MMBtu	2.63	2.59	2.62	2.60	2.62	3.01
ii.	In Pf/kWh	1.35	1.33	1.35	1.34	1.34	1.54
	Index: Lowest = 100	101.5	100.0	101.5	100.8	100.8	115.8
b.	*End-user prices in Pf/kWh excluding all taxes and VAT*						
i.	Domestic	4.62	3.81	3.85	4.79	4.64	4.55
	Index/BP	342	286	285	357	346	295
ii.	Commercial	3.35	1.65	3.59	3.46	3.75	3.40
	Index/BP	248	124	266	258	280	221
iii.	Med. ind. firm	2.94	1.35	2.29	2.16	2.63	2.21
	Index/BP	218	112	170	161	196	144
iv.	Large ind. firm	1.71	1.13	1.75	1.74	2.20	1.83
	Index/BP	127	85	130	130	164	119
v.	Large ind. int.	1.57	0.97	—	1.69	1.99	1.56
	Index/BP	116	73	—	126	149	101
vi.	Power stns	1.85	1.48	1.61	1.68	1.75	1.44
	Index/BP	137	111	119	125	131	94
vii.	Feedstocks	1.59	0.92	1.46	1.59	1.89	1.53
	Index/BP	117	69	108	119	141	99
c.	*Wtd average*	2.94	2.44	2.70	3.17	3.00	2.77
	Index/BP	218	183	200	237	224	180
d.	*Index to lowest*						
i.	Wtd average	120.5	100.0	110.7	129.9	123.0	113.5
ii.	Index in c.	121.1	101.7	111.1	131.7	124.4	100.0

Source: Peter Odell, 'Europe's gas consumption and imports to increase with adequate low cost supplies', *Energy Exploration and Exploitation*, Vol. 15, No. 1, 1997, pp. 35–54; end-user prices are from *European Energy Pricewatch*, and research by the consultancy Energy Advice.

ascribed only to higher profits or lower efficiencies in the respective gas transmission and distribution companies. Nevertheless, if they can surmount the entry barriers, there is plenty of commercial scope for new companies to enter the market, undercutting established players. The tangible experience which bears out this conclusion is the Wintershall story in Germany (see Chapter 5) whereby a new entrant has been able to enter the market by undercutting the prices of established companies, despite having to bear the capital cost of building new pipelines.

Longer-term perspectives: the recurring conundrums of reserves and costs

Thus far we have concentrated mainly on the short term, principally the next five years, in an attempt to see how competition may unfold in European gas markets. But one of the guiding principles over the past 30 years is that gas companies, principally producers and transmission companies, have to plan for the long term in order to ensure market expansion and security of supply. In support of this principle of long-term planning, three general assumptions or – perhaps more accurately – assertions, about European gas markets over the past 30 years have been:

(1)   that indigenous European gas reserves are 'running out';
(2)   that new gas field developments will inevitably be 'expensive' compared with previous developments;
(3)   that unless producers are given 'high' prices and are able to sign long-term take or pay contracts, they will not be prepared to develop new fields which will mean that, in the longer term, the gas market cannot be maintained or expanded.

These assertions continue to be part of the public position of many major players in European gas markets, and are bedrock assumptions upon which many gas scenarios and projections are based. However, in the light of historical experience and changing market circumstances, they should increasingly be questioned.

Reserves

Table 3.14 looks at remaining proven reserves of European countries and external suppliers from the late 1960s to the mid-1990s. Only in France is there compelling evidence that reserves are 'running out'. In Britain, Norway, the Netherlands, Germany and Italy the gas resource base remains obstinately robust in absolute terms and while there is some evidence that reserve to production ratios have declined over the past 15 years this is not compelling.

Moreover, a decline in reserve to production (R/P) ratios needs to be seen in the context of rising production – a development which in many countries was not thought possible. For example, in 1980 Germany produced 18.9 BCM and Italy 12.5 BCM in comparison to 21.9 BCM and 19.9 BCM in 1996 respectively. There appears to be an unofficial depletion policy in both countries (as there has been an official policy in the Netherlands) which maintains a stable relationship between production and reserves. Any liberalization process which might bring forward

Table 3.14: Remaining proven reserves in major European countries and external suppliers 1968–97, BCM (reserve to production ratio)

	1968	1981	1986	1991	1997
Norway		1314 (45)	2228 (82)	2300 (81)	3000 (70)
UK[a]	700	739 (16)	634 (13)	545 (9)	760 (8)
Netherlands	1990 (142)	1578 (17)	1815 (25)	1970 (24)	1765 (20)
Germany (West)	202 (31)	190 (10)	182 (12)	199 (12)	223 (10)[b]
Italy	180 (17)	175 (14)	290 (18)	328 (20)	290 (15)
Poland		120 (19)	96 (15)	161 (30)	149 (31)
Romania		125 (4)	180 (6)	130 (20)	389 (21)
Denmark		139	94 (49)	161 (30)	167 (26)
Algeria	2350	3174 (71)	3030 (57)	3300 (55)	3700 (49)
FSU[c]	9000	30500 (68)	37500 (58)	54530 (66)	56650 (77)

[a] 1969.
[b] Unified Germany.
[c] Former Soviet Union (principally Russia, Turkmenistan and Kazakstan).

Sources: 1968 figures from OECD, *Impact of Natural Gas in the Consumption of Energy in the OECD European Member Countries* (Paris: OECD, 1969), Table 5, p. 32 and Table 7, p. 35; other years from Cedigaz, *Natural Gas in the World* (respective years).

additional indigenous production could impact significantly on short-term availability of supply, as occurred in Britain when the British Gas monopsony was removed.[44]

It should also be remembered that the table cites only *proven* reserves. For example, UK remaining proven plus probable plus possible reserves at 31 December 1996 were 1,960 BCM, more than 2.5 times the proven figure of 760 BCM.[45] Despite the widespread use of 'proven reserves' as the major indicator of the remaining resource gas base in European countries, this measure has been shown to be almost irrelevant – France excepted – as a predictor of likely future discoveries and levels of production. What it emphatically has not meant, despite a general assumption which has continued in many minds up to the present day, is that a reserve figure for a specific year divided by production in the previous year can be presented as the number of years before that country's gas reserves 'run out'.

The experience of the past three decades makes it questionable whether useful information is conveyed either by the figures of 'proven reserves' or some wider definition of 'resources', except when applied to a specific gas field. When citing these figures in respect of an entire country, the statistics rarely relate the physical reserve availability to: deliverability, delivered costs of production and transmission to markets, and current gas market prices. When measured in these terms in 1997, Germany's 208 BCM of reserves might have been valued a great deal higher than Turkmenistan's 3,500 BCM. Few would go as far as Peter Odell's forecast that European gas production potential in 2025 could be 60% higher than in 1995.[46] However, the reserve conundrum is that gas reserves have continued to be discovered in and around Europe in sufficient quantities to extend current production levels for at least one decade, and in most countries several decades, into the future. On current evidence, it is as

---

[44] Production rose from around 55 BCM in 1991/92 to nearly 90 BCM in 1996, and is expected to be in the range 90–120 BCM by 2001. Ibid., 1995 and 1997, Appendix 7; and 1997, p. 56.

[45] UK Department of Trade and Industry, *The Energy Report: Oil and Gas Resources of the United Kingdom 1995, 1996 and 1997*, Vol. 2, Table 5.2, p. 45.

[46] Peter Odell, 'Europe's gas consumption and imports to increase with adequate low cost supplies', *Energy Exploration and Exploitation*, Vol. 15, No. 1, 1997, pp. 35–54.

likely that European energy balances will move beyond the fossil fuel era leaving significant gas reserves in the ground, as it is that the gas reserves available to European markets will 'run out'.

Costs

The 'supply push' scenario suggests that Europe's main suppliers will have the potential to bring up to 50–60 BCM of gas, additional to current contractual commitments, through existing transmission capacity at relatively low costs. Since the greater part of the investments connected with this infrastructure will have been sunk, there will be a significant incentive to maximize throughput. However, important questions remain as to the longer-term costs of delivering gas to European borders.

With the commercial confidentiality that surrounds the industry, calculations of costs have always been a relatively mysterious exercise. Over the past few years published literature has attempted to estimate costs of a wide variety of current and future gas supplies to European borders. The figures in Table 3.15 are from two different (widely quoted) sources incorporating different assumptions, reaching roughly similar conclusions regarding the general level of costs from major supply sources. For current suppliers, the costs delivered to the nearest European Union border appear to be (all in $/mmbtu): the Netherlands, substantially less than $1.00; Algeria, $1.00–2.00 for pipeline gas and $2.00–3.00 for LNG; Norway, $1.30–2.00 for older fields and $2.30–3.00 for developments completed in the mid-1990s; Russia, $3.20–4.00. For future baseload pipeline gas supplies, the costs are all higher than these figures with the exception of Britain's Interconnector at $2.10 and Libyan supply at $1.50–1.70. New LNG projects are estimated at $2.30–3.60. Since the figures cited are estimated in 1993 and 1995 dollars, all of these figures would be higher today. However, Table 3.15 does not do justice to the detail of the assumptions in these estimates which are broken down into production, transportation costs and transit fees, with each element given separately. Taking these figures at face value, Russian and some Norwegian supplies already appear to be uncompetitive at 1997 European gas prices. With the exception of British and Libyan pipeline gas and

Table 3.15: Estimated full costs of gas delivered to European borders

	Pauwels[a] 1993$/mmbtu	OME/IEA[b] 1995$/mmbtu
The Netherlands:		
low-cal	0.25	
hi-cal	0.75–1.60	
Norway:		2.3–2.9
Ekofisk	1.34	
Sleipner East	1.56–1.89	
Frigg	1.77	
Heimdal	1.82	
Troll	1.96–2.29	
Sleipner West	2.66–2.99	
Haltenbanken	2.92–3.25	
LNG (Barents)	4.17–4.20	
Algeria:		
Trans-Med	1.06	1.5–1.8
GME	1.39	1.5–1.8
LNG (France)	1.99	2.3–2.8
UK (Interconnector)	2.10	
Russia:		
Western Siberia	3.22	3.5–3.9
Yamal	3.37	3.0–3.6
Barents Sea	4.65	
Other pipeline:		
Iran	4.09	3.4–4.1
Turkmenistan	4.49	3.6–4.2
Qatar	4.70	3.7–4.4
Libya		1.5–1.7
Other LNG:		
Libya	2.43–2.71	2.3–2.8
Egypt	2.81	
Nigeria	2.97–3.40	3.1–3.6
Qatar	3.51	3.0–3.5

[a] Ranges represent landfall at different locations.
[b] Ranges represent discount rates of 10% and 15% for transportation costs.

Sources: Jean-Pierre Pauwels, *Géopolitique de l'approvisionnement energétique de l'Union Européenne au XXI siècle* (Brussels: Bruylant, 1994), Table IV.I, pp. 114–15; estimates of Observatoire Meditérranée Européenne, cited in International Energy Agency, *The IEA Natural Gas Security Study* (Paris: OECD, 1995), Table 3.16, p. 67.

possibly Libyan LNG, no new suppliers would seem to have a chance to compete in the present marketplace, let alone, the lower prices which a more competitive market which may bring in the future.

But the figures appear to be based on the full costs of setting up new grassroots production and transmission infrastructure, rather than for fully amortised infrastructure requiring only refurbishment and operating expenditures. This methodology makes Russian gas costs appear particularly high and reinforces a prevailing view held by Western observers during the Soviet period, that Soviet gas was sold at a loss in foreign markets. In a previous publication, this author attempted to compare a number of different estimates of the costs of Russian gas delivered to Europe and came to the conclusion that the cost of Siberian gas delivered to the export border was around $1.00 in 1990/91 dollars.[47]

The reason for quoting the figures in Table 3.15 is not to denigrate the efforts of their authors, but rather to make the (obvious but often neglected) point that cost estimates are highly dependent on the assumptions embodied within them. Costs of future developments depend very much on whether the gas is coming from existing fields, satellites of existing fields, or new grassroots projects (such as Yamal Peninsula and the Barents Sea). And also whether the gas is coming through existing pipelines needing refurbishment, new pipelines which can be built in modular form (i.e. in stages) from field to export border, new pipelines needing to be built in complete (and possibly multiple) strings from field to export border.[48]

More recent, but less comprehensive, figures for costs in the North Sea also suggest figures substantially below those in Table 3.15. Data for unit costs of new gas fields on the United Kingdom Continental Shelf show an interesting picture (Table 3.16). The cost of bringing new gas fields on stream has almost halved over the period 1980–96. Given the expectations of how costs would develop, this can only be regarded as an extraordinary outcome. It is no exaggeration to say that in 1980 such a development would not have been believed possible. This should serve as a timely

---

[47] Stern 1995, pp. 16–17 and 20–27.
[48] Ibid.

Table 3.16: Unit costs[a] of UKCS gas fields, 1996 (pence per therm)

Fields starting production:	
before 1980	8
1980–85	22
1986–90	18
1991–95	14
All fields in production	12.5
Fields under development at year-end 1996	11.5

[a] Including costs of exploration, development and operation during field life, excluding tax, royalty and costs of abortive exploration.

Source: UK Department of Trade and Industry, *The Energy Report: Oil and Gas Resources of the United Kingdom 1997*, Vol. 2, Table 2.4, p. 19.

warning that cost-reduction technology, driven by the commercial require-ments of a lower energy price environment, can produce unexpected results.

Another striking example of cost reduction has been seen in the development of subsea pipelines. A comparison by Statoil of the costs of bringing into operation the Zeepipe and Norfrapipe lines (which have generally similar parameters) shows that total costs for Norfra – built just two years later – had fallen by around 30%.[49]

Another development in the North Sea has also changed the way in which companies view the economics of gas projects. Gas condensate fields (containing a mixture of gas and liquids), and complex fields containing layers of gas and oil, have always been a feature of the industry. What has changed over the past decade has been the ability to develop these fields (through new drilling technology), maximizing the production of liquids – for which the marketing and hence the economic calculations are rather more straightforward. For fields containing both gas and liquids, it is therefore possible for the liquids to 'carry' a significant share of the economic cost, allowing the company to take a more relaxed view of the price at which it will sell the gas. Indeed in fields where the hydrocarbon content is overwhelmingly liquid with a relatively small gas share, the gas could be viewed as a 'free' commodity with all of

---

[49] Jacobsen, loc. cit. (note 5 above).

the production costs (and potentially also transmission costs to shore) covered by revenues from the liquids.

Both general cost reduction and the ability to spread development costs across liquids and gas have had a very significant and positive impact on Norwegian gas development. The development of the Troll field had always been thought to be extremely high cost, requiring gas prices in excess of $40/bbl oil equivalent. In the event, in the contract signed in mid-1986, at a time when world oil prices were at an historic low, and in 1996, when the development came on stream, European gas prices were more than 30% lower in nominal terms (and probably nearer 50% in real terms) than during the negotiations in the mid-1980s.[50] Yet there is no sign that the partners in the Troll field will be 'losing money' from the sale of the gas. Part of the reason for this may be that:

Troll is a 1.2 billion barrel oil field ... developments already approved or under consideration by the end of 1995 put at the Troll partners' disposal 946 million barrels of oil and 288 billion barrels of condensate. The extended flat Troll oil layer once though uneconomic in places is now accessible with modern horizontal drilling and subsea platform technology. The significance to gas markets is that a billion barrel oil bonus goes a long way towards gas price indifference.[51]

These isolated examples from the North Sea can clearly not be generalized across the entire range of gas developments to which Europe may have access over the next decade. The recurring conundrum of costs is that the conventional wisdom of their constant increase – despite its intuitive appeal – has been shown to be seriously flawed in the past, and should be questioned before being invoked for future gas development. It could be an over-statement to claim that the trend is towards constantly falling costs, but that possibility should not be ruled out for the next decade.

---

[50] Norwegian prices to continental European buyers quoted at $3.50–4.50/mmbtu during the period 1984–86, and $2.50-2.80/mmbtu in 1996. Cedigaz, *Natural Gas in the World*, 1987, p. 89 and 1996, p. 127.

[51] 'Message from Norway: Troll is an oil field', *Gas Matters,* September 1996, pp. 1–3.

Lower gas prices: causes and responses

The lower gas prices which have been envisaged are a direct consequence of supply push/demand pull forces. The competition which may result will give gas prices their own dynamic and significantly 'decouple' them from oil product prices to which they have been firmly shackled since the beginning of the European gas business. While this is a credible scenario, it should not be forgotten that oil prices also have their own dynamic, largely driven by supply/demand pressures. If, as is widely foreseen, oil prices weaken and drop below the $16–20/barrel range of the mid- to late 1990s, a significant fall in gas prices would be needed in order merely to keep gas competitive in some of its end-use markets.

A fall in gas prices, whether caused by the development of competitive gas markets or lower oil prices, or both, will raise the question as to whether the level to which they fall will be sufficient to cover marginal costs (of production and transportation) and maintain incentives to explore for (and produce) new supply. Despite the unsatisfactory and fragmentary nature of the data cited in this chapter, it appears that border prices in Continental Europe could fall significantly below $2/mmbtu (1997) with all the major suppliers continuing to cover operating costs. However, if border prices move down to a longer-term equilibrium price of around $2/mmbtu (1997), suppliers with significant gas reserves will need to consider whether they are content to allow their resource to stay in the ground, or whether they will seek ways of commercializing these resources at lower costs (almost certainly with lower margins). Table 3.15 would suggest that at this price level no new gas will be developed and that eventually as Europe 'runs short of gas', prices will rise. This is the scenario favoured by producers, as it fits in with their traditional position that unless buyers are willing to pay higher prices for new gas, producers will refuse to explore for, and develop, gas fields. But there is little historical evidence that such a claim has any foundation in reality, with the exception of the immediate aftermath of a major price fall. In North America where competition (and other developments) caused significant reductions in wellhead prices, exploration and development subsequently recovered and gas fields continued to be developed at much lower prices. In Britain, a strong recovery has yet to be seen in the wake of the collapse of gas prices in 1995. In 1994 and 1995 approval was given for 10 new gas developments, a figure which fell to two in 1996.[52]

If exploration and production companies really believed that gas price expectations were so low that their activities had become redundant, they would logically start to make large numbers of their staff redundant, or move to another part of the world to explore.[53] The fact that companies rarely act in this way suggests that gas exploration and production within and around Europe seems likely to endure at prices lower than those of mid-1997 due to a combination of cost reduction, availability of gas from condensate fields, acceptance of lower margins and incurable producer optimism that prices will be sufficient to warrant new development. Whether at a sustained border price as low as $2.00/mmbtu this would still prove to be the case can only be guessed. This author's guess is that it would.

However, over the next decade, any baseload project which is not robust at a border price around $2.00/mmbtu (1997) may need to be rethought by its investors.[54] Should this type of price environment persist for several years, new suppliers will find other ways of bringing their gas to markets. If they are unwilling or unable to do so, then demand will be choked off and prices will rise. On a longer timescale, up to 2010, it seems entirely possible that all four of the present suppliers to the European market will be able to make significant quantities of additional gas available to Continental European markets at costs (and hence prices) which certainly do not exceed price levels in 1997 (i.e. $2.50–3.00/mmbtu) and will probably be much closer to $2.00 (1997). This goes directly against the conventional wisdom that unless markets are able to offer prices of $3.00–4.50, producers will have no incentive to develop new fields and that long-term security of supply will be jeopardized.

---

[52] UK Department of Trade and Industry, op. cit., 1997, Table 6.1, pp. 48, 53. These are for new offshore gas fields only (i.e. not onshore fields and not incremental projects).

[53] UK Continental Shelf producers did move out of gas exploration during the 1970s when BGC showed no interest in buying gas. The 'problem' for explorers taking a definite decision that gas exploration is not worthwhile is that they may find gas when looking for oil.

[54] The term 'baseload' is important here. It is perfectly possible that niche LNG projects (such as Nigeria LNG and Atlantic/Trinidad) selling into specific markets can remain competitive since they will not necessarily face gas-to-gas competition.

To claim that reserves have already been established, and that more will be discovered and produced to provide gas supplies to Europe, at significantly higher demand levels at lower price levels than experienced in 1997, may appear overly complacent. However, over the past three decades as far as reserves are concerned, and since 1980 as far as prices are concerned, European gas markets have largely reflected those realities; realities which nobody – with the exception of Peter Odell – believed were possible. Nobody can say for sure that the next decade will produce a similar pattern. The proposition which has been advanced in this chapter is that for at least the next five years, and possibly the next decade, the most likely outcome is ample supplies at lower prices.

Conclusions: supply push/demand pull

Market pressures will move European gas markets decisively towards gas-to-gas competition in the period up to 2000. The principal reason for this is the coincidence in timing of a number of major pipeline projects – from Britain, Russia, Algeria, and Norway – all of which will be completed, and/or expanded, in the period 1998–2000, which will allow their owners to move volumes into European markets, additional to those which have already been purchased on long-term contracts, at relatively low cost.

The 'supply push' pressures on European gas markets during the immediate post-1998 period appear very great; but in northwest Europe they appear irresistible and short-term. Existing suppliers have significant quantities of relatively low-cost gas and spare capacity in existing facilities. As such, this is not a new phenomenon. Additional gas supply and spare transmission capacity in facilities have always existed (although the extent of either commodity has been hard to document), but even if the owners of the gas have wished to sell more (which has not always been the case) the owners of the capacity have had strong incentives to restrict its use in order to protect their markets. What is new is that, for the first time, a group of sellers from Britain with both gas and capacity are actively seeking a short-term outlet for gas. While they are not deliberately seeking to break down the current market equilibrium in Continental Europe, they have no significant incentive to preserve it. Traders from Britain and North

America are invading, causing Continental European companies to try and set up similar businesses.

The beginning of a gas trading mentality among the major gas transmission companies has already been demonstrated in the behaviour of Gasunie and British producers. In addition, the German companies Ruhrgas and Wingas aspire to the status of traders as evidenced by their efforts to become suppliers of third party gas to central/east European countries, as the latter try to diversify away from Russian supplies.[55] The aspiration of companies to become gas traders is likely to further undermine the traditional management of European gas markets.

All the major existing suppliers and transmission companies would wish to retain the present traditional gas market system and gas contractual arrangements. However, despite the fact that not all may have publicly acknowledged impending change, all have anticipated the onset of gas-to-gas competition and harbour fears that unless they move to prevent the encroachment of others, they may lose market share to a 'preemptive strike'. These fears appear to be greatest between Russian and Norwegian suppliers in northwest Europe. Competition between the Netra system (owned by established German and Norwegian companies) and Russian gas from the Belarus–Poland system (owned within Germany by Gazprom and Wingas) is likely to be (and arguably has already been) the first head-on clash between major players. The opening up of central/east European gas markets to competition for non-Russian supplies is shaping up to be another major forum for competition. Although none of the major current players is in favour of liberalization, the very expectation that gas-to-gas competition is inevitable places pressure on suppliers to 'get in first' and claim market share. Such moves will of course greatly hasten the onset of liberalization.

Large consumers – in particular power generators and chemical companies – are likely to have the commercial power (by virtue of the size of their demand) to take advantage of low-priced gas on offer, and to solicit such supply, thereby 'pulling' it into the market. If gas companies try to prevent them, they are likely to have:

---

[55] 'Norway's Czech-Mate for Russian gas', *Gas Matters*, April 1997, pp. 1–7.

- the political influence to put pressure on governments to accelerate the liberalization of gas markets, particularly if liberalization of electricity markets is proceeding at a faster pace;
- the financial power to threaten to build new pipelines, and if necessary to implement that threat.

These large consumers may have a strong incentive to break up the existing managed market arrangements in order to achieve lower prices through competition. Individual large customers in specific countries will start the demand–pull for the gas likely to be on offer from suppliers, but two other groups of consumers will rapidly become aware of the results of their success:

- competitors in other countries;
- smaller industrial customers in the same country.

These two groups will sustain the demand–pull pressures such that any strategy on the part of gatekeepers to 'bribe' a small number of very large customers into acquiescence by means of low prices is unlikely to succeed in anything other than the short term. It will be very difficult for governments and gatekeepers to make the case that, despite being aware of gas on offer at attractive prices, industrial customers must continue to purchase from their traditional merchants. If eligibility for direct purchase is made dependent on annual volume thresholds (see Chapters 4 and 5), customers will seek to find ways around this by aggregation of sites, 'marriages of convenience' between companies and other devious means. All in all, it is hard to imagine that customers using 5–10 million cubic metres per year will be willing to wait around until 2010 before they can choose their supplier, simply because this is the best that the European Commission could persuade a qualified majority of member states to agree to at the time the Gas Directive was passed.

This chapter has taken a relatively short-term focus. Five years, and even 10, is a short time for major gas developments, and this analysis therefore stands accused of being overly shortsighted. In the type of market which it has been suggested is likely to evolve in this short term, it is highly unlikely that multibillion dollar greenfield projects – such as gas from the Yamal Peninsula and a pipeline from Iran or Central Asia to Europe – can be developed with traditional long-term contracts containing high take or pay provisions. The standard response is that without such developments, the long-term security of supply for European gas markets will be jeopardized. (Longer-term security of supply is dealt with in Chapter 6.) It is not possible to argue definitively either for or against this proposition, but only to suggest that market players (and potentially governments) may have to grapple with this issue as and when supply availability begins to tail off and prices start to rise. However, what is more likely from a 1998 perspective is that the investors and bankers involved in these projects will need to be more innovative, and take significantly greater risks if they want their projects to get under way over the next decade. In summary, for the next decade, the risk of sitting on unsaleable gas reserves looks much greater than the risk of being unable to obtain access to affordable gas supplies.

Chapter 4

International Institutional Frameworks: The European Union and the Energy Charter

The European Union, the Single Market and liberalization[1]

In the run-up to the completion of the internal market at the end of 1992, energy arrived late on the political agenda and proved a very difficult area for the member states to make any significant progress. The view of the gas and electricity industries was that nothing needed changing – and the involvement of Brussels was neither necessary nor welcome. Some of these views were a reflection of the need to protect substantial profits, others were simply a fear of change. The political view in most member states – aside from mavericks like the British who had already moved a considerable way down the liberalization road – was that a large number of industry and trade union groups would be antagonised, and that the benefits did not appear sufficiently substantial to make such an effort worthwhile. Governments and companies expressed their concerns in the language of security of supply and the need to protect public service obligations.

The chronology shows that the passage of Price Transparency and Gas and Electricity Transit Directives was achieved during the first three years of the Commission's work in this area. The stumbling block was a move towards any kind of serious liberalization. In an attempt to find some common ground, the Commission set up consultative committees for the gas and electricity industries which reported their findings in 1991. Both were inconclusive, simply registering the large amount of disagreement between the Commission and the industry. However, even at that early stage in the process, it was evident that the electricity industry was

---

[1] For the detail of the early debate on the Single Energy Market and the failed Directive, see Jonathan P. Stern, *Third Party Access in European Gas Industries: Regulation-driven or Market-led?* (London: RIIA, 1992).

Box 4.1: EU liberalization initiatives for gas and electricity industries: a chronology

1985:	Single European Act largely excludes energy sector
May 1988:	Publication of the Commission's paper on 'The Internal Energy Market'
July 1990:	Price Transparency Directive enters into force
December 1990:	Electricity Transit Directive enters into force
May 1991:	Gas Transit Directive enters into force
February 1992:	Draft Directive published on 'Common Rules' for gas and electricity industries [exclusive rights, 'unbundling', and 'third party access' (TPA)]
1993:	Parliament pursues concepts of 'negotiated TPA' and 'harmonization' measures
May 1994:	Common Rules Draft Directive is lost with dissolution of Parliament and Commission; new Commission recommences by concentrating on Common Rules Directive for Electricity
February 1997:	Common Rules Directive for Electricity enters into force
December 1997:	Political agreement reached on a Common Rules Directive for Gas

prepared to concede that liberalization could bring efficiencies and advantages to the industry. This allowed the electricity debate to move to the detail of how liberalization could be introduced, and on what timetable. By contrast, many of the established actors in European gas industries still regarded the introduction of liberalization as the equivalent of the end of civilization. They may not have gone quite so far as to claim that its outcome would leave consumers freezing and starving in their homes, but this was the impression they left on their audiences. As far as the Commission was concerned, the gas gatekeepers were the ultimate liberalization refuseniks.

With this degree of industry opposition and little political support, it rapidly became clear that the Draft Directive on 'Common Rules' for gas and electricity (published in February 1992) could not succeed. It is possible that the issues of 'unbundling' (separation of accounts for different functions of integrated companies) and abolition of 'exclusive rights' (to construct facilities, import and export) could have been resolved. But no progress could be made on the question of access to facilities, so called 'third party access' (TPA). Amendments from the

Economic and Social Committee of the Parliament and redrafting by DGXVII produced the concept of 'negotiated TPA' – a four-point plan involving:

- non-discriminatory licensing of construction of production, transmission and distribution facilities;
- negotiated access for 'eligible consumers' defined as industrial with a annual consumption of 100 GWh (electricity) and 25 million cubic metres (gas) and distribution companies;
- separation ('unbundling') of accounts between different activities for vertically integrated undertakings;
- designation of responsibility for transmission operators which would ensure maintenance and development of the system in a given area.

The 1992 Draft Directive was lost with the dissolution of Parliament and the Commission in May 1994. However, the important conclusion from the 1988–94 period was that the gas and electricity industries would need to be separated in terms of liberalization proposals.

The Electricity Directive

The new Commission immediately pursued the concept of 'negotiated third party access' for the electricity industry. While liberalizers were critical of this formulation as insufficient to promote competition, it proved too radical for the French, who, in 1994, countered with their 'single buyer' proposal, a concept which appeared simply to be a defence of the monopoly status quo, and in particular the centralized state-owned French utility structure, utilizing public service and security of supply arguments as reasons for rejecting any rapid or radical change.

At the end of 1995, as the Commission continued its work to harmonize the 'negotiated TPA' proposal with the single buyer approach, the Energy White Paper was published reaffirming the centrality of energy liberalization:

> The prime objective will be to liberalise the internal market for electricity and natural gas. The completion of this objective is central to the development of

general energy policy guidelines which should facilitate the working of the integrated market. (para 4.2.2)

However, it was to be another year before the Electricity Directive was finally adopted.[2] The compromise between the negotiated TPA and single buyer systems is that member states will be allowed to adopt either system as long as they lead to equivalent economic results. The major provisions of the Directive are that:

- integrated companies must provide 'unbundled' (i.e. separate) accounts for each of the different functions (generation, transmission, and distribution);
- access will be allowed for the very largest consumers (more than 100 gigawatt hours per year). A minimum share of the market which must be open to competition will be set and progressively increased over a 6-year period, based on market shares set by the Commission. Consumers falling within the competitive sector will be decided by national governments;
- very little guidance is given regarding the regulation of the industry or on the issue of tariffs. The Directive refers to 'a competent authority' for the resolution of disputes. While tariffs must be non-discriminatory and transparent, there is no guidance regarding the methodology of how they should be calculated;
- the Commission will enforce reciprocity between the two different systems, e.g. a member state will not be able to block access to a customer if that customer would be deemed to be eligible for access in the system of the member state seeking access.

The timetable for implementing the Electricity Directive is relatively relaxed. In 2006 only around one-third of the total EU market is foreseen to be open to competition. The Commission will then review the Directive and consider the case for a further opening of the market.

---

[2] *Concerning Common Rules for the Internal Market in Electricity*, Directive 96/92EC of the European Parliament and of the Council of 19 December 1996, *Official Journal of the European Communities*, No. L 27/20, January 1997.

Box 4.2: Timetable for the Electricity Directive

19 February 1997:	'Implementation date' i.e. date of entry into force
19 February 1999:	Directive must be transposed into national laws (with the exception of Greece, Belgium and Ireland). First market opening based on a 40 GWh threshold becomes legally enforceable
1 January 2000:	Market opening based on a 20 GWh threshold becomes legally enforceable
1 January 2003:	Market opening based on a 9 GWh threshold becomes legally enforceable
1 January 2006:	Commission reviews Directive and considers further opening

The Gas Directive

In the later part of 1996, as the final decisions were being made on the Electricity Directive, a draft proposal for a Gas Directive was circulated by the Irish Presidency of the EU.[3] At that time there was considerable hope that, using a similar blueprint, a Gas Directive could be signed during the first half of 1997 (the Dutch Presidency). Predictably, this proved much more difficult than anticipated. Despite several Dutch attempts at a compromise, no agreement could be reached even though many substantial provisions had been removed from the previous Irish proposal.[4] In July 1997 the Luxembourg Presidency took over a draft which was well advanced, but still had significant areas of disagreement. However, in December 1997 a political agreement was reached, expected to enter into force in mid-1998, taking into account any amendments which may be required by the European Parliament.[5] Assuming this

---

[3] Presidency Compromise Proposal, SN 4325/96, Brussels, 15 October 1996.

[4] Presidency Compromise Proposal for an Amended Proposal for a European Parliament and Council Directive Concerning Common Rules for the Internal Market in Natural Gas, 24 March 1997. Compared with the Irish draft, this proposal no longer included rights of 'eminent domain'; obligations to build transmission capacity on demand; rights of producers and suppliers to gain access to systems to supply their own premises.

[5] This chapter and its appendix take the details from the outcome of the Energy Council meeting of 8 December 1997. This produced a Consolidated Text from the General Secretariat of the Council: *Directive 97/EC of the European Parliament and of the Council Concerning Rules for the Internal Market in Natural Gas*, SN 4930/97, Brussels, 10 December 1997.

occurs without any major reversals, the provisions of the Directive should be transposed into national legislation by the middle of the year 2000.

The Gas Directive is similar to its electricity forerunner, with one very important difference. The basic distinction in gas is that member states will have to make a choice between a system of 'negotiated access' and 'regulated access'. (The 'single buyer' concept does not appear in the Gas Directive.) 'Negotiated access' would require transportation companies to negotiate 'voluntary commercial agreements in good faith' with eligible customers wishing to use the system. 'Regulated access' would give eligible customers the right to use transportation systems on payment of published, regulated tariffs.

Appendix 4.1 contains the detail of the Gas Directive. Here, we review the most significant obstacles to the passage of the Directive during the 1996–7 discussions. Four issues were paramount.

(1) The degree and speed of competition

A gradual opening of markets was always foreseen, but opening up all users with an annual consumption greater than 25 million cubic metres would constitute a massive share of the total gas market in some countries, but only a modest share in others (see Table 4.1). The final proposal is for a combined minimum and maximum market opening to competition. A minimum percentage of the market must be opened on the basis of eligible consumers, with the member state retaining discretion to limit that percentage if it would exceed a defined maximum level. Article 18 (paras 3–5) requires a minimum opening of the market of at least 20% of the annual gas consumption of the national gas market. This will increase to 28% five years after the entry into force of the directive and 33% five years later. But if the definition of eligible customers results in an initial opening greater than 30%, the member state may modify the definition of eligible customers in a way that reduces the market opening to a maximum 30%; a figure which increases to 38% five years after the Directive comes into force and to 43% five years later.

Table 4.1: Share of total consumption of all power generators, 1996 (%)

	Industrial demand thresholds in million cubic metres/year		
	> 25	>15	>5
Austria	50.2	53.1	58.2
Belgium	39.3	42.7	47.1
Denmark	61.5	62.1	65.0
France	19.6	24.5	31.6
Finland	91.0	92.7	93.8
Germany	31.0	35.0	44.0[a]
Greece	0	0	0
Ireland	75.0	77.0	81.0
Italy	38.0	38.0	44.0
Luxembourg	43.4	48.7	48.2
The Netherlands	40.5	41.5	42.5
Portugal	0	0	0
Spain[b]	29.0	42.0	80.0
Sweden	39.2	31.1	35.3
United Kingdom	28.8	31.1	35.3
EU15[c]	33.2	36.4	42.3

[a] Estimate.
[b] CHP included in industrial use.
[c] Weighted average based on Eurostat figures for total gas consumption in 1996.
Source: Annex to EU Gas Directive.

(2) Customers eligible to request access

Article 18(2) designates eligible customers in two categories:

(i) gas-fired power generators, irrespective of their annual consumption level; however, and in order to safeguard the balance of their electricity market, the Member States may introduce a threshold, which may not exceed the level envisaged for other final customers, for the eligibility of combined heat and power producers.

(ii) other final customers consuming more than 25 million cubic metres per year on a consumption site basis. This threshold is reduced to 15 million cubic metres/year five years after the Directive comes into force and 5 million cubic metres/year five years later.

(3) How to safeguard current take or pay contracts

Article 25 of the Directive allows companies to request a 'derogation' (i.e. temporary exemption) from access provisions if it encounters (or considers it would encounter) 'serious financial difficulties because of its take or pay commitments'. Companies will have to apply to their governments or a 'designated competent authority' (see below) and the latter will be required to notify the Commission. Article 25(2) then states that:

> Within four weeks from its receipt of this notification, the Commission may request that the Member State or the designated competent authority concerned may amend or withdraw the decision to grant a derogation. If the Member State or the designated competent authority concerned does not follow this request within a period of four weeks, a final decision shall be taken expeditiously in accordance with procedure 1 of Article 2 of Council Decision 87/373 of 13 July 1987 laying down procedures for the exercise of implementing powers conferred on the Commission.

(4) How to protect 'emergent markets'

'Emergent markets' had to be defined and allowed a derogation, for a limited period. Article 26 defines emergent markets and the conditions under which derogations apply as follows:

> Member States not directly connected to the interconnected system of any other Member State and having only one main external supplier may derogate ... A supplier having a market share of more than 75% shall be considered a main supplier. This derogation will automatically expire from the moment at least one of these conditions no longer applies. Any such derogation shall be notified to the Commission ... This derogation will automatically expire from the moment the Member State no longer qualifies as an emergent market.

Not only member states but regions within individual countries may be eligible for derogations:

> Where implementation of this Directive would cause substantial problems in a geographically limited area of a Member State, in particular concerning the

development of the transmission infrastructure, and with a view to encouraging investments, the Member State may apply to the Commission for a temporary derogation ... A derogation may only be granted if no gas infrastructure has been established in this area, or has been so established for less than 10 years. The temporary derogation may not exceed ten years after the first supply of gas in the area. (paras 3 and 4)

Other issues

At a late stage in the negotiations on the Directive, the question of access to upstream pipelines and facilities entered into the discussions. Regarded by some as the 'revenge' of non-producing EU nations on producers (particularly the British who had pushed very hard for liberalization measures), Article 23 allows that the eligible customers described earlier:

wherever they are located, are able to obtain access to upstream pipeline networks, including facilities supplying technical services incidental to such access ... except for the parts of the such networks and facilities which are used for local production operations at the site of a field where the gas is produced.

In other respects, the Gas Directive is similar to its electricity counterpart. It contains a similar provision (Article 12) that vertically integrated companies must provide separate accounts for the functions of transmission, distribution, and storage; and where appropriate consolidated accounts for non-gas activities.

Regulatory issues

Another similarity is in the treatment of regulation where Article 22 – the only article which deals specifically with regulation – consists of a single four-line paragraph:

Member States shall create appropriate and efficient mechanisms for regulation, control and transparency so as to avoid any abuse of a dominant position, in particular to the detriment of consumers, and any predatory behaviour. These mechanisms shall take account of the provisions of the Treaty, and in particular Article 86 thereof.

In terms of negotiating access conditions, the Directive places regulation in the context of dispute resolution in Article 21:

> Member States shall designate a competent authority, which must be independent of the parties, to expeditiously settle disputes concerning negotiations and refusal of access within the scope of this Directive. The competent authority shall present its conclusions without delay, if possible within twelve weeks of the introduction of the dispute. Recourse to this authority shall be without prejudice to the exercise of rights of appeal under Community law.
>
> In the event of cross-border disputes, the dispute settlement authority shall be (the one) covering the system of the (company) which refuses use of or access to the systems. Where in cross-border disputes, more than one such authority cover the system concerned, the authorities shall consult with a view to securing that the provisions of this Directive are applied consistently.

There is nothing in the Directive which gives any guidance as to the detail of tariff methodology or design, or of access conditions. Nor is there any attempt to define market behaviour which may be considered 'predatory', or negotiating behaviour which could be construed as failing the test of 'good faith' or 'abuse of a negotiating position', In terms of regulatory institutions, the Directive speaks of a 'competent authority', without any suggestion of the type of competence which may be required. The only reference to institutional relationships is in the context of dispute resolution in the upstream sector where the authority is required to be 'independent of the parties'.

The Directive allows for very few instances in which the European Commission itself is allowed to perform any regulatory functions. Where the Commission has a role, it is principally in terms of approving derogations which may be allowed in respect of emergent countries or regions (Article 26), and take or pay contracts (Article 25). Articles 21 and 23 dealing with access are very specific in limiting issues to national dispute resolution authorities, thereby excluding any role for the Commission. The only

Box 4.3 Estimated timetable for the Gas Directive[6]

February 1998:	Common position reached by member states
Mid-1998:	'Implementation date' or date of entry into force
Mid-2000:	Directive must be transposed into national laws (with the exception of those countries and regions granted derogations). First market opening for consumers with an annual consumption in excess of 25MMcm – equating to a minimum of 20–30% of a country's national consumption – becomes legally enforceable
Mid-2003:	Market opening for consumers with an annual consumption in excess of 15MMcm – equating to a minimum 38% of a country's national consumption – becomes legally enforceable
Mid-2008:	Market opening for customers with an annual consumption in excess of 5MMcm – equating to a minimum 43% of a country's national consumption – becomes enforceable.

other contexts in which a role is allowed for the Commission is under crisis conditions (Article 24) and to adjudicate in potential disputes between a company operating within one system of access, but requesting access in a member state operating the alternative system (Article 19).

Conclusions

After nearly a decade of debate on a gas liberalization directive, the Commission finally reached a political agreement at the end of 1997. It has not only been an extremely long and hard road, but also the resulting Directive is a relatively weak document in comparison to the hopes and aspirations of the late 1980s. This general outcome is largely attributable to the degree of opposition from gas companies and the support which they mustered from their governments. But two of the crucial battles – specification of methodologies for setting pipeline tariffs and charges for other services, and any regulatory basis for enforcing competition and access provisions – were lost in the early 1990s, even prior to the failure of the 1992 Draft Directive. The insistence on the principle of subsidiarity

---

[6] The actual dates will depend on the final 'implementation date' which will be when the Directive 'enters into force' – 20 days after its publication in the *Official Journal of the European Communities* (Article 30). This will depend on the speed of its passage through the European Parliament.

removed any basis for discussion of detailed regulation or tariff methodologies. From an institutional perspective, the use of the term 'competent authority' combined with a concentration on 'settlement of disputes', gives the impression of an arbitration body, rather than a specialized regulatory authority. The stipulation that the competent authority must be 'independent of the parties' could have interesting connotations in the upstream sector, where governments tend to be among the interested parties and, in the Dutch and Norwegian sectors, are major owners of gas fields and pipeline networks. Thus, it is only by inference that the Directive makes any suggestion that regulation should be independent of government. How to erect their own regulation and tariff superstructures, on the very low base provided by the Directive, will be entirely at the discretion of member states, and (as we shall see in Chapter 7) this is possibly the major reason why, in many countries, progress will not be rapid.

If competition is not proceeding satisfactorily, or if companies have specific complaints that they are not receiving protection from national regulatory authorities, both the Commission and companies have the option of taking cases to the European Court. However, past experience suggests major drawbacks to this course of action:

- the time required for these cases to be heard invariably stretches into years. During this period, the fast-moving market situation may render the specific commercial opportunity irrelevant to the company, not to mention the executive time and expense involved in bringing the case;
- the European Court has, in the past, seemed relatively unsympathetic to the Commission's attempted demonopolisation measures and unwilling to legislate in situations where it believes that the Council and the member states should rule on a political solution.[7]

Another reason why progress towards liberalization will not be rapid is that the definition of eligible customers and minimum market openings

---

[7] See for example the Court's ruling on statutory energy import and export monopolies. Leigh Hancher, 'Import/export ruling: Court favours Member State discretion on PSOs', *Financial Times, EC Energy Monthly*, November 1997, pp. 7–10.

falls some way short of ensuring that this percentage of the market *must* be taken over by competitors to the established merchant transmission companies. Barriers to entry could ensure that nothing happens in some member states, particularly those where governments have no enthusiasm for liberalization, for at least the first five years following implementation. This is the distinction between 'letting markets work' and 'making markets work', which was seen in the early years of the British experiment. If barriers to entry are sufficiently high to prevent change, then strong government and regulatory commitment to change will be required. If that commitment is absent, little is likely to happen quickly. However, in countries where electricity liberalization is progressing rapidly – either due to the Directive or for other reasons – the power sector may drive gas liberalization because of the synergies between the two in both gas-fired power generation, and joint electricity/gas distribution.

These conclusions are not intended to suggest that the Directive is not, and will not be a worthwhile piece of legislation in favour of liberalization. The Directive provides both a yardstick by which member states can measure their progress, and excludes indefinite procrastination by those governments which oppose liberalization. As we shall see in Chapter 5, anticipation of the Directive has already caused significant changes in the organization and behaviour of a number of gas industries. But (as with all other EU legislation) its effectiveness will depend on how it is transposed into national legislation and then interpreted by member states. While the effect of the Directive is likely to be positive, in itself it falls far short of being a significant driver for liberalization in European gas markets. What will happen increasingly will be specific developments in individual countries.

The Energy Charter Treaty and gas transit issues[8]

The concept of a European energy charter was advanced by Dutch Prime Minister Lubbers at the 1990 European Council Meeting in Dublin. The

---

[8] For background see Julia Doré and Robert De Bauw, *The Energy Charter Treaty: Origins, Aims and Prospects* (London: RIIA, 1995); for the text see *The Energy Charter Treaty and Related Documents* (Energy Charter Secretariat, Brussels, 1996).

original concept was to create a formal cooperation agreement between western Europe, eastern Europe and the former Soviet Union, whereby investments in, and transit of energy resources would be guaranteed by all parties to the charter, thereby lessening commercial risks for investors and energy importers.

In December 1991, 51 states, including virtually every European country, all the states of the former Soviet Union, and other non-European members of the OECD (the United States, Canada, Japan and Australia), agreed the European Energy Charter. However, by 1991 both the geographical context and the substance of the Charter had significantly changed. The addition of non-European signatories had widened the geographical focus, while the substance of the Charter had broadened to include environmental dimensions of energy trade and in particular energy efficiency.[9]

Three years after agreeing the European Energy Charter, the Energy Charter Treaty (ECT), and a Protocol on Energy Efficiency and Environmental Aspects were signed in December 1994 by an overwhelming majority of relevant countries. The Treaty came into force on 16 April 1998, having been ratified by the necessary 30 countries (Table 4.2). Ratification had not yet been achieved by key countries such as the Russian Federation and Ukraine (the inability of the United States and Canada to sign and ratify being less relevant), but there were reasonable prospects of a satisfactory outcome in both cases.

Table 4.2: Countries which had ratified the Energy Charter Treaty by January 1998

Albania	Denmark	Latvia	Slovenia
Armenia	Finland	Liechtenstein	Spain
Austria	Georgia	Luxembourg	Sweden
Azerbaijan	Germany	Moldova	Switzerland
Bulgaria	Greece	The Netherlands	Tajikistan
Croatia	Kazakstan	Portugal	Turkmenistan
Cyprus	Kyrgyzstan	Romania	United Kingdom
Czech Republic	Italy	Slovakia	Uzbekistan

Source: Energy Charter Secretariat, Brussels, 16 January 1998.

---

[9] Also included in the original conception was a nuclear power protocol but this failed because of insufficient support.

The ECT is concerned with a range of energy and energy-related environmental activities, but for the purposes of this study, the transit provisions are the most important. The ECT is potentially very significant in that it would require contracting parties to transit gas across their territories for other parties on terms which, if they could not be agreed between the parties, would be subject to binding dispute resolution. If signatories wished to argue that their facilities were insufficient or unavailable, they would be required to give a convincing and detailed account of these problems in a spirit of cooperation in order to reach a solution. The opening paragraph of the transit provisions contained in Article 7 of the Treaty states that:

> Each Contracting Party shall take the necessary measures to facilitate the transit of energy ... consistent with the principle of freedom of transit and without distinction as to the origin ... ownership ... or discrimination as to pricing ... and without imposing any unreasonable delays, restrictions or charges.

The usual excuse of insufficient capacity is dealt with in para. 4:

> In the event that transit ... cannot be achieved on commercial terms ... the contracting parties should not place obstacles in the way of new capacity being established.

If parties cannot agree (para. 7) the issues will first be referred to the Secretary General who, within 30 days will appoint a conciliator. If within 90 days of being appointed, the conciliator has failed to reach agreement then a resolution procedure will be recommended, and interim tariffs and other conditions will be instituted. Crucially during this period, Article 6 states that:

> A Contracting Party ... shall not, in the event of a dispute ... interrupt or reduce ... the existing flow of energy ... prior to the conclusion of dispute resolution procedures ... except where this is specifically provided for in a contract or other agreement ... or permitted in accordance with the conciliator's decision.

The Charter process has been subjected to a number of criticisms by governments and companies:

- initially the Charter was criticized as an attempt to monopolize Russian resources for west European consumption;
- individual governments such as the United States, Canada and Norway will probably stay out of the Treaty for a range of reasons including internal politics, complications arising from national legislation, and particularly stringent definitions of national sovereignty;
- energy companies were either:
  - hostile to the Charter on the grounds that it would introduce access to pipelines 'through the back door'; or create 'another level of bureaucracy';
  - indifferent on the grounds that the commercial contracts which they would sign would supersede any provisions offered by the Charter.

Most of these arguments have been defused or dropped, and none of the potential non-signatories will affect the significance and usefulness of the Charter as far as the future of European gas markets is concerned. But the inclusion of both the Russian Federation and Ukraine is crucial, with Belarus and Turkey also important countries yet to ratify.

The relationship of the ECT to the liberalization of energy markets is an interesting one. So politically sensitive was the issue of liberalization and access to pipelines when the Charter was being negotiated, that in order for Continental European governments to agree the text, a quasi disclaimer was inserted into the Charter's objectives to the effect that the Charter 'does not impose privatization or third party access'.[10] Despite the definition of the term 'transit' having been specifically distanced from the notion of liberalized access to networks, the concluding document of the December 1991 agreement notes that:[11]

> The signatories recognise that transit of energy products through their territories is essential for the liberalisation of trade in energy products ... They stress the importance of ... interconnection ... To this end, they will ensure the compatibility of technical specifications governing the installation and operation of such networks.

---

[10] Energy Charter Secretariat, op. cit., para. 5 of 'Objectives', p. 13. The same paragraph reaffirms national sovereignty over resources and the rights of governments to determine policies in relation to their resources.

[11] Ibid., Title II Implementation, para. 3, p. 222.

The crucial element of the Charter for gas markets is that it is the only institution with a sufficiently wide geographical membership to allow a resolution of existing transit problems, and future gas transit issues, both between the countries of the former Soviet Union, and between those countries and those within the European space. The other existing gas transit agreement is the 1991 EU Transit Directive.[12] The CIS countries have signed a transit agreement relating to oil and oil products, but not to gas.[13] However, even the existence and harmonization of CIS and EU agreements would still leave a geographical/ institutional gap in terms of central and east European countries. This is the strength of the Energy Charter's geographical reach.

While much of the gas transit in Europe has been unproblematic, some has not. In the post-Soviet era, gas transit has held up much better than could reasonably have been expected. Yet (as we saw in Chapter 3) there have been significant problems in the transit of Russian gas through Ukraine to a range of European countries. For the future, the apparent refusal of Gazprom to transit gas from Central Asian countries – especially Turkmenistan and Kazakstan (but not excluding Uzbekistan) – through Russia to European countries is a significant issue which could be addressed within the framework of the Charter. Also the determination of Gazprom to create an undersea route for a new pipeline to Turkey suggests its lack of confidence in relying on a less expensive route through the Caucasus (Georgia and Armenia).

As far as Russian gas through Ukraine is concerned, the problems which were experienced in the immediate aftermath of the break-up of the Soviet Union have lessened in the period since 1995. However, these problems have not gone away, and no long-term basis has been established which would enable the future to become more predictable. As far as transit of gas from Turkmenistan and Kazakstan is concerned, the refusal of Russia's Gazprom to countenance the transit for gas which would then compete with Russian gas in European markets is entirely logical from a

---

[12] Council Directive of 31 May 1991, *Official Journal of the European Communities*, No. L147/37, June 1991.

[13] *Agreement on Realisation of Coordinated Policy in the Sphere of Crude Oil and Oil Products Transit through High Pressure Transmission Lines*, Moscow, 12 April 1996.

commercial standpoint.[14] However, it is fundamentally contrary to the terms of the Treaty and is an example of the type of anti-competitive behaviour by merchant transmission companies which has been a hallmark of the European gas market over the past decades.

The centrality and the conflicting interests of Gazprom (and the Russian government) in facilitating transit for these, potentially interlocking, sets of trades is particularly interesting. In the case of ensuring transit westward (through Ukraine and other countries), it would benefit the Russian side enormously to have a legally enforceable transit regime with rapid and agreed international dispute settlement procedures. Indeed the existence of such a regime might in itself serve as a guarantee that it would never need to be invoked, and would give significant security comfort to European customers of Russian gas. It is not clear that Gazprom would consider this guarantee to be worth the risk of the potential competition which could be unleashed by allowing the construction of new pipelines (probably alongside existing pipelines) for the transit of Central Asian gas to Europe.[15] However, given that in the future, Central Asian gas could provide a low-cost addition to Russian gas supplies, Russian ratification could be viewed as a means of solving a current problem (Ukraine) while not necessarily conceding any crucial commercial advantage.

The ratification of the Russian and Ukrainian governments is an essential first step for the ECT to assume much greater relevance for the future of European gas markets. Without Russian and Ukrainian ratification, the provisions of the EU Transit Directive will probably remain the benchmark by which these issues are judged. But EU membership, even with its foreseen enlargement, remains far too limited a geographical context for transit within the European gas arena. The geographical reach of the existing ECT signatories – with the ultimate addition of North African countries – will be necessary to provide the

---

[14] 'Gazprom declines Turkmen and Kazakh gas outlets to the West', *Gas Matters*, September 1997, p. ix.

[15] From Central Asia 'transit' would probably involve carriage in Russian and Ukrainian pipelines to the western part of Ukraine. Thereafter it would require the building of new capacity between western Ukraine and European customers.

institutional framework to address current and emerging problems. For gas transit in the East Asian region, China, Mongolia and Korea will need to be added to the signatories in order to provide an appropriate framework for dealing with the emerging gas market in that region.[16]

Distinctions between 'transit' and 'access' are likely to become less easy to identify in the future. For as long as transit can only be requested by owners of high-pressure pipeline systems – which are named in the EU Transit Directive and may eventually be named in the ECT – the two concepts can be separated. However, if it can be represented that this is a discriminatory regime by which owners of high-pressure pipelines can gain access to networks which can be denied to others, there may be legal pressure for change.

Whether the ECT will succeed in providing a workable and enforceable transit regime remains uncertain. The Treaty has the membership and the remit to play an extremely important role, but ratification by the Russian Federation and Ukraine remains crucial. With these two countries on board, the Treaty could play a central role in facilitating gas supply and maintaining gas security from and through the countries of the former Soviet Union. As far as its practical powers to enforce transit are concerned, it is difficult to disagree with Roggenkamp's conclusion that:

> Ultimately the practical impact of Article 7 of the ECT not only depends on enactment in national legislation but also on the working of the various dispute settlement procedures. Therefore it remains to be seen whether this provision will provide the rules necessary to actually achieve transit, or whether, like Article V of the GATT, it will remain a dead letter.[17]

However, European gas markets include a large geographical space over which European Union rules and directives can never provide more than helpful guidance. If parties are genuinely seeking an international legal code with enforceable dispute resolution procedures, the ECT is the only existing framework in which they can place their trust.

---

[16] Keun-Wook Paik, 'Towards a north east Asian energy charter', *Energy Policy*, Vol. 20, No. 5, pp. 433–43.

[17] Martha M. Roggenkamp, 'Transit of networkbound energy: a new phenomenon? Transit examined from the Barcelona Transit Convention to the Energy Charter Treaty', *World Competition*, Vol. 19, No. 2, December 1995, pp. 119–46

Appendix 4.1 *The Gas Directive**

The Gas Directive is organized into seven chapters. What follow are extracts from the Directive that are particularly relevant to this study.

Chapter I focuses on the scope and definitions of terms used in the Directive. The most important of these is the term 'natural gas undertaking' which means:

> any legal or natural person carrying out at least one of the following functions: production, transmission, distribution, supply, purchase and storage of natural gas, including liquefied natural gas, and which is responsible for the commercial, technical and/or maintenance tasks related to those functions, but shall not include final customers.

Included at a late stage of the negotiations was the separate identification of 'upstream pipeline networks' (Article 2(2)): 'any pipeline or network of pipelines operated and/or constructed as part of an oil or gas production project, or used to convey natural gas from one or more such projects to a processing plant or terminal or final coastal landing terminal'.

Chapter II is entitled *General rules for the organisation of the sector*. Article 3(2) entitles member states to:

> impose on natural gas undertakings, in the general economic interest, public service obligations which may relate to security including security of supply, regularity, quality and price of supplies and to environmental protection. Such obligations must be clearly defined, transparent, non-discriminatory and verifiable … Member States which so wish may introduce the implementation of long term planning, taking into account the possibilities of third parties seeking access to the system.

Article 3(3) allows Member States to decide:

> not to apply the provisions of Article 4 with respect to distribution insofar as the application of these provisions would obstruct the performance, in law or in fact, of the obligations imposed on natural gas undertakings in the general economic interest and insofar as the development of trade would not be affected to such an extent as would be contrary to the interests of the Community. The interests of the Community include, inter alia, competition with regard to eligible customers in accordance with this Directive.

Article 4 requires non-discriminatory licensing of companies by member states or 'any competent authority they designate':

- to build and operate pipelines and other facilities;
- to supply gas as well as to wholesale customers.

Article 4(3) requires member states to:

---

* This appendix is based on the text of the Energy Council meeting of 8 December 1997. This produced a Consolidated Text from the General Secretariat of the Council: *Directive 97/EC of the European Parliament and of the Council Concerning Rules for the Internal Market in Natural Gas*, SN 4930/97, Brussels, 10 December 1997.

ensure that the reasons for any refusal to grant an authorisation are objective and non-discriminatory and are given to the applicant. Reasons for such refusals shall be forwarded to the Commission for information. Member States shall establish a procedure enabling the applicant to appeal against such refusals.

Article 4(4) gives further protection:

> For the protection of newly supplied areas and efficient operation generally ... Member States may decline to grant a further authorisation to build and operate distribution pipeline systems in any particular area once such pipeline systems have been, or are, proposed to be built in that area and if existing or proposed capacity is not saturated.

The combination of the provisions in Articles 3 and 4 gives member states the right – demanded by France – largely to exclude the distribution sector from competition.

Article 5 concerns technical compatibility of systems:

> Member States shall ensure that technical rules establishing the minimum technical design and operational requirements for the connection to the system of LNG facilities, storage facilities, other transmission or distribution systems, and direct lines, are developed and made available. These requirements shall ensure the inter-operability of systems and shall be objective and non-discriminatory.

Chapter III concerns transmission, storage and LNG. Article 7 requires that companies must:

(1) operate, maintain and develop under economic conditions secure, reliable and efficient transmission, storage and/or LNG facilities, with due regard to the environment;

(2) not discriminate between system users or classes of system users, particularly in favour of related undertakings;

(3) provide [to other companies] sufficient information to ensure that the transport and storage of natural gas can take place in a manner compatible with the secure and efficient operation of the interconnected system.

Article 8 concerns the safeguarding of commercially sensitive information.

Chapter IV concerns distribution and supply and Articles 9, 10 and 11 simply repeat, for distribution, the obligations contained in Articles 7 and 8.

Chapter V concerns unbundling and transparency of accounts. Article 12 gives:

> Member States or any competent authority they designate, including the dispute resolution authorities [see Article 21(2) and Article 23(3)] ... the right of access to the accounts of ... [companies] ... which they need to consult in carrying out their functions ... [Authorities] ... shall preserve confidentiality of commercially sensitive information ... [but] ... Member States may introduce exemptions from the principle of confidentiality if this is necessary for the competent authorities to carry out their functions.

Article 13 concerns the keeping of accounts by gas companies, the publication of accounts and the form in which different activities shall be accounted. In particular, para 3 states that:

> integrated [companies] shall, in their internal accounting, keep separate accounts for their natural gas transmission, distribution and storage activities, and, where appropriate, consolidated

accounts for non-gas activities, as they would be required to do if the activities in question were carried out by separate undertakings, with a view to avoiding discrimination, cross-subsidisation and distortion of competition. These internal accounts shall include a balance sheet and a profit and loss account for each activity. Where ... access to the system is on the basis of a single charge for both transmission and distribution, the accounts for transmission and distribution may be combined.

Significantly, companies are not require to account separately for production activities.

Chapter VI concerns access to the system. Article 14 allows member states to select either negotiated or regulated access as long as 'both procedures shall operate in accordance with objective, transparent and non-discriminatory criteria'.

Article 15 defines the terms of negotiated access:

(1) Member States shall take the necessary measures for [gas companies] or eligible customers either inside or outside the territory covered by the interconnected system to be able to negotiate access to the system so as to conclude supply contracts with each other on the basis of voluntary commercial agreements. The parties are to be obliged to negotiate access to the system in good faith.

(2) The contracts for access to the system must be negotiated with the relevant natural gas undertakings. Member States shall require natural gas undertakings to publish their main commercial conditions for the use of the system within the first year following the implementation of this Directive and on an annual basis every year thereafter.

Article 16 defines regulated access:

Member States opting for a procedure of regulated access, shall take the necessary measures to give natural gas undertaking and eligible customers either inside or outside the territory covered by the interconnected system a right of access to the system, on the basis of published tariffs and/or other terms and obligations for use of that system. This right of access for eligible customers may be given by enabling them to enter into supply contracts with competing gas undertakings other than the owner and/or operator of the system of a related undertaking.

Article 17 deals with the basis on which access may be refused:

(1) Natural gas undertakings may refuse access to the system on the basis of lack of capacity or where access to the system would prevent them from carrying out the public service obligations ... which are assigned to them or on the basis of serious economic and financial difficulties with take or pay contracts having regard to Article 25 ... Duly substantiated reasons must be given for such a refusal.

(2) Member States may take the measures necessary to ensure that the natural gas undertaking refusing access to the system on the basis of lack of capacity or a lack of connection shall make the necessary enhancements as far as it is economical to do so or when a potential customer is willing to pay for it. In circumstances where Member States apply paragraph 4 of Article 4 (see above), Member States shall take such measures.

Article 18 deals with customers eligible to request access:

(2) Member States shall take the necessary measures to ensure that at least the following customers are designated as eligible customers:
   - gas fired power generators, irrespective of their annual consumption level; however, and in order to safeguard the balance of their electricity market, the Member States may introduce a threshold, which may not exceed the level envisaged for other final customers, for the eligibility of combined heat and power producers. Such thresholds shall be notified to the Commission.
   - other final customers consuming more than 25 million cubic metres per year (MMcm/year) on a consumption site basis. This threshold is reduced to 15 MMcm/year five years after the Directive comes into force and 5 MMcm/year five years later.

(3) Member States shall ensure that the definition of eligible customers … will result in an opening of the market equal to at least 20% of the total annual gas consumption of the national gas market.

(4) The percentage mentioned in paragraph 3 shall increase to 28% of the total annual gas consumption of the national gas market five years after the entry into force of this Directive, and to 33% of the total annual gas consumption of the national gas market ten years after the entry into force of this Directive.

(5) If the definition of eligible customers … results in a market opening of more than 30% of the total annual gas consumption of the national gas market, the Member State concerned may modify the definition of eligible customers to the extent that the opening of the market is reduced to 30% of more of the total annual consumption of the national gas market. Member States shall modify the definition of eligible customers in a balanced manner, not creating specific disadvantages for certain types or classes of eligible customers, but taking into account existing market structures.

(6) Member States shall take the following measures to ensure that the opening of their natural gas market will be increased over a period of ten years:
   - the threshold set in paragraph 2 … for eligible customers other than gas fired power generators, shall be reduced to 15 million cubic metres per year on a consumption site basis five years after the entry into force of this Directive, and to 5 million cubic metres per year on a consumption site basis ten years after the entry into force of this Directive.
   - the percentage mentioned in paragraph 5 shall increase to 38% of the total annual gas consumption of the national gas market five years after the entry into force of this Directive and to 43% … ten years after the entry into force.

(7) In respect of emergent markets, the gradual opening of this Article shall start to apply from the date the derogation expires.

(8) Distribution undertakings, if not already specified as eligible customers … will have the legal capacity to contract for natural gas in accordance with Articles 15 and 16 for the volume of natural gas being consumed by their customers designated as eligible within their distribution system, in order to supply those customers.

(9) Member States shall publish by 31 January of each year the criteria for the definition of eligible customers … This information, together will all other appropriate information to justify the fulfilment of market opening under this Article will be sent to the

Commission ... The Commission may request a Member State to modify its specifications if they create obstacles to the correct application of the Directive as regards the good functioning of the internal natural gas market. If the Member State concerned does not follow this request within a period of three months, a final decision will be taken in accordance with ... procedures for the exercise of implementing powers conferred on the Commission.

Article 19 takes into account reciprocity between those operating systems of regulated and negotiated access: this is identical to the provisions of the Electricity Directive:

(1) To avoid imbalance in the opening of gas markets during the period referred to in Article 28:
  (a) contracts for the supply of gas under the provisions of Articles 15, 16 and 17 with an eligible customer in the system of another Member State shall not be prohibited if the customer is considered as eligible in both systems involved;
  (b) in cases where transactions as described in (a) are refused because of the customer being eligible in only one of the two systems, the Commission may oblige, taking into account the situation in the market and the common interest, the refusing party to execute the requested gas supply at the request of the Member State where the eligible customer is located.
(2) ... the Commission shall review the application of paragraph 1(b) on the basis of market developments taking into account the common interest. In the light of experience gained, the Commission shall evaluate this situation and report on possible imbalance in the opening of gas markets with regard to this paragraph.

Article 20 deals with the construction of 'direct lines' i.e. pipelines complementary to the interconnected system.

(1) Member States shall take the necessary measures to enable:
  – natural gas undertakings established within their territory to supply the customers described in Article 18 ... through a direct line.
  – any such eligible customers within their territory to be supplied through a direct line by natural gas undertakings.
(2) Member States must provide objective, transparent and non-discriminatory criteria for authorisations to construct and operate direct lines.
(3) Member States may make authorisations to construct a direct line subject either to the refusal of system access on the basis of Article 17 or to the opening of a dispute settlement procedure under Article 21.

Article 21 deal with disputes over access to the system:

(1) Member States shall ensure that the parties negotiate access to the system in good faith and that none of them abuses its negotiating position to prevent the successful outcome of those negotiations.
(2) Member States shall designate a competent authority, which must be independent of the parties, to expeditiously settle disputes concerning negotiations and refusal of access

within the scope of this Directive. The competent authority shall present its conclusions without delay or if possible within twelve weeks of the introduction of the dispute. Recourse to this authority shall be without prejudice to the exercise of rights of appeal under Community law.

(3) In the event of cross-border disputes, the dispute settlement authority shall be (the one) covering the system of the natural gas undertaking which refuses use of or access to the systems. Where in cross-border disputes, more than one such authority covers the system concerned, the authorities shall consult with a view to securing that the provisions of this Directive are applied consistently.

Article 22 deals with regulation:

Member States shall create appropriate and efficient mechanisms for regulation, control and transparency so as to avoid any abuse of a dominant position, in particular to the detriment of consumers, and any predatory behaviour. These mechanisms shall take account of the provisions of the Treaty, and in particular Article 86 thereof.

Article 23 deals with upstream pipeline networks:

(1) Member States shall take the necessary measures to ensure that natural gas undertakings and customers required to be eligible under Article 18, wherever they are located, are able to obtain access to upstream pipeline networks, including facilities supplying technical services incidental to such access ... except for the parts of such networks and facilities which are used for local production operations at the site of a field where the gas is produced. The measures shall be notified to the Commission in accordance with the provisions of Article 29.

(2) Such access shall be provided in a manner determined by the Member States in accordance with the relevant legal instruments. Member States shall apply the objectives of fair and open access, achieving a competitive market in natural gas and avoiding any abuse of a dominant position, taking into account security and regularity of supplies, capacity which is or can reasonably be made available, and environmental protection. The following may be taken into account:

   (a) the need to refuse access where there is an incompatibility of technical specifications which cannot be reasonably overcome;

   (b) the need to avoid difficulties which cannot be reasonably overcome and could prejudice the efficient, current and planned future production of hydrocarbons, including that from fields of marginal economic viability;

   (c) the need to respect the duly substantiated reasonable needs of the owner or operator of the upstream pipeline network for the transport and processing of gas and the interests of all other users of the upstream pipeline network or relevant processing or handling facilities who may be affected; and

   (d) the need to apply their laws and administrative procedures, in conformity with Community law, for the grant of authorisation for production or upstream development.

(3) Member States shall ensure that they have in place dispute settlement arrangements, including an authority independent of the parties with access to all relevant information,

to enable disputes relating to access to upstream pipeline networks to be settled expeditiously, taking into account the criteria in paragraph 2 and the number of parties which may be involved in negotiating access to such networks.

(4)   In the event of cross-border disputes, the dispute settlement arrangements for the Member States having jurisdiction over the upstream pipeline network which refuses access shall be applied. Where in cross-border disputes, more that one Member States covers the network concerned, the Member States concerned shall consult with a view to securing that the provisions of this Directive are applied consistently.

Chapter VII contains the *Final Provisions* of the Directive. Article 24 deals with emergency measures which Member States may take:

(1)   In the event of a sudden crisis in the energy market and where the physical safety or security of persons, apparatus or installations or system integrity is threatened, a Member State may temporarily take the necessary safeguard measures.

(2)   Such measures must cause the least possible disturbance in the functioning of the internal market and must not be wider in scope than is strictly necessary to remedy the sudden difficulties which have arisen.

(3)   The Member State concerned shall without delay notify these measures to the other Member States and to the Commission, which may decide that the Member State concerned must amend or abolish such measures, insofar as they distort competition and adversely affect trade in a manner which is at variance with the common interest.

Article 25 deals with take or pay provisions in gas contracts:

(1)   If a natural gas undertaking encounters (or considers it would encounter) serious financial difficulties because of its take-or-pay commitments accepted in one or more gas purchase contracts, an application for a temporary derogation from Article 15 and/or Article 16 of this Directive may be sent to the Member State concerned or the designated competent authority. Applications shall, according to the choice of Member States, be presented on a case by case basis either before or after refusal of access to the system. Member states may also give the natural gas undertaking the choice to present an application either before or after refusal of access to the system. Where a natural gas undertaking has refused access, the application shall be presented without delay. The applications shall be accompanied by all relevant information on the nature and extent of the problem and on the efforts undertaken by the gas undertaking to solve the problem.

If alternative solutions are not reasonably available and taking into account the provisions of paragraph 3, the Member State or the designated competent authority may decide to grant a derogation.

(2)   The Member State, or the designated competent authority, shall notify its decision to grant a derogation to the Commission without delay, together with all relevant information with respect to the derogation. This information may be submitted to the Commission in an aggregated form, enabling the Commission to reach a well-founded decision. Within four weeks from its receipt of this notification, the Commission may request that the

Member State or the designated competent authority concerned may amend or withdraw the decision to grant a derogation. If the Member State or the designated competent authority concerned does not follow this request within a period of four weeks, a final decision shall be taken expeditiously in accordance with procedure 1 of Article 2 of Council Decision 87/373 of 13 July 1987 laying down procedures for the exercise of implementing powers conferred on the Commission.

The Commission shall preserve the confidentiality of commercially sensitive information.

(3) When deciding on derogations referred to in paragraph 1, the Member State, or the designated competent authority, and the Commission shall take into account, in particular, the following criteria:

(a) the objective to achieve a competitive gas market;

(b) the need to fulfil public service obligations and to ensure security of supply;

(c) the position of the natural gas undertaking in the gas market and the actual state of competition in this market;

(d) the seriousness of the economic and financial difficulties encountered by natural gas undertakings and transmission undertakings or eligible customers;

(e) the dates of signature and terms of the contract or contracts in question, including the extent to which they allow for market changes;

(f) the efforts made to find a solution;

(g) the extent to which, when accepting the take-or-pay commitments in question, the undertaking could reasonably have foreseen, having regard to the provisions of this Directive, that serious difficulties were likely to arise;

(h) the level of connection of the system with other systems and the degree of inter-operability of these systems; and

(i) the effects the granting of a derogation would have on the correct application of this Directive as regards the good functioning of the natural gas market.

A decision on a request for a derogation concerning take-or-pay contracts concluded before entry into force of this Directive should not lead to a situation in which it is impossible to find economically viable alternative outlets. Serious difficulties shall in any case be deemed not to exist when the sales of natural gas do not fall below the level of minimum offtake guarantees contained in gas purchase contracts or in so far as the relevant gas purchase take-or-pay contracts can be adapted or the natural gas undertaking is able to find alternative outlets.

(4) Natural gas undertakings not having received a derogation referred to in paragraph 1 shall not refuse, or shall no longer refuse, access to the system because of take-or-pay commitments accepted in a gas purchase contract. Member States shall ensure that the relevant provisions of Chapter VI of this Directive are respected.

(5) Any derogation granted under the above provisions must be duly substantiated. The Commission shall publish the decision.

(6) The Commission shall, within five years from the entry into force of this Directive, submit a review report on the experience of the application of this Article, in order to allow the Council and the European Parliament to consider, in due time the need for adaptations of this Article.

Article 26 concerns derogations which may be granted to emergent markets:

(1) Member States not directly connected to the interconnected system of any other Member State and having only one main external supplier may derogate from Article 4, Article 18 paragraphs 1, 2, 3, 4, and 6 and/or Article 20 of this Directive. A supplier having a market share of more than 75% shall be considered a main supplier. This derogation will automatically expire from the moment at least one of these conditions no longer applies. Any such derogation shall be notified to the Commission.

(2) A Member State, qualifying as an emergent market, which because of the implementation of the Directive would experience substantial problems, not associated with the contractual take-or-pay commitments referred to in Article 25, may derogate from Article 4, Article 18 paragraphs 1, 2, 3, 4, and 6 and/or Article 20 of this Directive. This derogation will automatically expire from the moment the Member State no longer qualifies as an emergent market. Any such derogation shall be notified to the Commission.

(3) Where implementation of this Directive would cause substantial problems in a geographically limited area of a Member State, in particular concerning the development of the transmission infrastructure, and with a view to encouraging investments, the Member State may apply to the Commission for a temporary derogation from Article 4, Article 18 paragraphs 1,2,3,4, and 6 and/or Article 20.

(4) The Commission may grant the derogation referred to in paragraph 3, taking into account, in particular the following criteria:
    – the needs for infrastructural investments, which would not be economical to operate in a competitive market environment;
    – the level and pay back of investments required;
    – the size and maturity of the gas system in the area concerned;
    – the prospects for the gas market concerned;
    – the geographic size and characteristics of the area or region concerned;
    – the socio-economic and demographic factors.
    A derogation may only be granted if no gas infrastructure has been established in this area, or has been so established for less than 10 years. The temporary derogation may not exceed 10 years after the first supply of gas in the area.

(5) The Commission shall inform the Member States of those applications prior to taking a decision referred to in paragraph 4, taking into account the respect of confidentiality. This decision, as well as the derogations referred to in paragraphs 1 and 2 shall be published.

Article 27 concerns harmonization requirements:

(1) The Commission shall submit a report to the Council and the European Parliament, before the end of the first year following the entry into force of this Directive, on harmonisation requirements which are not linked to the provisions of this Directive. If necessary, the commission shall attach to the report any harmonisation proposals necessary for the effective operation of the internal gas market.

(2) The Council and the European Parliament shall give their views on such proposals within two years of their submission.

Article 28 concerns developments after the implementation of the Directive:

The Commission shall review the application of this Directive and submit a report on the experience gained on the functioning of the internal market in natural gas and the implementation of the general rules mentioned in Article 3 in order to allow the Council and the European Parliament, in the light of experience gained, to consider, in due time, the possibility of provisions on further improving the internal market in natural gas, which would be effective 10 years after the entry into force of the Directive.

Article 29 concerns the timetable for bringing the Directive into force:

Member States shall bring into force the laws, regulations and administrative provisions necessary to comply with this Directive no later than 2 years from the date specified in Article 30. They shall forthwith inform the Commission thereof.

When Member States adopt these provisions, they shall contain a reference to this Directive or shall be accompanied by such reference on the occasion of their official publication. The methods of making such reference shall be laid down by the Member States.

Article 30 states that 'This Directive shall enter into force on the 20th day following that of its publication in the Official Journal of the European Communities'.

There is also an Appendix to the Directive containing 'Statements in the Council's Minutes' in which the Commission and individual member states made their own attempts to clarify specific points in respect of individual Articles in the Directive. Here we make reference to only a few of these statements.

Re: Articles 8(2) and 11(2): The Council and the Commission state that the provisions of Articles 8(2) and 11(2) shall not imply any duty on undertakings to change their legal structure or create new companies.

Re: Article 18: The Council and the Commission consider that, since Member States are allowed to decide on a more extensive opening of the market, the concept of site may also apply, if a Member State so chooses, where firms belonging to the same industrial group or consumers forming a consortium or coming from the same industrial zone conclude natural gas supply contracts which in aggregate exceed the eligibility thresholds laid down in Article 18(2) and (6).

The Council and the Commission consider that other final customers consuming less than 25 million cubic metres of gas per year on a consumption-site basis but having a gas-fired power production unit and/or a combined heat and power installation are only to be eligible for the volume of gas required for this power and/or heat and power production.

Chapter 5

National Institutional Developments: Competition and Liberalization Experiences

This chapter reviews the beginning of liberalization and regulation experiments in Europe. It begins with the most advanced of these experiments in Britain and then looks at a number of national developments in both importing and exporting countries. The theme of these experiences is not simply the focus of this study – competition and liberalization – but the wider context of institutional change which is permeating the industry throughout the Continent.

Britain: regulation-driven competition and liberalization[1]

The development of competition, liberalization and regulation

Box 5.1 summarizes a complex history of competition in the British gas industry in four phases. During Phase 1, 1982–88, despite the passage of legislation and regulation, and the creation of a regulatory Office of Gas Supply (Ofgas) there was little change in BG's monopoly/monopsony position. Phase 2, 1988–94, saw a determined effort by the government and regulatory authorities (Ofgas, the Office of Fair Trading and the Monopolies and Mergers Commission) to 'manage' competition into existence by a series of regulatory measures designed to bring new entrants into the gas market.[2] This was achieved by forcing BG into the following sequence of measures:

---

[1] This section draws heavily on the author's article, 'The British gas market ten years after privatization: a model or a warning for the rest of Europe?', *Energy Policy*, March 1997, pp. 387–92. It is important to stress that all of the competition and liberalization developments described here have occurred in the 'British' gas market, rather than 'UK', which includes Northern Ireland, a region which – with its emerging and monopolistic gas market – will probably have to seek a derogation under the EU Gas Directive.

[2] M. Parker and J. Surrey, *UK Gas Policy: Regulated Monopoly or Managed Competition?*, STEEP Special Report No. 2, 1994, Science Policy Research Unit, University of Sussex.

Box 5.1: The evolution of competition and liberalization in Britain: four major phases

Phase 1. 1982–88: Monopoly and monopsony
  –1982 Oil and Gas Enterprise Act creates the possibility for competition
  –1986 Gas Act privatizes British Gas (BG) and creates the regulatory office (OFGAS)

Phase 2. 1988–94: Managed competition
  –1988 Monopolies and Mergers Commission (MMC) report forces BG to publish price schedules
  –1990 First contract for transportation signed (Quadrant Gas)
  –1991 Office of Fair Trading (OFT) report forces reduction of BG's market share in industrial market and expands the competitive sector
  –1992 'Release gas' programme commences
  –1993 MMC report recommends: demerging of BG's trading activities from transportation; delaying competition in the residential market until after 2000. Government rejects MMC recommendations.
  –1993 BG's share of the non-residential market falls to 70%

Phase 3. 1994– present: Self-sustaining competition
  –late 1994/early 1995 surplus of supply over demand, spot market evolves
  –April 1995 sharp price reductions/distress sales
  –1995 suppliers/shippers in substantial commercial difficulty
  –1995 BG's share of the non-residential market falls to 35%, causing substantial 'take or pay' problems. Obligation to price according to schedules suspended
  –1997 (February) BG 'demerges' into two companies: Centrica (British Gas Trading), and BG plc (exploration and production, British Gas transportation and international activities)
  –1997 (June) Monopolies and Mergers Commission Report recommends new regime for transportation tariffs with separate storage tariffs

Phase 4. 1996–98: Evolving competition in the residential market
  –1996 (April) first 'trial area' opened to competition
  –1997 further 'trial areas' opened
  –1998 remainder of the residential market to be opened in stages by June 1998

- publishing schedules for industrial gas prices (from which the company was not allowed to deviate);
- 'releasing' to new entrants some of the gas which it had purchased under long-term contracts.

- expanding the competitive sector of the market such that only residential and small commercial customers remained within the BG monopoly, while restricting BG's share of the contestable market to 55%.

During 1994 (Phase 3) self-sustaining competition took hold and the market no longer needed managing as BG's share fell extremely rapidly. At the same time, a surplus of gas supply developed and prices fell sharply. BG was locked into long-term 'take or pay' contracts at higher prices and began to experience serious financial problems. In early 1996 it was announced that the company would be 'demerged' into a trading business (renamed 'Centrica'), and a transportation, exploration and international business (renamed BG plc), and this was achieved in February 1997.[3] In June 1997 a new charging regime for transportation and storage tariffs was decided by the Monopolies and Mergers Commission (MMC), after BG had refused to accept Ofgas' proposals. The final phase of competition (Phase 4), opening up the residential gas market, commenced in April 1996, with the first 'trial area'. After the first year of the trial around 20% of customers had changed to other suppliers. It is planned that additional areas of the residential market be opened up such that by June 1998, the entire market will be open to competition.[4]

Stepping aside from the detail of this story, three groups of issues are critical to any appreciation of why the British system has evolved in this way: the changing context of government policy, the growing importance of regulation, and the impact on major players.

The context of government policy

One of the most interesting aspects of the original privatization of the British Gas Corporation was the government's stubborn insistence that

---

[3] Aside from its gas trading business (which in Britain trades under the name of British Gas) Centrica also owns the Morecambe Bay gas fields, a very significant resource base from which to serve its customers. BG plc (which outside Britain trades under the name of British Gas) has significant exploration properties on the UKCS and around the world. Both companies have capacity rights in the Interconnector pipeline.

[4] *Further extension of competition*, a consultation document, Ofgas, July 1997.

competition would emerge despite the universally held view (even by the government's supporters) that it would not. Few observers believed that successive governments would subsequently have the determination to enforce competition by their own actions, and via the regulator, especially since this required overturning the entire policy context of privatization. Even fewer could have expected that such action would be met by ineffectual protests from BG's management and shareholders, as the competition framework which had been set out in the privatization prospectus was virtually torn up.[5] This change in the policy context was marked by:

- an extremely rapid timetable for the preparation and passing of legislation, regulation and other key policy instruments. This rapid timetable required the 'railroading' of measures through the legislative process, with severe restrictions on discussion, even within parliament;[6]
- a complete reversal in the culture of providing certainty of decision-making. The traditional policy context in which all circumstances – however extreme – would be covered by a combination of gas industry and government measures and contingency plans, rapidly vanished. The government largely abdicated responsibility as the industry embarked on a 'voyage of discovery' with little certainty as to its eventual destination;

---

[5] The only note in the privatization prospectus was that the company would be subject to normal competition law (including review by the MMC). By December 1992 – barely six years after privatization – Ofgas stated that, 'We believe that the terms of the offer for sale ceased to have any moral or legal standing several years ago'. G. McGregor, *Separation of British Gas' Transportation and Storage Business* (London: Ofgas, 1992), p. 15.

[6] This process began with the original 1986 legislation where the Select Committee responsible for inquiring into the regulation of the industry found itself forced to read the detail in the *Financial Times* newspaper, because the official documents were produced at such a late stage (*Regulation of the Gas Industry First Report of the Energy Committee*, Session 1985/6 HC15, London: HMSO, 1986, p. 32). Another example of this haste was the government's response to the 1993 Monopolies and Mergers Commission Report – a 1,000-page document and the most wide-ranging regulatory inquiry into a privatized utility yet seen, which had taken more than a year to prepare. The Department of Trade and Industry published its response in a 6-page press release issued two days before the Christmas holiday. This was the only document issued to explain that the government was rejecting the main MMC proposals and had decided to commence the opening up of the residential market to competition just over two years from that date.

- a switch of responsibility from parliament and ministers to Ofgas. The principal consequence of the government's position has been the transfer of almost all of its former duties to the regulatory authority. Thus the provisions of the 1995 Gas Act confer very wide powers of discretion over the industry upon the Director General of Ofgas – appointed for a 5-year period by the Secretary of State for Trade and Industry. The notable exception is in the area of offshore regulation where the government has jealously guarded its regulatory power, refusing even to allow Ofgas jurisdiction over the terminals where gas is landed.

The regulatory model

The original model of British utility regulation has been succinctly summarized as follows:

> Observation of the operation of regulatory systems overseas, especially in the United States, led the Government to seek to develop a quicker and less bureaucratic system of regulation. This was centred on the idea of a single independent regulator for each industry, operating without undue bureaucracy and supported by a small staff. The regulator would be appointed by the Government and the Government would retain important responsibilities in a number of areas. But in carrying out his or her allotted functions, each regulator would be independent of the Government in the performance of his or her duties.[7]

The reference to 'a quicker and less bureaucratic system' was advanced as 'light-handed' regulation and believed to be greatly superior to the huge North American professional regulatory bureaucracies. This concept has come under increasing strain over the past decade. We have already noted that the 1995 Gas Act transferred significant responsibilities from the government to the regulatory authority. The post-1993 period – when it was decided to open up the residential market to competition – placed considerable pressures on a relatively small staff required to devise and implement the complex and innovative opening of the residential gas

---

[7] National Audit Office, *The Work of the Directors General of Telecommunications, Gas Supply, Water Services and Electricity Supply,* HC 645 (London: HMSO, 1996, para. 2.3, pp. 6, 7.)

market on an extremely rapid timetable, at the same time as its regular duties.[8] Problems have arisen with regard to the original regulatory model in terms of:

- the apparent lack of accountability of a single, unelected person appointed for a 5-year term with enormous decision-making power;
- the independence of the regulatory authority – a difficult concept to interpret in the British context;
- the question of whether the Office should be staffed with permanent and technically trained personnel. Aside from the Director General, the Office has traditionally been staffed with civil servants seconded for periods of 3–5 years;
- the resolution of overlaps with other regulatory bodies, principally the Office of Electricity Supply (OFFER) but also, as noted, the Department of Trade and Industry which is in charge of offshore gas (and oil) regulation;
- the continuing appropriateness of 'price cap' (RPI-X) regulation as the dominant regulatory methodology, particularly in relation to transportation charges.

All of these issues have, to some extent, contributed to the problems experienced over the past decade. For an industry to experience four major competition regulatory investigations within a decade is unprecedented. A common way of explaining these events is in the personalization of the relationship between the regulatory authority and BG. Certainly during the tenure of the first director general the adversarial nature of exchanges between BG and Ofgas grew to legendary proportions. This adversarial climate abated during the early years of the second director general's tenure, but then flared again in the run-up to the 1996 MMC reference. These highly public exchanges were probably a symptom (rather than a cause) of a regulatory framework, whereby a small office is required to

---

[8] In 1994/95, the staff of Ofgas was 68, compared with Oftel 162, Ofwat 178, Offer 215. By 1998 Ofgas staff had grown to 130 people. Ibid., Figure 8, p. 30.

devise, implement and oversee fundamental and innovatory change at breakneck speed.

The impact of competition on industry actors

British Gas   The clearest impact of competition was on British Gas itself, which ceased to exist as an entity in February 1997. As far as employees were concerned, the impact was mixed: top executives – despite the unpleasant press coverage they received – saw their salaries increase significantly and retired on generous pensions. The rest of the workforce fared less well: at privatization, the company employed 90,000. At demerger, just over a decade later the workforce had shrunk to 36,000. For management and shareholders, the crucial issue has been how a company which, at privatization supplied 100% of gas to final consumers and which appeared to have been given a 25-year franchise to supply all but the largest industrial customers, allowed its share of the non-residential market to be reduced to 35%, and its entire franchise market to be opened up to competition within 12 years.

Shippers and suppliers   During the phase of managed competition, it was relatively easy to gain market share and sell gas at a profit. Until mid-1995, BG was required to publish price schedules and progressively to give away its share of the industrial market. The first phase of the 'release gas' programme only required new shippers to present sufficient financial credentials to sign up for gas and sell on at a small profit. However, after 1994 and particularly as gas prices collapsed in the spring of 1995, this became a much more difficult and risky business. Shippers and suppliers which purchased gas in the early 1990s on long-term contracts with take or pay conditions have (like BG) encountered serious problems which were solved only after litigation.[9] Others have suffered significant losses.

By late 1997 aside from Centrica (British Gas Trading plus Accord Energy), 13 companies held market shares greater than 1% in the non-

---

[9] The two principal cases were between Enron and the owners of the 'J Block' field and between National Power and United Gas.

residential sectors. These included eight producer affiliates, one power generation company, three regional electricity company (REC) affiliates, and one very small independent.[10] It is clear that, aside from the very large REC affiliate, producers dominate the gas market. During 1997 several joint ventures serving the industrial market broke up including Quadrant (Shell and Esso), Alliance (BP, Statoil and Norsk Hydro) and Kinetica (Conoco and PowerGen) with some companies withdrawing from the market. In the residential market a number of new alliances were forged between energy and non-energy companies.[11] Further activity of this kind can be anticipated.

Customers　　In the decade following privatization, all classes of customer saw a significant fall in real gas prices. For residential customers (and all others using less than 2,500 therms per year) the decline has been 24–27%. For industrial customers, the decline has been greater than 50%.[12] These are impressive figures, widely quoted by government officials and Ofgas. The official index of industrial fuel prices for 1996 (1990 = 100) shows gas at 66.1 compared with coal at 82.6, heavy fuel oil at 125.7, and electricity at 105.3.[13] The same index in 1994, as gas-to-gas competition was starting in the industrial market, showed that with the exception of electricity, gas prices (relative to 1990) were significantly higher than prices of competitive fuels (relative to 1990). It also shows that, relative to 1990, 1996 gas prices had returned to the levels of 1979, whereas other

---

[10] These figures are based on a sample of customers. They identify companies with more than 1% in any of the three non-residential sectors: interruptible, above 25,000 therms, below 25,000 therms. Figures from John Hall Associates quoted in *UK Gas Report* (*Financial Times*), 24 November 1997, p. 14.

[11] For example the merger of Amerada Hess residential marketing operations with those of SWEB; the marketing alliances of Yorkshire Electricity and Southern Electric with the supermarket chains Asda and Argos (respectively); Northern Electric with SAGA (a company which markets a range of products to elderly people). Also members of trades union organizations forming a marketing group, and local authorities joining together to purchase gas.

[12] National Audit Office, op. cit.

[13] *Digest of UK Energy Statistics* (London: HMSO, 1997), Table 85, p. 186. The gas index for the first three quarters of 1997 was at a similar level, but the indices of competing fuels had fallen somewhat.

fuels were still significantly above 1979 levels. In terms of prices therefore, the coming of gas-to-gas competition has caused substantial falls, both with respect to competitive fuels and in comparison with gas prices in other European countries (see Table 3.13).

Aside from prices, the question of service standards became problematic with BG's difficulty in billing and invoicing – partly due to the introduction of new information technology systems, and partly the 'teething troubles' of a new system – reaching crisis proportions during 1996.[14] Although concerns have been raised regarding the conduct of suppliers in the residential market, it is too early to evaluate performance with regard to public service obligations – particularly in the area of indebted customers and services to vulnerable groups. The issue of how different classes of customer will weigh the benefits of lower prices against different levels and qualities of service delivery remains to be seen.

Achievements and unresolved problems

The British experiment has produced a number of achievements of which the most important are that:

- a competitive and extremely dynamic market has been created, even if its early development owed more to the management of government and regulatory authorities than to the forces of supply and demand. All market sectors, including a corner of the residential market, have been opened to competition, and by early 1998 no disasters had occurred, despite the dire warnings of technical experts;
- prices paid by (particularly industrial) consumers have declined substantially. In the post-1994 period this can be largely attributed to the introduction of competition.

But there were also a number of unresolved problems:

- regulation: how the regulatory regime will evolve in terms of institutions, methodologies, priorities and timetables for implementing further liberalization measures;

---

[14] Gas Consumers Council, *1996 Annual Report.*

- common carriage: whether the unique 'common carriage' regime is sustainable;[15]
- decline in standards of service and social consequences: concerns about the decline in BG's standards of service may simply be due to the enforced speed of the transition to a more competitive market, but it is difficult to be certain about how rapidly the situation will improve. Indeed as the residential market is opened up, with the problems of adjusting to a system where large numbers of customers may change their supplier (possibly more than once), service quality may deteriorate further. Public service (especially social) obligations are an area where the ability and willingness of suppliers to fulfil their obligations, and the ability of Ofgas (or any other organization) to police their performance, remains uncertain;
- information technology: the ability of information technology systems to deal with system balancing and large numbers of customers changing their supplier, especially during the introduction of residential competition.

One problem which appeared to have been resolved by late 1997 was that of contractual liabilities arising from the introduction of competition. All of BG's contracts contained take or pay clauses placing long-term purchase obligations on the buyer. Most of these were entered into when BG had 100% of the market and an absolute obligation to provide a secure supply. With BG's market share much reduced, the company was unable to take the volumes foreseen under these contracts and incurred serious financial penalties. By the end of 1997 British Gas and its successor company Centrica, the heir to these contractual liabilities, had completed the renegotiation of those contracts at a cost to shareholders exceeding £750 million.[16]

---

[15] Common carriage is a system whereby when the capacity of a pipeline system is oversubscribed, the requirements of all shippers are scaled back on a pro rata basis. The most common system is 'contract carriage' where capacity is (commonly) allocated on a 'first come first served' basis.

[16] 'Centrica completes its renegotiation of take or pay supply contracts', *UK Gas Report*, 16 January 1998, p. 5. For a general account of this problem, see M. Stoppard, *Today's Gas Glut and Yesterday's Contracts: The British Gas Predicament* (Oxford: Oxford Institute for Energy Studies, 1996).

Policy on international trade

Despite constant homilies about the merits of free trade and free markets from British politicians since 1980, international trade in gas remained completely controlled by the government. The latter repeatedly refused to allow any further import contracts for Norwegian gas to be signed, as of 1984.[17] Denial of imports was replaced by a determination to export gas as the government forced companies to form a committee (chaired by a British civil servant) to create (what eventually became) the Interconnector pipeline project between Britain and Belgium.[18] Any attempt to sponsor alternative export lines – for example the Britannia field whose owners tried desperately to obtain permission for their own export line direct to the Continent – was rejected. For the Interconnector pipeline, the government dictated the direction of gas flow, the route, the ownership structure (which could not be dominated by a single entity), and (a large part of) the commercial rules governing the pipeline. Only in April 1997, after construction of the Interconnector was well under way, did the government finally agree on a revision of the Frigg Treaty which will allow new gas to be piped through the existing system. The UK and Norwegian governments have also signed a framework agreement on other cross-boundary lines which will avoid the need for a separate treaty for future cases.[19]

While the main reason for the policy on trade was the promotion of maximum possible UKCS production on the fastest possible timetable, for taxation and balance of payments reasons the issue of liberalization has been of some importance. The creation of a grid-to-grid connection with a Continental European country (Belgium), capable of carrying 20 BCM per year with fragmented (and tradeable) ownership of capacity, will constitute a considerable step forward in gas trading. The Interconnector was intended to provide a means by which the British could export both their gas and their liberalization philosophy to the Continent.

---

[17] J. P. Stern, 'After Sleipner: a policy for UK gas supplies', *Energy Policy*, February 1986, pp. 9–14.
[18] A useful summary of the Interconnector project can be found in James Allcock, 'The Interconnector: its origins and prospects', Gastech 1996 Conference Proceedings.
[19] 'Fraser's Frigg footnote', *Gas Matters*, May 1997, pp. 30–31. John Michell, 'North Sea Gas Trade and Regulation in a New Era of Cooperation', a paper to the European Autumn Gas Conference, Barcelona, 4 and 5 November 1997.

Lessons from the British experiment

The development of competition and the decline in prices, despite being the most often-quoted lessons of the British experiment, may not be the most important. For the development of competition, liberalization and regulation in Continental Europe, it may be of greater significance that:

- the anti-competitive structure of the British gas industry required a period of 12 years from the passage of first legislation to the arrival of self-sustaining competition. This is a lengthy period considering the passage of legislation, massively proactive regulation and a relatively compliant dominant player;
- once it had been acknowledged in 1991 that competition had failed and could not succeed without a major change in market structure, the regulatory act of requiring the dominant player to withdraw from nearly half of the contestable market caused self-sustaining competition to develop within a 3-year period;
- despite the initial proposition of 'light-handed regulation', the development of self-sustaining competition has required significant regulatory complexity. Even a specialized gas regulatory office has had great difficulty in overseeing and implementing such complexities;
- once the monopsony power of the gatekeeper performing the supply/demand balancing role was removed, producers/suppliers quickly oversupplied the market, causing a sharp fall in purchase prices.

Finally, the impact of the privatization of the electricity industry cannot be underestimated.[20] At the same time as events in the gas industry were unfolding, a very large amount of baseload gas-fired generation was being constructed in Britain. Private electricity generation and distribution companies were becoming major actors in all segments of the gas chain. The impact of developments in electricity markets, including electricity regulation, on the liberalization of British gas markets continues to be enormous.

Thus, one of the most important lessons is the swiftness of institutional

---

[20] John Surrey (ed.), *The British Electricity Experiment. Privatisation: the Record, the Issues, the Lessons* (London: Earthscan, 1996).

change and market structure which has taken place in Britain starting in 1990. Institutionally, there have been significant numbers of new entrants (some of which have already disappeared from the market). The roles of many companies have changed and broadened to cover other parts of the chain (again some have failed to profit from these activities and already withdrawn) and different ranges of services. The dominant player in the market, British Gas, has ceased to exist and a large part of its market share has been taken by others. From a position of almost zero in 1990, power generation customers account for nearly 20% of the gas market and this share will probably exceed 30% by 2010. From a market dominated by long-term contracts and confidential prices, short-term trades are now growing in importance and short-term prices – quoted daily and several months ahead on the International Petroleum Exchange Market – have become an important marker for all gas sales.

In summary, the British gas market in 1998 is unrecognizable from that of a decade earlier.

The Netherlands: from opponent to leader

The implacable opposition of Shell and Exxon (the owners of the Groningen field) and the Dutch government to liberalization proposals in early debates on these issues hardly suggested that the Netherlands would be in the forefront of radical change in this area.[21] However, the 1995 Dutch White Paper on energy policy may prove to be a landmark document in the liberalization of Continental European gas and electricity industries.[22] For the first time, the government of a Continental European country set out a policy for radical liberalization of both energy utility industries, starting with third party access to networks for large consumers, with an intention to extend access to smaller consumers in the future.

---

[21] See for example, Gasunie *Annual Report*, 1991 and 1992, p. 5. It is important to stress the opposition of Shell and Exxon in respect of the views of Dutch producers. Other producers had spoken in favour of liberalization.

[22] Ministry of Economic Affairs, *Third White Paper on Energy Policy* (The Hague: 1996). Although we are focusing here on the liberalization provisions, it is important to recognize that the major focus of the White Paper is sustainability, and specifically the Dutch response to the challenge of climate change.

Structural changes in energy utility markets

The White Paper summarized the intended changes in the gas and electricity markets as follows:

- decision making will change from being 'supply driven' to 'demand driven';
- network functions will be disengaged from production and supply/ distribution, the exception being in gas where transmission and sales will remain under the Gasunie management;
- access to networks on non-discriminatory terms will be allowed;
- independent monitoring (regulation) of network functions will be implemented;
- there will be a transitional process towards freedom of choice for all consumers;
- captive customers will continue to receive government protection;
- electricity generation, trade and supplies to non-captive customers are to be liberalized;
- energy utilities will separate their functions, creating single-function utilities as well as utilities with combined functions (e.g. generation, supply and service);
- greater competition will be promoted, not necessarily following Europe, but stimulating competition within the Netherlands.

Table 5.1 summarizes some of the detail of these changes which will take place in the gas and electricity industries. While our concern here is with the impact on the gas industry, the main energy focus of the White Paper was the electricity industry. The document was produced because of the requirement for government to report to Parliament on the progress of the 1989 Electricity Act. As the White Paper was being prepared, the Minister of Economic Affairs decided to adopt similar measures for the gas industry.

The gas industry

The Dutch gas industry is the biggest in Europe in terms of production, exports and low-cost accessible reserves. The discovery of the giant Groningen

Table 5.1: Principal changes to statutory framework and other preconditions

Electricity	Situation in 1996	Within five years
Generation	private generators free distributors >25MW approval by SEP minimum capacity public utilities	free
Transmission	transmission not transparent	non-discriminatory grid access independent regulation
Trade	exports free (not distributors) imports free (not distributors) maximum tariffs	exports/imports free non-captives free captives protected (coverage plans, maximum tariffs)
Decentralised capacity	cogeneration and renewables equal mandated feedback to distributor, payment for 'avoided costs'	differentiated for cogeneration and renewables Cogeneration>2MW: free market cogeneration<2MW: regulated at market value
	private joint ventures: only with local distributor	joint ventures: freedom of choice renewables: stimulatory feedback payment
New distribution grids	not regulated	regional decision based on nationwide criteria
Gas		
Production	free (based on permit)	free (based on permit)
Transmission	not regulated	free non-discriminatory grid access, independent regulation, 'negotiated access'
Trade	producers must sell gas to Gasunie for domestic market	producers free non-captives free captives protected (coverage plans, maximum tariffs)
New distribution grids	not regulated	regional decision based on nationwide criteria

Source: Third White Paper on Energy Policy, 1996, p. 96

field in the late 1950s gave rise to exportable surpluses of gas, which allowed natural gas industries to be created in many Continental European countries. The Groningen discovery also provided the incentive to explore for gas more widely in the North Sea. Dutch gas exploration, production and exports have been relatively tightly controlled by government policy. However, this control has been exercised by means of informal instructions; there is no legal restriction on access to high-pressure pipelines and, in the past, Gasunie has allowed access for specific producers to sell to specific customers.

The Dutch government required Gasunie – the merchant transmission company – to operate a very strict depletion policy in order to maintain security of supply for domestic gas consumers. Remaining reserves must be adequate to cover 25 years of Dutch domestic gas demand plus export contract commitments.[23] The Ministry of Economics has the power to earmark gas of Dutch origin for domestic use. For the gas (and electricity) market, the White Paper envisages a gradual move towards liberalization. Non-discriminatory 'negotiated' access to Gasunie's transmission system will be introduced immediately for non-captive customers with an annual demand above 10 million cubic metres. Captive customers with an annual demand below 170,000 cubic metres will continue to be supplied by their distribution company. Intermediate customers with an annual demand of 170,000–10 million cubic metres will be given an opportunity to become non-captive over the next 5 years. As Table 5.2 shows, this means that 40% of the gas market could be immediately liberalized and within 5 years, this figure could rise to 60%. As far as the domestic market is concerned, there are important elements of continuity with current policy. Exploration and production policy will remain tightly controlled by the government in terms of allowed production levels. The 25 years' reserve coverage of internal demand will be retained, although this will be inter-preted more flexibly than in the past, allowing for a change in policy towards international trade.

---

[23] For background to Dutch gas policy see Javier Estrada, Arild Moe and Kare Dahl Martinsen, *The Development of European Gas Markets: Environmental, Economic and Political Perspectives* (Chichester: John Wiley, 1995), pp. 204–11.

Table 5.2: Captive, intermediate and non-captive gas and electricity customers

	% of market	
	Gas	Electricity
Captive	40	40–45
Intermediate	20	30
Non-captive	40	25–30

Source: *Third White Paper on Energy Policy*, 1996, p. 84.

The impact of Dutch liberalization measures could be significant for the European gas market. Dutch exports amount to some 40 BCM per year, making the country the largest external supplier after Russia. However, there is an important distinction between Groningen gas exports – which have a lower gross calorific value (9.24 kilowatt hours per standard cubic metre) than the majority of gas traded in Europe (10.78–11.55 kWh/Sm³) – and exports of Dutch offshore gas with a higher calorific value (10.01 kWh/Sm³). This difference in calorific value has meant that gas from Groningen and offshore fields has been marketed through two separate pipeline networks, both within the Netherlands and throughout Europe. France, Belgium and Germany receive low and high CV gas from the Netherlands, while Italy and Switzerland receive only high CV gas. Traditionally all production for domestic Dutch use had to be offered to Gasunie, but this did not apply to exports. Nevertheless, over time Gasunie has come to manage all export contracts. In addition, despite being a major exporter, Gasunie also imports small quantities of Norwegian (and more recently British) gas on long-term contracts. Both Gasunie and the Dutch government have also insisted that the country's long-term future will see an increase in gas imports as domestic reserves become further depleted. Less than six months after publication of the White Paper, Gasunie announced a contract with Gazprom, allowing for an import of 4 BCM of Russian gas per year, with associated services to promote security for buyers of Russian gas in Europe.[24]

---

[24] 'Gasunie opens new markets to Gazprom', *Gas Matters*, June 1996, pp. 1–2.

Developments since the White Paper

By the end of 1997 contracts between large industrial and power-generation customers and British producers through the Interconnector pipeline had already seen Gasunie sign transportation agreements to deliver gas to Dutch distribution companies and power generators (see Chapter 3). In addition, industrial users with a demand greater than 10 million cubic metres/ year had a realistic opportunity to choose their supplier. Discussions were under way to introduce a similar choice for customers with an annual consumption of 170,000 cubic metres, accounting for 64% of the Dutch market, by 2002; by 2007, the residential gas market would also be liberalized.[25] At the time of writing, such proposals are only in the discussion phase. But they are a great deal more radical than anything under consideration elsewhere in Continental Europe.

Yet there is little indication as to how this radical liberalization will be implemented. The White Paper recognized that liberalization measures would require a new regulatory framework. However, this framework was discussed only in the following rather general terms:

(1)   at least once every four years a report will be published assessing the energy market with respect to security, sustainability, competitiveness and environment;

(2)   a transparent statutory and administrative framework is required for existing and new electricity, gas and heat infrastructure. As well as access to networks, the issue of construction of new infrastructure will also be dealt with;

(3)   statutory arrangements for liberalization of electricity and gas markets will be devised, with rights and duties of suppliers *vis-à-vis* captive customers;

(4)   regulation will relate first to network access issues and supplies to captive customers. This regulation will be permanent. There will also be government regulation of supplies to captive customers which will cease when these customers no longer have the status of 'captives'.[26]

---

[25] 'Dutch unveil competition plans', *International Gas Report*, 9 January 1998, pp. 20–21.
[26] White Paper, op. cit., pp. 115 and 137.

In late 1997 the Electricity Act was passed which included provisions for regulation of the electricity and (potentially) the gas industry. At the time of writing, this was being formulated but it appeared that the new regulatory body would be part of the Ministry of Economic Affairs for at least 5 years, at the end of which it would become either independent or part of the (newly created) Competition Office.[27] The general impression is that Dutch regulation will be reactive rather than proactive, and that regulators will not intervene unless absolutely necessary.

Origins and consequences of the Dutch position

As far as the liberalization of Continental European gas and electricity industries is concerned the Dutch White Paper has already proved to be a landmark document. This was the first example of a government of an important Continental European country (and EU member state) publishing a policy document which included a commitment to radical liberalization of both major energy utility industries. However, alongside this commitment, there are questions to be asked about the strategy and tactics of the Dutch government.

First, it is interesting to examine the reasons behind the sea change in Dutch government policy. Five major points seem to have been particularly influential in the decision making of the new government:

- the apparent willingness to exchange a reduction of upstream revenues (from taxation) for the competitive advantage to industry which would result from a fall in gas prices to consumers;
- the fact that the electricity situation, particularly in respect of over-capacity in cogeneration, required a major reform. There is evidence that gas was considered as an afterthought to electricity;[28]
- the fact that the British–Belgian Interconnector pipeline would be likely to make the Dutch position against liberalized access increasingly

---

[27] 'Electricity in the Netherlands: balancing liberalization with defence', *Financial Times, EC Energy Monthly*, August 1997, pp. 6–8.
[28] Gertjan Lankhorst, *The Dutch White Paper: What it Means for the European Gas Industry*, a paper to the European Autumn Gas Conference, Copenhagen, November 1996.

untenable and prevent Dutch producers and Gasunie from realizing significant commercial opportunities;

• the arrival of a new Minister of Economics (Wijers) who was strongly in favour of liberalization.

• the Dutch Presidency of the EU (the first six months of 1997).

Throughout the White Paper there are references to conditions which may be used to guide the pace of liberalization. First, the speed of a European Union commitment to liberalization measures, and the regulation of utilities. Second, and related to the first, an issue of 'reciprocity' of measures within other European Union member countries. The White Paper gave the impression that the progress of Dutch liberalization reforms will be conditional on the progress of EU legislation and regulation, and the willingness of other European countries to introduce similar liberalization measures. In that respect, discussions which were taking place at the end of 1997 were extremely radical in comparison to those being held in other countries in Continental Europe. Under these proposals, liberalization of the Dutch residential gas market could be taking place at the same time as other EU member states are reducing eligibility thresholds to 5 million cubic metres/year.

However, before leaving the impression that the Dutch will inevitably hurtle down a liberalization path similar to the British, two caveats should be noted. First, the Dutch White Paper was principally about sustainability and climate change policy. It will be interesting to see whether, as they unfold, the Dutch sustainability and liberalization initiatives in the White Paper will be compatible or conflicting. Unless new entrants in the gas and electricity markets can be persuaded to concentrate their competitive activity in the area of conservation and efficiency packages, rather than simply offering reduced prices (which may remove the incentive of consumers to save energy), liberalization could prove to be the enemy of energy conservation. Second, Dutch liberalization initiatives have been strongly identified with a particular government and a particular minister. Political changes within the Netherlands could see changes in the country's liberalization agenda.

Germany: pipeline competition with strong resistance to liberalization[29]

In November 1989, as the fall of the Berlin Wall signalled the beginning of the reunification of Germany and the end of the postwar era in Europe, an equally dramatic event occurred in the German gas industry. Wintershall, a hitherto small West German gas producer, announced that it planned to build a pipeline – the Midal line – from Emden (the landfall of Norwegian gas supplies to Continental Europe) via Kassel to Ludwigshafen, the headquarters of Wintershall's parent company, the chemicals giant BASF.[30] This action followed fierce price disputes between BASF and its supplier Ruhrgas over a period of years.[31] These disputes essentially focused on the prices which BASF had to pay as a result of the *Anleg-barkeitsprinzip* – pricing according to the market value of competing fuels for a specific industrial customer (see Chapter 2). During this period, BASF took the decision that it would need to become directly involved in the gas market in order to improve its commercial position *vis-à-vis* the transmission companies. The events of 1989–91 changed the political landscape, presented opportunities which could not have been imagined, and opened up a new chapter in the German gas industry.

The announcement of the intention to build the Midal line amounted to 'a declaration of war' on the market domination of Ruhrgas in West Germany.[32] With the reunification of Germany, however, the gas industry of the former German Democratic Republic (GDR) became available for acquisition. In July 1990 'the pre-emptive strike' of Ruhrgas and BEB, purchasing 35% and 10% respectively of the East German transmission company VNG, appeared to signal the 'takeover' of the eastern part of Germany by entrenched dominant companies in the Federal Republic.[33]

[29] The early paragraphs of this account are reproduced from the author's earlier work: *Third Party Access in European Gas Industries: Regulation-driven or Market-led?* (London: EEP/RIIA, 1992), pp. 88–89.

[30] 'Wintershall plans major German trunkline', *IGR*, 10 November 1989, pp. 1–2.

[31] 'German giants engage in a little hardball', *Gas Matters*, 30 November 1991, pp. 3–5.

[32] Burkhard Richter, 'Recent developments in Germany concerning competition in the gas industry', *Oil and Gas Law and Taxation Review*, No. 4, 1989/90, pp. 91–96.

[33] In the German Democratic Republic the gas transmission company was known as Schwartze Pumpe. The new company formed after reunification was named Verbundnetzgas

This was reinforced when the chairman of Ruhrgas was asked by the East German government to renegotiate the terms of the Yamburg contract.[34]

However, in October of 1990, Wintershall – which had been left complaining about its relatively small 15% stake in VNG – announced a coup: a cooperation agreement with Gazprom at the heart of which was a joint venture company to market Russian gas in the eastern part of Germany.[35] (Gazprom apparently first proposed a similar arrangement to Ruhrgas and was rebuffed.) This allowed Wintershall to bring these transmission aspirations to fruition by building the Stegal pipeline carrying Russian gas from St Katharinen on the German/Czech border, to join the Midal line south of Kassel (Map 5.1).[36] There ensued a large and well-publicized price dispute between VNG and WIEH (but in reality between Ruhrgas and Wintershall) which centred on charges for transit fees and provision of related services.[37]

These events need to be placed in the context of the debate over the introduction of competition and foreign investment into the industries of the former GDR, and German industrial politics.[38] However, in the context of this study they mark the beginning of gas-to-gas competition in a united Germany. Since 1990 a frenzy of pipeline construction has been evident in Germany, a development which has seen the building of competing pipeline systems by Ruhrgas/VNG – concentrating on expanding the role

---

(VNG) AG. For an assessment of Ruhrgas' position, see Arild Moe, 'Natural Gas in the Federal Republic of Germany, the position of Ruhrgas', *International Challenges*, Vol. 8, No. 4, pp. 47–55.

[34] These activities caused a furore and an investigation by the European Commission's competition directorate. Sara Knight, 'Ruhrgas sparks cross-border row', *Financial Times*, 6 July 1990.

[35] The name of the original joint venture was Wintershall Erdgas Handelshaus (WIEH). Subsequently an additional joint venture, Wingas, was formed for transmission and marketing of gas within Germany. With the exception of sales to VNG, WIEH became the joint venture's marketing arm in central/eastern European countries.

[36] For a Wintershall account of events, see Peter L. Menzel, 'Europe's Changing Energy Markets', a paper to the *Gas Daily* Conference, London, 21 and 22 May 1992.

[37] For details, see 'The battle for East Germany goes behind closed doors', *Gas Matters*, 16 December 1991, pp. 1–4.

[38] For an account which places these events in the wider context of reunification, see Barbara Lippert and Rosalind Stevens-Ströhmann et al., *German Reunification and EC Integration: German and British Perspectives* (London: RIIA/Pinter, 1993), Chapter 7.

Map 5.1: New German gas pipelines

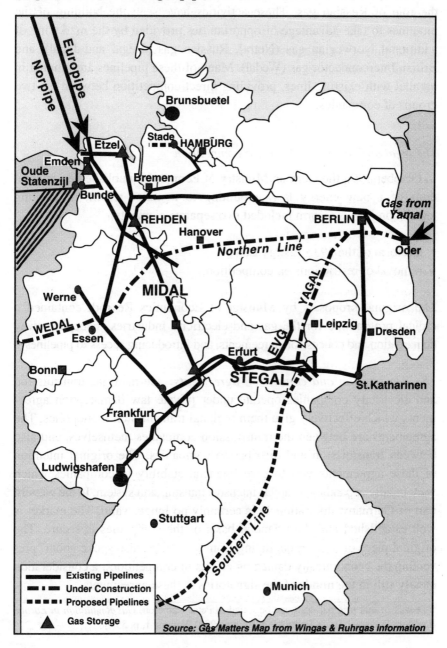

Source: Gas Matters Map from Wingas & Ruhrgas information

of Norwegian gas in Germany; and Wingas – concentrating on expanding the role of Russian gas. These activities have seen the building of the pipelines to take advantage of opportunities provided by the marketing of additional Norwegian gas (Netra), Russian gas (Stegal and Jagal), and British Interconnector gas (Wedal). Many of these pipelines are running in parallel with existing lines, providing direct competition between the two groups of companies.

The legal and regulatory basis for competition

In October 1993 the German Ministry of Economics published an internal draft of a new energy law amounting to a major reform of existing legislation.[39] This reform included two separate elements:

- a reform of the 1935 Energy Law;
- removal of restrictions on competition.

The original proposals by Minister of Economics Rexrodt contained a radical programme for the gas and electricity industries, sweeping away demarcation and concession agreements, and introducing access to pipelines.

The demarcation and concession agreements German gas transmission and electricity companies operate under private law demarcation agreements which effectively give them regional transmission monopolies. The agreements are between the transmission companies themselves, and also between transmission and distribution companies. The original intention of these agreements was to give financial stability to companies which were rapidly expanding a capital-intensive transmission system. In the western part of Germany, this rationale is certainly no longer valid. The market is well established and the financial basis of the companies is secure. The original piece of legislation, dating from the 1930s, also spoke about 'preventing the economically damaging effects of competition', a consideration clearly still in the minds of the signatories to these agreements.

---

[39] Details of that original draft can be found in Peter Cameron, *Gas Regulation in Europe* (London: Financial Times Energy Publishing, 1995), Volume 1, p. 55.

Along with the demarcation agreements, the regulatory structure of the industry has traditionally featured 'concession agreements' whereby municipal authorities granted exclusive rights to companies to construct a network and supply gas and electricity within a specific area. (The municipal authority retains the right to grant 'eminent domain' or 'wayleaves' to a company – usually the municipal distributor.) Concession agreements thus ensured that no consumer within this specified area could purchase gas or power from any alternative supplier. This was another part of the financial stability package for both transmission and distribution companies, ensuring that neither could face competition from alternative suppliers. Contracts between transmission companies and those customers within the concession area typically require the customer to take additional quantities of gas only from the transmission company. Even where there is not a complete ban on third party supplies, the contract requires the customer to notify the transmission company giving the latter either rights of first refusal or other means of intervention.[40] This type of arrangement has not been resisted by municipalities because it has allowed them to charge extremely high prices for gas and electricity in order to subsidize other services (such as transportation and leisure facilities) which they provide to local communities.[41]

While the original demarcation agreements were of indeterminate duration, the 5th Amendment to the Law against Restrictions on Competition 1989:

- limited their maximum duration to 20 years;
- terminated any agreement already in force for more than 20 years by 1 January 1995 at the latest;
- provided that a demarcation agreement overlapping with the end of a concession agreement would terminate automatically with the end of the concession agreement.

---

[40] 'RWE, Thyssengas agree to surrender exclusivity clauses', *European Gas Markets*, 23 May 1997, p. 4.
[41] For the financial aspects of concession agreements and their impact on municipal finances in Germany, see 'Rexrodt relaunches German reform drive', *Gas Matters*, May 1996, pp. 5–8.

It was hoped that this amendment to the law would give rise to strong competition in gas and electricity industries starting in 1995. In the event, as we shall see, it has given rise to major litigation and attempts by transmission companies to integrate vertically with distribution companies.

Competition and access: landmark cases

In its efforts to introduce greater competition, the German government has been supported by the Federal Cartel Office (FCO), the principal competition regulatory body. In 1994 an exceptionally frank speech by the President of Germany's FCO noted the shortcomings of the country's electricity and gas industries:

> in practice, the German market consists of regional monopolies with little or no supply competition ... the lack of competition has negative effects on the national economy as a whole – the extraordinarily high level of energy prices in Germany is a burden for industry and its international competitiveness.
>
> In their defence, the energy companies often argue that they might not be able to guarantee security of supply if more competition were introduced. But this argument is not very convincing. The system of energy supply in Germany was created at a time when security of supply might have been a real problem ... today, electricity and gas networks cover virtually the whole country and sufficient production facilities are in place. With the achievement of this objective, the question is now whether the regional monopoly model put in place in order to create and develop the system is still appropriate.[42]

Since 1991 landmark legal cases began to test the parameters of existing German competition law with respect to the gas and electricity industries.

The Ruhrgas–Thyssengas demarcation agreement [43] As just noted, demarcation agreements were due to expire in 1995 and the first of these agreements was between Ruhrgas and Thyssengas. An attempt by these two

---

[42] Dieter Wolf, 'Competition, Liberalization and Privatization – a German Perspective', a paper to the Royal Institute of International Affairs Conference, Emerging Policies for European Energy, December 1994.

[43] Cameron, op. cit., Vol. 1, pp. 59–60.

companies to renew their agreement at the end of 1994 was blocked by the FCO. The agreement allowed the two companies to supply customers in each other's areas, thereby excluding other suppliers; prevented Thyssengas from supplying in any other company's supply area, thereby further protecting Ruhrgas' interests in those areas; and allowed the two companies to deliver gas jointly to four local utilities.[44]

The Federal Cartel Office had declared this agreement (and by implication all other demarcation agreements) incompatible with Article 85(1) of the EU Treaty. The basis for that judgment was that because Thyssengas imports more than half its gas from the Netherlands, and Ruhrgas purchases part of its gas from other member states, the demarcation agreement can be considered to 'limit trade between member states and impede competition within the boundaries of the common market'. In contrast to German competition law, EU law does not provide for exemptions from the ban on cartels for demarcation and concession contracts in the energy sector. The parties (Ruhrgas and Thyssengas) appealed to the Berlin Court of Appeals which referred the matter to the European Court for a decision as to whether the FCO is competent to apply Article 85 to the German gas and electricity industry. A ruling has yet to be made, but the case looks likely to be overtaken by the passage of the new German energy law.

The Selfkant case   The small municipality of Selfkant, located within the demarcation area of Thyssengas, had been attempting to expand its gas distribution system. In 1993 Gasunie (the Dutch merchant transmission company) and Thyssengas (an important customer of Gasunie) refused to allow Selfkant to purchase gas from Mega (a Dutch gas supplier and affiliate of Gasunie). After taking its case to the Commission, Selfkant eventually obtained offers of supply both from the Dutch exporter and from the authorized Thyssengas subsidiary (Aachen Westgas).[45]

Third party access: the Weissenborn case   The major German gas companies – led by Ruhrgas – always maintained that access was not only

---

[44] 'Ruling soon on German demarcation case', *Gas Matters*, October 1996, pp. 7–9.
[45] Cameron, op. cit., Vol. 1, p. 61.

undesirable, but also contrary to constitutional protection of property rights. There had also been a serious legal debate as to whether TPA would be contrary to German competition law. Although the Law on Restrictions against Competition states that the denial of transportation rights constitutes a *prima facie* abuse of a dominant position, this principle had never been tested because of the demarcation agreements between the transmission companies. It was not foreseen that Wintershall would succeed in entering the gas market by forming a joint venture with Russia's Gazprom, which would both build pipelines and market gas in Germany. As a new entrant, Wingas was not party to any agreements and therefore not required to respect the demarcation areas.

In 1992 a paper manufacturer (Weissenborn), supplied by Erdgas Südsachsen, which in turn purchased gas from VNG, signed a contract with WIEH at a lower price. The latter then requested VNG to transport its gas to Weissenborn's premises. (As mentioned, VNG's ownership is dominated by Ruhrgas 35% and BEB 10%, but Wintershall also owns a 15% share and Gazprom 5%.) When VNG refused, on the grounds that access would not have been necessary if VNG had bought the gas from WIEH and resold it to Weissenborn, the case was referred to the FCO.

The FCO supported the case for TPA, ruling that it was 'not incompatible with Germany competition law'. VNG immediately appealed in the regional court in Berlin which overturned the FCO. Undeterred, the FCO appealed this judgment to the Federal Bundesgerichthof (highest administrative) Court which ruled, against the findings of the Federal Cartel Office, that, in this particular case, VNG did not have to carry gas for WIEH to the paper company in Lower Saxony. This ruling was made on the basis that VNG had made an offer to the customer which matched WIEH's offer. Therefore, since the offers were similar, the Court saw no basis for allowing WIEH to use VNG's pipeline network.[46]

Thus the ruling neither established a precedent, nor conclusively settled the debate between:

---

[46] Ibid., pp. 60–61; 'German Cartel Office: If at first you don't succeed...', *Gas Matters*, March 1995, pp. 4–6.

- the FCO which believed that the ruling established the compatibility of TPA with German competition law on the basis that:
  - TPA should be negotiated (not enforced);
  - TPA does not constitute a hindrance to the pipeline owner's basic constitutional right of freedom of economic activity;
  - the obligation to permit TPA, in order to create competition, does not constitute an unreasonable promotion of competition to the pipeline owner's disadvantage;
- VNG which believed that:
  - gas supply companies are not in principle obliged to grant TPA;
  - refusal to permit TPA can be contested only if it constitutes abuse of a dominant position.

The legal problem for those seeking access was that the Court did not give any indication as to the circumstances in which it would be prepared to grant access. The practical problem was that since the case demonstrated that access can be legally defeated if an existing supplier is prepared to match the offer made by a new supplier, others were dissuaded from making further attempts. If consumers believe that they can force their current supplier to reduce prices by threatening to take gas from an alternative supplier using TPA (even if they have no real intention of doing so) this could have a significant impact on the future behaviour of both consumers and suppliers. However, the impact may be limited if the case has to be litigated before the existing supplier can be coerced into offering better terms. It is significant that, following this case, Wintershall agreed a demarcation agreement with VNG in eastern Germany which seemed to imply a recognition that competition by means of access through pipelines would not be possible.

Competition developments in transmission and marketing

Aside from these major cases, the perception of impending institutional and regulatory change has focused the minds of all market players. According to the CEO of the production and transmission company BEB:

Clearly, with the changes in the German legal framework, and in particular the proposed ending of the system of demarcations, the market will become more fluid. We are looking outside our traditional areas in Germany, and of course we are looking beyond the borders of Germany.

However, BEB has clear views on the limits of competition, even without demarcation areas:

> In the future there may be a re-allocation of supply areas between Ruhrgas and BEB ... But for us, there is a basic principle of competition here: we do not sell the same gas twice. We do not sell to Ruhrgas and then try to sell it to Ruhrgas' customers.[47]

It is also clear that in some instances there has been no need for legal or regulatory intervention in order to guarantee access to pipelines. In 1996, BEB sold some spot gas to the Polish Oil and Gas Company (PGNiG) and requested transportation through VNG's system. VNG initially refused on the basis that it should be allowed to perform the merchant function of buying from BEB and selling to PGNiG. However, it eventually agreed to transport the gas. The CEO of BEB drew the conclusion that:

> In long term relationships you have these occasional disputes, but there was no real problem between us and VNG. They are a first class company and we have a general understanding with them that we will cooperate in a number of areas.[48]

However, in resolving this transportation problem, it was undoubtedly helpful that BEB owns 15% of VNG and is also a shareholder in Ruhrgas which owns another 25% of the company. It also provided a stark contrast to an episode nearly 10 years earlier in which Ruhrgas refused to transport

---

[47] The statement that 'we do not sell the same gas twice' is a direct quote from the judge's reasoning in the Weissenborn case. Apart from the issue of a matching offer, Wintershall's request for access was refused because the judge found that Wintershall and VNG had bought gas from the same source (Gazprom) and that Wintershall would sell to both VNG and a VNG customer. The judge (somewhat confusingly) construed this potential situation as 'selling the same gas twice'. 'BEB prepares for change', *European Gas Markets*, 24 April 1997, pp. 6–7.

[48] Ibid.

Norwegian gas to Austria as part of the Troll contracts. After protracted negotiations, Ruhrgas purchased the gas and 'resold' it to Statoil on the German/Austrian border.[49]

Another notable example is the experience of Bayerngas, the regional Bavarian transmission company. Following the loss of its largest single industrial customer (the chemical company Wacker-Chemie) to Wingas in 1996, the company's Chief Executive noted the impact on the company:

> We lost it for a variety of reasons, including the price. But for us the most important thing was that Wacker was a wake-up call; it really did make the whole company sit up and take notice.[50]

It may therefore not have been a coincidence that Bayerngas then signed a contract with Wingas in 1997 which will allow for the purchase of up to 15% of its supplies, despite the fact that Ruhrgas, hitherto the company's sole supplier, was in the process of significantly raising its shareholding in Bayerngas. Other regional transmission companies, which had been exclusively supplied by Ruhrgas, have also begun to include Wingas in their portfolios, in particular Westfälische Ferngas and VEW, two of Germany's largest regional suppliers.[51] These developments could probably have only taken place with the agreement of Ruhrgas, thereby releasing the regional companies from their exclusive purchase obligation. The purchases from Wingas do not involve displacing Ruhrgas sales, rather they allow that incremental purchases of gas – up to a certain percentage of total requirements – can be made by the regional companies and municipalities.

One way in which the German regulatory authorities are attempting to break down the barriers of the concession agreements is to use their approval of shareholding exchanges as a bargaining counter. The purchase of 50% of transmission company Thyssengas' shares by the electricity company RWE was conditional upon the transmission company removing

---

[49] 'Ruhrgas holds out against transporter status', *World Gas Report*, 19 June 1987, p. 1.
[50] 'Exciting times for Germany's Bayerngas', *Financial Times International Gas Report*, 21 March 1997, pp. 6–8; 'Bayerngas revamp finalised', ibid., 27 June 1997, p. 14.
[51] 'Wingas makes inroads on rival Ruhrgas', ibid., 16 May 1997, p. 3. 'VEW, Westfaelische Ferngas create new German gas major', *European Gas Markets*, 10 April 1997, p. 4.

exclusivity clauses from its contracts.[52] The RWE investment in Thyssen-gas is again part of a trend of German electricity companies becoming involved in the gas industry, both within Germany and elsewhere in Europe.

Vertical integration by means of purchasing equity in other energy companies, particularly between those companies involved in demarcation and concession agreements, is another area where competition authorities have begun to impose limits. In 1997 the FCO blocked a merger between Westfälische Ferngas and VEW Energie, which would have created the third largest transportation company after Ruhrgas and Wingas, on the grounds that it would have given the resulting company an excessively dominant position in North Rhine–Westphalia. Interestingly the parties did not appeal the decision following the Bundesgerichtshof Court's rejection of two attempted electricity investments by RWE and PreussenElektra. The Court made clear that acquisitions of this kind will in future be based on three criteria:

(1)   dominant energy companies will need to keep their equity shares in distribution companies below 20%;
(2)   this equity participation must be limited in time;
(3)   the equity agreement must not include a clause which would allow the new shareholder to veto the distribution company's choice of suppliers; choice of generation decision; decision to extend its distribution activities into neighbouring regions.[53]

Mindful of the increasing competition and impending legal/regulatory changes within Germany, German companies have begun to extend their activities elsewhere in Europe. This applies not simply to the purchase of equity in other European gas companies – for example the Ruhrgas' and Bayernwerk's purchase of equity in Hungarian gas distribution companies and RWE taking a share in the Prague gas works, and Bayernwerk.

---

[52] 'RWE, Thyssengas agree to surrender exclusivity clauses', *European Gas Markets*, 23 May 1997, p. 4.
[53] 'German cartel office bans merger of WFG and VEW', and 'Berlin court ruling upsets energy majors' strategy', *Gas Matters*, September 1997, pp. iii–iv and August 1997, pp. x–xi.

German gas companies are beginning to supply gas to other countries: Ruhrgas to MOL (Hungary) and BEB to Distrigaz (Belgium), Dangas (Denmark) and in negotiation with both Transgas (in the Czech Republic) and PGNiG.[54]

An example of a more aggressive foreign approach by German companies is the Ruhrgas contract (starting in 1999) to supply Austrian distribution companies at Linz and Salzburg, breaking the monopoly of the Austrian transmission company OMV.[55] This does not involve issues of access since Ruhrgas will build a new pipeline to deliver the gas. It is uncertain whether Ruhrgas took this action as a result of the Wingas/OMV pipeline supplying the Wacker-Chemie plant which had been taken from Ruhrgas' customer Bayerngas. However, as a further retaliation, it has been suggested that the OMV/Wingas pipeline may be expanded within Bavaria to try and expand market share, almost certainly at the expense of Ruhrgas.[56] This kind of overt competition between two major European transmission companies, Ruhrgas and OMV, breaks all the established rules of European gas commerce and is a clear indication of the dawning of a new, more competitive era.

Lessons from Germany

Events in the German gas market since 1991 clearly demonstrate that gas-to-gas competition has arrived in the country, although by the rather unusual method of building parallel pipeline networks to compete for customers. With ferocious resistance from established gas companies to government and regulatory attempts to introduce liberalized access to pipelines, the first development has been competition between transmission companies largely selling Russian gas. The emergence of Wintershall as a

---

[54] BEB has already signed a contract for winter peak supplies to Czech Transgas. This may be the forerunner of a more permanent contractual relationship. 'BEB, VNG and Transgas sign contract for winter gas deliveries into Czech Republic', *European Gas Markets*, 28 November 1997, p. 4.

[55] 'Ruhrgas price cut breaks Austrian monopoly', *Gas Matters*, January 1997, p. 1; 'Ruhrgas plans Austria Anschluss', ibid., February 1997, p. 4.

[56] 'OMV to help Wintershall', *International Gas Report*, 18 April 1997, p. 7.

major player in German gas transportation and marketing, disturbing the long-established status quo, was due to a number of factors:

- the reunification of Germany followed by the collapse of Soviet communism which created an entirely different German market and removed many of the ideological objections to the import of Russian gas;
- the inability of BASF to obtain what it considered to be satisfactory terms for supply to its chemical plants due to the *Anlegbarkeitsprinzip* pricing which in turn created sufficient incentive for BASF to make such huge investments and allowed WIEH/Wingas to undercut the prices of the incumbent merchant companies and persuade customers to switch supplier;
- the special relationship with Gazprom which, with the creation of the WIEH and Wingas joint ventures, brought to Wintershall's pipeline projects the credibility which they had hitherto lacked. Norwegian producers have repeatedly declined to sell gas to the Wintershall joint ventures, giving rise to allegations of unfair practices and a case brought under EU competition authorities (see Norway later in this chapter);
- the financial power of Wintershall's parent company, BASF, which allowed the financing of the Stegal and Midal pipelines prior to signing contracts for a majority of the throughput of the pipeline, and prior to settling equity ownership of the assets.

But while Wintershall began as a 'revolutionary' actor in the German market, by the mid-1990s it had begun to find its place in a changed status quo, establishing a vertical demarcation agreement with VNG in East Germany, having won a superior court case against the FCO.[57] While this did not signal the end of Wintershall's support for liberalization, it was a pragmatic commercial move necessary to increase the load factor of its pipelines. The company certainly retains an interest in offering *lower* prices than those charged by the long-time incumbents. But the need to amortise its investments in new pipeline infrastructure means that, as

---

[57] A vertical demarcation agreement is where Wintershall, having agreed to sell to VNG, cannot then sell to VNG's customers. 'Setback for liberalization plans as court approves demarcation', *Financial Times, EC Energy Monthly*, 26 February 1996.

presently constituted, German competition will not deliver the lowest possible prices. Yet Wingas has continued to be a catalyst for change in Germany, providing regional transmission companies and municipalities with their first experience of supply diversification. This is having a significant effect on wholesale prices with municipalities which – despite not being free to purchase their supplies – are increasingly using the threat of competition to reduce purchase prices from their traditional supplier.[58]

The type of pipeline-to-pipeline competition could not have taken hold in Germany without very significant existing margins in the gas transmission sector. Had BASF/Wintershall not been able to foresee their ability to build the infrastructure and still sell significantly below the prices being offered by the dominant companies, they could not have afforded to take such a major commercial step. The objection of liberal economists to the German pipeline-to-pipeline model is that, in requiring two sets of pipelines to be built, it imposes significantly higher costs and lower efficiencies than competition through access. While this may be an unassailable theoretical position, it is unlikely to be relevant to German legal and political circumstances in 1997, until the owners of pipelines choose, or are forced, to provide access to their systems.

Pipeline-to-pipeline competition has brought lower prices to German industrial customers, and as such it has been a welcome development for both politicians and competition authorities. The resistance of the established gas transmission companies to legal and regulatory changes which would introduce liberalization has continued in parallel with the development of competition. Yet despite their resistance, it is clear that companies are positioning themselves both at home and abroad for anticipated changes. This includes attempted joint ventures and alliances between gas and electricity companies in both German and foreign markets.

Alongside the evolution of national legislation, the FCO has been fighting a range of competition cases, with mixed success, testing out the boundaries of German law and the applicability of European law. The government and regulatory institutions appear neither radical in their

---

[58] The CEO of Wingas noted that the Bremen municipality achieved a significant reduction in its gas costs, just by using the threat of a Wingas purchase, which did not take place. 'Wintershall in '96 profits surge', *International Gas Report*, 18 April 1997, pp. 14–15.

goals, nor in any great hurry to achieve them. Their actions suggest a patient strategy of incremental change in legal and regulatory frameworks, using national and EU legal instruments to achieve their goals. Since 1993 the government has been trying to pass new energy legislation, to sweep away the monopoly elements of demarcation and concession agreements and provide some degree of access to pipelines supervised by the Federal Ministry of Economics.[59] This legislation seems likely to be passed during 1998, but it will not include any provision for access, other than that provided by the EU Gas Directive. The likely adoption of negotiated access will mean that the FCO will remain in charge of gas regulation.

In terms of market structure, the authorities have had some success in limiting the degree of attempted horizontal and vertical integration in the gas and electricity industries by which companies have tried to pre-empt the removal of demarcation and concession agreements. As long as the gas industry continues to move in the direction of greater competition and liberalization the competition authorities appear to be content. This patience seems to be a combination of *Realpolitik* – that this is the most that can be achieved in the current political situation – and a belief that future market developments in Germany will set the stage for the desired degree of liberalization, making legislation and regulation much easier to enact.

The most important goal of both government and regulatory authorities is achieving price reductions for an industrial sector which has for some time been paying some of the highest gas prices in Europe. The first step towards competition – eliminating demarcation and concession agreements – can go a considerable way towards achieving across-the-board price reductions for industry. Assuming that this can be achieved, the German authorities may then turn their attention to questions of liberalization with negotiated access as the first step in this process.

From the point of view of competition and market structure, it is as yet uncertain whether the traditional market dominance of Ruhrgas is simply being replaced by the duopoly of Ruhrgas and Wingas, each company allied to a major producer (or set of producers): Wingas with Gazprom;

---

[59] In fact the draft energy legislation is more directly concerned with the electricity industry than with gas. It will transpose into German law many of the provisions of the EU Electricity Directive (see Chapter 5).

Ruhrgas with Statoil and other Norwegian producers. With each company also becoming closely associated with certain distribution companies – partly through equity investments by these companies – the German gas market could become divided into two increasingly vertically integrated blocs: 'forces of Ruhrgas' versus 'forces of Wingas'.[60] It is likely that this kind of vertically integrated duopoly will turn out to be too simple a structural projection of what is likely to become an extremely complex market.

The geographic and economic centrality and influence of Germany within Europe are such that developments in the German gas market cannot but have a significant affect on surrounding countries, and possibly in the wider Europe. Significant development of *competition* in German gas markets will reduce prices to industry and could give rise to similar competitive pressures in neighbouring countries. Development of *liberalization* would not only remove powerful gas industry opponents to this kind of change within the European Union as a whole, but could transform them into proponents for faster change elsewhere in Europe.

Spain: anti-competitive structure with rapidly emerging liberalization

The Spanish gas industry, a relatively small but rapidly growing gas market, presents an interesting contradiction in terms of competition and liberalization in European gas markets. Gas Natural is the overwhelmingly dominant gas transmission and distribution company, selling gas to around 90% of the Spanish market. The company was formed in 1991 by a merger of the country's two largest distribution companies with Repsol's gas distribution business. In 1994 Gas Natural purchased 91% of the equity of Enagas – the monopoly transmission company. The creation of Gas Natural appeared to be a defensive privatization measure by political and commercial interests, partly intent on preventing foreign incursion into the industry, partly consolidating against EU-inspired liberalization measures. Gas Natural's major shareholders are the oil and energy group Repsol with 45.3% and the Catalan savings bank La Caixa with 25.5%.

So it came as some surprise when, following the election of a new

---

[60] Estrada et al., op. cit., p. 345.

Spanish government, immediate legislation, followed by a Royal Decree published in September 1996, established access to pipelines and LNG facilities for users of 1.2 million cubic metres per day.[61] However, not only was this a very high threshold, but the legislation was also hedged about with qualifications which would allow Gas Natural/Enagas to refuse access. This was followed in December 1997 by the Electricity Act, which provided for a significantly faster liberalization in that sector. The electricity industry is significantly more diversified than gas, with more players in generation and distribution as well as a greater mixture of public and private ownership.

First shots in the liberalization war were fired as a result of developments in the power sector. In early 1997 Repsol and Gas Natural signed a cooperation agreement with the generating company Iberdrola covering power generation, cogeneration and foreign projects (specifically in Latin America).[62] This was a clear challenge to the state-owned generator Endesa which, with its allies (oil company) Cepsa and Banco Central Hispano (BCH), had been attempting to form a rival consortium which could build gas-fired power plants in Spain.[63] The situation is further complicated by the 41.2% shareholding of the French company Elf in Cepsa, which could have given the French company a very strong position to seek access to the Spanish grid. This aspiring consortium approached Gas Natural for access and was apparently rebuffed. At that point, Endesa appears to have made efforts to join the Repsol/Iberdrola/Gas Natural consortium – a proposal which also did not appear to be well received.[64] By the end of 1997 Gas Natural appeared to have broken with Repsol/Iberdrola in announcing a construction programme of 10 gas-fired power stations by 2007, the first two of which will be built by 2000 at Algeciras

---

[61] The July 1996 legislation allowed much greater scope for access than the subsequent September measures. Royal Decree 2033/96, 6 September 1996. *EU Gas Directive*, House of Lords Select Committee on the European Communities, HL Paper 35 (London: The Stationery Office, 1997), pp. 72–4.

[62] 'Major Spanish gas/power accord sealed', *International Gas Report*, 7 February 1997, pp. 1–2.

[63] 'Spanish battles escalate to gas warfare', ibid., 7 March 1997, pp. 1–2.

[64] 'Focus on Spain', *European Gas Markets*, 23 May 1997, p. 3.

and Malaga.[65] This programme would make Gas Natural the fifth largest generator in Spain.

Gas Natural's actions may have been triggered by the December 1997 publication of the Hydrocarbons Bill which presages a faster opening up of the market than foreseen by the EU Directive because of the structure of Spanish industrial gas consumption (see Table 4.1). The government has forecast that the customers eligibility thresholds of 25, 15 and 5 million cubic metres will, in the case of Spain, give rise to market openings of 40%, 50% and 65%, and the government will not modify these openings (as it is entitled to do under Article 18(5) (see Appendix 4.1). The Bill, which is expected to become law during 1998, may also propose a market opening in advance of the likely EU date (mid-2000).[66] What is still uncertain is whether the government will move to create a separate gas regulatory authority to oversee liberalization, or whether this will be added to the duties of the existing Spanish Electricity Regulatory Commission (CSEN).[67] What is clear is that the government's main liberalization objective is to reduce the prices of both electricity and gas to industry, and some have speculated that in pursuit of that aim, the government may opt for regulated, rather than negotiated access.[68] The partial privatization of Endesa and liberalization of electricity is seen as having an important role in reducing electricity prices, which in turn is important for maintaining the competitiveness of Spanish industry.

This rather brief account of the Spanish experience highlights a contradiction between a consolidation of the structure of the gas industry (a directly anti-competitive and protectionist act) followed by the relatively rapid, but admittedly relatively restrictive, introduction of liberalization legislation. Following a failed attempt by a powerful rival energy

---

[65] 'Spain's Gas Natural steps up power drive', *International Gas Report*, 9 January 1998, p. 7.

[66] 'Spain plans to outstrip EU', ibid., p. 19.

[67] Sebastia Ruscalleda i Gallart, 'Regulating Gas and Electricity in a Changing Environment', a paper to the 12th Annual European Autumn Gas Conference, Barcelona, 5 November 1997.

[68] 'EU Gas Directive' op. cit., para. 222, p. 80; Tom Burns, 'Spain's sell-off policy pays dividends', *Financial Times*, 1 August 1997; 'Spain leads the way with liberalization decree', *European Gas Markets*, 16 January 1998, p. 7.

(electricity and oil) conglomerate to gain access to pipelines, further legislation is to be introduced to open the market still further. Whether the eventual outcome of this process will be faster and more successful progress towards liberalization has yet to be seen. But the determination of the present government to drive down gas and electricity prices to industrial customers by a combination of privatization and liberalization may be decisive in determining future developments in the Spanish gas industry.

Russia: institutional change and uncertainty

As was noted in Chapter 3, the Russian gas production and transmission company, RAO Gazprom, produces 95% of the country's gas. From Siberia westwards, Gazprom has a transmission and wholesale monopoly of all large customers, including distribution companies.[69] The Russian gas export company, VEP Gazexport, is a wholly owned subsidiary of Gazprom. Gazexport is the sole exporter of Russian gas outside the former Soviet Union. (Exports to former Soviet republics are handled by a different division of Gazprom.)

Gazprom is owned 40% by the Russian government, 50% by employees and Russian citizens (through a voucher privatization), 10% by the company itself (9% of which has been allocated for offer to foreign investors).[70] Gazprom in the person of Chairman Rem Vyakhirev votes 35% of the government's 40% share in the company and this arrangement will continue, but according to an agreement reached in April 1997 the Chairman is required to make a quarterly report to a 10-person committee headed by the Energy Minister.[71] Gazprom's relationship with successive Russian governments have been periodically difficult, despite the fact that the company's former chairman, Victor Chernomyrdin, has been Russian Prime Minister since 1992. Perennial disagreements have centred on:

---

[69] Gazprom's institutional evolution from Ministry of the Soviet Gas Industry to 1996 is covered in Valery Kryukov and Arild Moe, *Gazprom: Internal Structure, Management Principles and Financial Flows* (London: RIIA, 1996).

[70] The 50% held by Russian citizens is divided into several groups, see ibid., Chapter 7 for details.

[71] 'Russia's reformers put squeeze on Gazprom', *Gas Matters*, May 1997, pp. 5–7.

- from the government side, constant arguments about the amount of tax which Gazprom should pay;
- from Gazprom's side, arguments about how payment arrears (often by government departments and companies) should be set against taxation.

The company's principal short-term problem is non-payment, and the volume of barter trade which has to be accepted as payment by domestic customers. Large-scale non-payment began in 1992 and steadily increased as prices were raised massively towards 'market levels'. During 1994–95, payment arrears by Russian customers were around 50% of receivables. Since 1996 this picture has been complicated by the widespread appearance (or to be strictly accurate, reappearance) of barter trade. Despite the fact that in 1996 Gazprom's accounts were for the first time published according to international accounting standards, it is extremely difficult to disentangle accurate statistics regarding receivables.[72] In the first quarter of 1997 Gazprom reported that it received payment for only 45% of gas delivered and only 6% of those payments were in cash. Non-payment is a highly political issue, given the unemployment and social unrest which could result from payment enforcement and a crucial financial issue, given the sums of money involved. The trade-off between how much tax Gazprom should pay, and the extent to which it should be allowed to enforce payment, has been and continues to be, a running battle between the company and the government. In June 1997 a Presidential Decree lowering industrial gas prices by 40% was published, but this price cut will only apply to those companies which have paid all of their federal and local taxes and which are up to date in their payments to Gazprom.[73] For our purposes, resolution of the non-payment issue will have, as we shall see, an extremely important bearing on future restructuring and liberalization of the gas industry.

---

[72] Gazprom's 1996 IAS accounts state that 57% of accounts receivable settled during calendar year 1996 were in the form of barter trade or inter-enterprise transfer.
[73] *Eastern Bloc Energy*, July 1997, p. 4.

Restructuring, liberalization and regulation

Gazprom has eight major production subsidiaries, three of which, located in Siberia, account for around 80% of production, each centred on a single major field: Nadymgazprom (Medvezhe), Urengoygazprom (Urengoy) and Yamburggazodobycha (Yamburg). Until 1997 the company's 14 transmission subsidiaries were responsible for transportation and sales of gas throughout Russia. In the early part of 1997 a restructuring of the company was announced whereby all gas sales would be handled by a newly created marketing subsidiary, Mezhregiongaz. This, and other reform measures (see later), mean that the transmission subsidiaries have become transportation-only companies with no merchant function.[74]

At the beginning of 1997 it was announced that a newly created Federal Energy Commission would set regionally differentiated gas prices for industrial and residential customers. The idea was that the Commission would eventually be responsible for regulating transmission tariffs. Gazprom then announced an internal restructuring, akin to a corporatization of the company. This was accelerated by the April 1997 changes in the Russian government which once again brought to the fore younger economic reformers intent on reining in the power of the Russian monopoly utilities and increasing tax receipts from these companies. The clearest report on the reforms envisaged by government suggested a three stage process:

(1)   reforms to be completed during 1997 include regionally differentiated gas prices; a unified system of transmission pricing for independent producers and Gazprom subsidiaries; encouraging new investors (domestic and foreign) to develop new fields and pipelines; transparency of production and transportation costs; accounting and reporting procedures for Gazprom subsidiaries; establishing tariffs and conditions for access to pipelines (including a Commission to look at

---

[74] For more details on the Gazprom reorganization, see Arild Moe, 'The Reorganization of Gazprom: Scope and Impact' and Valery Kryukov, 'Gazprom – Financial Flows and Management: the Need for Internal Transparency', proceedings of the conference, Reform in the Russian Gas Industry: Regulation, Taxation, Foreign Investment and New Export Prospects, Royal Institute of International Affairs, London, 20–21 November 1997.

access for independent producers); tendering for rights to develop gas fields favourably located with respect to existing pipelines;

(2) reforms to be completed during 1998 include bringing residential prices up to those paid by industrial customers; transferring authority for local transmission tariffs to regional energy commissions;

(3) reforms to be completed during 1999–2000 include separation of production from transmission with contracts between different subsidiaries; regulation of transmission tariffs.[75]

Assuming these reforms are implemented, they would amount to Gazprom being transformed into a full open-access transportation company before the end of the century. But it would be unwise to make this assumption too readily. Both the scope and timetable of the reforms appear extremely ambitious, and are unlikely to be met. The institutions and personalities responsible for implementing the reforms are subject to frequent change. The roles of the Federal Energy Commission, Anti-Monopoly Committee, Ministry of Fuel and Energy, and the offices of the Prime Minister and Deputy Prime Minister seem to become more and less influential on a monthly basis. By early 1998 conventional wisdom seemed to suggest that Gazprom's leadership had 'seen off' the latest group of economic reformers who were the authors of the utility reforms and whose political longevity seemed to be in doubt. It would, however, be wrong to be cynical about the future reform of Gazprom. Not only has a degree of liberalization already taken place in Russia, but the way in which this develops will have an extremely important impact on European gas markets.

Likely restructuring and liberalization reforms: the relevance for European gas markets

Although the reform programme is likely to prove overly ambitious, some progress has been made towards the creation of corporatized production and transmission units trading by means of transfer prices. The key question in the first stage will be the extent to which the transmission

---

[75] 'Russia sets monopoly restructuring programme to year 2000', *Interfax Petroleum Report*, 2–9 May 1997.

companies will turn over all of their sales functions to the newly created marketing division (Mezhregiongaz) thereby becoming transmission-only companies. To the extent this does happen, transmission tariffs will need to be devised and implemented which will be a major step towards restructuring and liberalization.

Almost irrespective of the progress of internal restructuring, government pressure for Gazprom to be demerged (rather than 'broken up') into smaller entities is likely to continue and intensify in the coming years. This will be due less to any likely government conversion to the tenets of competition and liberalization, and more to the increasing threat which successive Russian politicians will perceive arising from the financial and political power of Gazprom. The current liberalization and restructuring programme will assist any eventual demerger into separate production and transmission companies.[76]

Yet the political, financial and institutional complexities of such a restructuring should not be minimized. Production is highly concentrated, both geographically and corporately (in the hands of three production associations) in Siberia. A structure of demerged production companies selling their gas through an open access transmission system (controlled by either a single company or multiple companies) would place significant power and wealth in the hands of three new companies in the Yamal–Nenets region of Siberia. This may not be attractive to Moscow politicians who, despite their problems with Gazprom, at least live in the same city as its senior management. Moreover, until the problem of non-payment and non-cash payment by Russian customers is resolved, or at least reduced to manageable proportions, the effect of demerger could be to plunge many of the newly independent production and/or transmission companies into immediate bankruptcy. The production companies would depend on a form of payment sufficiently liquid to allow them to cover their costs, plus payment of tariffs to the transmission company (or companies) and emerge with a tangible profit. A production-only company (or companies) would be much less well equipped than Gazprom to deal with large-scale

---

[76] There are, of course, a number of different options depending on how many production and transmission companies eventually demerge from the current structure.

non-payment, late payment, and/or a large proportion of barter goods exchanged for gas. These difficulties would almost certainly lead either to their inability to pay their transmission tariffs (with dire consequences for the transmission companies), and/or to serious financial problems within their own organizations.

However, when non-payment and barter problems have been resolved, or reduced, demerger will become a viable option. Competition and liberalization will be accelerated due to the reduction in gas demand within Russia, arising from bankruptcy and the start of conservation and efficiency measures which will greatly inflate the existing 'bubble' of excess supply.[77] Competition between producers for a shrinking market – and potentially between transmission companies competing to utilize available pipeline capacity – would provide ideal conditions for a strongly competitive market. Given the geographical concentration just noted, however, the potential for collusion between existing producers may be equal to, or greater than, the potential for competition.

But if Russian and foreign companies are given opportunities and incentives to open up smaller gas fields, and perhaps revisit older fields (where recovery could be increased with more advanced technology), with the prospect of delivering their production direct to consumers in Russia and beyond, competition between suppliers could rapidly become fierce. This would also be a major opportunity for Central Asian gas producers – freed from the embrace of a vertically integrated Gazprom – to negotiate directly with a range of customers, Russian and non-Russian, with their gas being delivered by transmission-only successor companies.

But if the demerger of Gazprom's production and transmission units could be considered positive for the Russian domestic gas market, it would hugely complicate existing exports to Europe.[78] All of the current long-term contracts are held by Gazprom (with Gazexport being the negotiating partner), and stretch into the next decade and beyond. In terms

---

[77] Jonathan P. Stern, *The Russian Gas 'Bubble': Consequences for European Gas Markets* (London: EEP/RIIA, 1995).
[78] Exports to former republics are not as complicated since they are negotiated on an annual basis.

of revenue earnings, these are the crown jewels of Gazprom's current assets valued at $185bn by the company.[79] The demerger of Gazprom would cause immense difficulties in terms of which entity would continue to hold the contracts. If a residual Gazprom company still existed after the production and transmission assets had been demerged into different companies, there would be no guarantee that the entity will have sufficient financial means to purchase sufficient gas from production companies for the management of 150–200 BCM/year of long-term contract gas. If there were no residual Gazprom company, the existing long-term contracts would presumably be allocated between the successor production companies. Such an allocation might amount to a complete renegotiation of contracts for around one-third of European gas demand – a highly destabilizing prospect for European markets. It is this prospect, probably more than concerns about a supply disruption for political or technical reasons, which would give rise to major security of supply fears in Europe in respect of Russian gas. While this is not an argument for indefinite retention of Gazprom's current vertically integrated structure and *de facto* export monopoly, structural change within the company raises problems which require careful consideration. Protagonists of restructuring Russia's gas industry will need to ensure that the proposals which they are advancing take these considerations into account and provide convincing solutions to potential contractual problems with European gas companies. This will not be an easy task.

Norway: institutional challenges

One of the curiosities of the Norwegian gas industry is that this major European supplier has not used any gas in its domestic energy balance for 25 years. While this situation will change in the future, the institutional structure of Norwegian gas export sales is coming under strain as competitive pressures mount.

---

[79] Presumably this figure is a valuation of the revenues which will be received from current long-term contracts over their remaining contractual life. 'Gazprom to use 2–3% of investment shares as convertibles', *Interfax Petroleum Report*, 28 November – 4 December 1997, p. 11.

Aside from major international companies operating in the Norwegian offshore sector, the Norwegian participants are Statoil – the state oil and gas company; Norsk Hydro – a company with private investors but with 51% state ownership; Saga Petroleum – a private company owned mainly by Norwegian interests (in which the Norwegian state owns a 'golden share', in order to prevent unwelcome takeovers). A further important aspect is an accounting distinction between resources held by state-owned companies and the 'State's Direct Financial Interest' (SDFI), established at the beginning of 1985. The SDFI in all fields and pipelines is operated by Statoil, but gives the Norwegian state an immediate and important interest in decision-making.[80] SDFI interests are considerable:

> The SDFI alone has 4700 million barrels of proven oil reserves and 1200 BCM of proven gas reserves spread in 21 fields. It also has interests in 7 oil and gas pipelines (50% of the total). In 1992 the SDFI alone accounted for 45% of all offshore investments. If the SDFI and Statoil's interests are combined, the state's share is 50.3% in fields already earmarked for development and 51.8% for all fields that are at the planning stage. Their combined control of commercial reserves is 68% and their share of total petroleum production between 1994–97 is 63%.[81]

This state dominance of gas resource ownership has been reinforced by gas (export) sales arrangements which, since 1986, have been dominated by the Gas Negotiating Committee or GFU – a tripartite body under the leadership of Statoil consisting of that company, Norsk Hydro and Saga Petroleum.[82] The guidelines for the GFU were set out as follows:

---

[80] 'The essence of the arrangement is that a part of Statoil's gross income from each individual project is transferred directly to the State, while a corresponding part of Statoil's expenses on each individual project is covered by the State through SDFI', Ministry of Petroleum and Energy, *Norwegian Petroleum Activity*, Fact Sheet 97, p. 10.
[81] Javier Estrada et al., *The Development of European Gas Markets: Environmental, Economic and Political Perspectives* (Chichester: John Wiley, 1995), p. 228; see Table 2.1 for SDFI gas production.
[82] For pre-1986 arrangements, see Javier Estrada et al., *Natural Gas in Europe: Markets, Organization and Politics* (London: Pinter, 1988), pp. 223–29.

The Committee is to act as a permanent advisory body for the Ministry of Petroleum and Energy in questions associated with the disposal of natural gas reserves and evaluations of which fields can most expediently be developed or exploited to deliver natural gas under new contracts ... Preparation and implementation of gas sales negotiations are to take place under the direction of the committee under Statoil's supervision ... It is the authorities' task to decide which fields are to be developed. Clarification with potential buyers concerning which fields are to be included in a gas sales agreement can therefore take place only after the authorities have decided on this.[83]

This centralization of decision-making in Norwegian state hands, with no serious opportunity for any outside input, caused widespread resentment among foreign companies operating in Norway. In 1993 decision making was widened with the creation of the Gas Supply Committee or FU whose role would be to 'function as an advisory body to the government with regard to the development and exploitation of gas fields and pipelines.'[84]

The Norwegian government regards the GFU/FU system as the chosen agent of the nation's sovereign control over its resources, and essential for optimising the management of those resources. The GFU negotiates sales contracts, the FU then recommends which fields should be developed to fulfil these contracts, and these recommendations are then passed to the Ministry. The Norwegian Parliament is asked to endorse the final decision. The issue of whether this system can survive in a competitive European gas markets and will eventually be replaced by a more liberal system, will be significant for the development of competition in European gas markets. There are three specific issues:

(1)   whether the GFU/FU system man be considered anti-competitive within the framework of the European Economic Area Treaty;[85]

---

[83] *Petroleum Activity in the Medium Term*, Report to the Storting No. 46 (1986–87), Chapter 11.

[84] The FU consisted of the ten largest gas resource holders in the Norwegian sector – the three GFU members and seven foreign companies. This was subsequently expanded to 12 companies. Report to the Storting No. 2 (1992–93), Chapter 2.

[85] With the Norwegian people's (second) rejection of EU membership in the 1993 Referendum, it is Norway's membership of the European Economic Area, which has a Treaty of Association with the EU, that is relevant here.

(2) whether a bureaucratic and slow-moving decision-making process whose stated purpose is to contribute to the management of resources, defined as optimization of the totality of the Norwegian oil and gas resource base from a variety of fields, can cope with a market in which decisions are increasingly likely to be needed within days (and possibly within hours) if existing market share is to be defended and new customers to be won

(3) whether the role of Statoil as representative of the state's direct economic share (SDFI) in the fields is still appropriate and tenable, given the size of the state as a potentially independent player in Norwegian gas sales.

The first of these issues was raised in June 1996, following a complaint from the German company Wintershall arising from its inability to purchase gas from the Norwegian company (and GFU member) Saga Petroleum, because of GFU objections. The complaint alleged a price-fixing cartel which led to a joint investigation by DG IV (the EU Competition Directorate) and the EFTA Surveillance Authority (ESA) into the activities of the three members of the GFU: Statoil, Norsk Hydro and Saga.[86] Since all of the gas is sold to companies in EU member states, the matter lies within the Competition Directorate DG IV's powers, but it was required to request the ESA to investigate Norwegian companies. The European Economic Area (EEA) Agreement, to which Norway is a party, incorporates EU competition rules.

The Norwegian government does not consider that the EEA Agreement is applicable to the GFU as a resource management institution. However, the ESA may disagree and may find the GFU/FU arrangements to be fundamentally anti-competitive and indeed consider the prevention of gas-to-gas competition as one of their main aims. In the event of such an outcome, the Norwegian government would come under severe pressure to abandon GFU/FU system.[87] It may, in any case, find that the commercial

---

[86] For background see 'Gas joint selling deals: DGIV, Britannia and the GFU', *FT, EC Energy Monthly*, 15 November 1996, pp. 7–8; 'Did the Norwegian dawn raids presage a new dawn?', *European Gas Markets*, February 1997, p. 6.

[87] Presumably Norway could withdraw from the EEA if the decision were to go against it, but this would be a very major step to protect a system which may in any case prove untenable in the future.

requirements of a competitive market make the present system untenable.

Given their resistance to changing institutional arrangements for gas sales, it is not surprising that successive Norwegian governments have been among the most implacable opponents of EU gas liberalization initiatives. This is curious from a policy perspective, given that Norwegian liberalization initiatives in the electricity sector are the most advanced in Europe.[88] While it may be relatively easy from an internal Norwegian perspective to separate the gas and electricity industries – because of the lack of a domestic gas market – from an international perspective, its policies appear completely contradictory. This may be yet another factor which weakens the Norwegian government's case for retaining the GFU.

Concern about European liberalization initiatives has prevented the unitization and liberalization of the Norwegian offshore pipeline network – an essential step towards optimising the throughput of an increasingly complex set of pipelines delivering gas from an increasing number of fields. The 'GasLed' concept was first advanced in late 1995 as a way of 'unitizing' the ownership of the offshore gas pipeline systems, and producing a single transmission tariff for gas delivered to Continental Europe.[89] Different variants were discussed, with the idea that the some of the systems – Ekofisk, Statpipe, Norpipe, Zeepipe, Norfrapipe and Europipe – might not initially be included in the GasLed concept.[90]

A White Paper was expected on the concept in the Spring of 1996, but government apparently considered that GasLed would undermine the present GFU system and Norwegian arguments against liberalization, and refused to allow any further discussions. This must be seen as a lost opportunity to prepare for a more competitive market conditions which will require more transparent and straightforward calculations of capacity availability and charging in Norwegian transmission systems.

It is difficult to understand how the Norwegian authorities can genuinely believe that the GFU/FU system has a long-term future. From the point of

---

[88] Atle Midtun and Steve Thomas, *Theoretical ambiguity and the weight of historical heritage: a comparative study of the British and Norwegian electricity liberalization,* Centre for Electricity Studies, Norwegian School of Management, Report No. 1, 1997.

[89] 'Oslo mulls pipe system plans', *Financial Times International Gas Report,* 24 November 1995, p. 15.

[90] 'Focus on Norway', *European Gas Markets,* January 1996, p. 3.

view of Norwegian national interest, it would be better to replace this system with something which appears less all embracing, rather than be faced with an adverse judgment from European competition authorities. While the abandonment of the GFU/FU system would probably not threaten ongoing contractual arrangements, it would increase the pressure from individual producers – both Norwegian and non-Norwegian – to market gas discoveries on an accelerated timetable.[91] However, such pressure could be strongly resisted by the Norwegian Parliament whose approval of individual field and pipeline developments, hitherto regarded as a 'rubber-stamping' exercise, would immediately become a much more serious element of the process. In a small country where a majority of the population and the political classes regard environmental and sustainability issues as matters of genuine priority, it is entirely possible that new development requests might be denied.

The other consequence of abolishing the GFU might be further to strengthen the pre-eminent position of Statoil, both in its own right and as operator of the SDFI. If the Norwegian government were to be deprived of its chosen resource management vehicle, it might respond by reinforcing the position of both Statoil and the SDFI in terms of licence awards and field development approvals, and carrying out its long-expressed 'threat' to limit new gas development.[92]

Either of these responses would curtail expansion of Norwegian gas exports, beyond what has already been contracted. This would be good news for other suppliers to European gas markets, but not necessarily good news for Norwegian Continental Shelf sellers. By contrast, dismantling of the GFU/FU system with no corresponding government restrictions would almost certainly lead to an increase in Norwegian gas exports by individual license holders, both Norwegian and non-Norwegian. In that scenario, the market power of Statoil, particularly if granted free rein to operate the SDFI, could be so overwhelmingly dominant that the

---

[91] There is no reason why the GFU should not be allowed to hold the existing contracts which have been signed. New contracts would simply be on a different basis.

[92] For an account of Norwegian gas export history in which these threats have surfaced periodically, see Jonathan P. Stern, 'Norwegian gas exports: past policy, current prospects and future options', *Energy Policy*, January/February 1990, pp. 55–60.

differences between the new and existing structures might not be so great.

Institutional developments in a wider European context

The gas markets which have received a relatively lengthy treatment in this chapter seem to the author to be those where significant change has occurred, and still is occurring which is both important in its own right, and may trigger significant developments elsewhere. This is not to suggest that important changes are limited to these countries. Indeed an important part of the argument advanced in this study is that change is occurring everywhere in Europe. The following brief overview is an attempt to highlight significant developments elsewhere on the Continent.

Italy: privatization with limited liberalization

The privatization of ENI has been fundamentally anti-liberalization in its failure to demerge the main corporate components of the conglomerate – AGIP and SNAM – into separate entities. However, significant changes are on the horizon in the Italian gas industry, although one of the principal drivers is similar privatization and liberalization in the electricity industry. As early as 1995 the gas transmission company SNAM was required to publish a transmission tariff, although the definition of those eligible for access to the system was limited to (electricity generator) ENEL and independent power producers operating on its behalf.[93]

In November 1996 the Autorità per l'energia electrica e il gas was established as an independent public body and started work in April 1997.[94] The regulatory authority is responsible for ensuring access to networks, setting tariffs, service quality, all aspects of concessions and dispute resolution. At the same time, the long-standing exclusive right of ENI to conduct exploration, production and storage in the Po Valley (the main producing area in the country) was abolished.[95]

---

[93] 'SNAM's transport tariff can be cheaper than Britain's', *Gas Matters*, March 1995, pp. 23–25.
[94] 'Italy cleans up its gas laws: hello regulator, goodbye monopoly', ibid., January 1997, pp. 1–4.
[95] Oliveiro Bernadini, 'The Italian Authority for Electricity and Gas Regulation', a paper to the 12th European Autumn Gas Conference, Barcelona, 5 November 1997.

During the debates on the EU Gas Directive, the Italian government tended to be in the camp of the conservatives, but in the wake of agreement on the text, there seemed to be some new enthusiasm with indication that the government would allow smaller industrial users to combine the volumes in order to become eligible for direct purchase. Whether this type of activity will be linked to a finding by the national anti-trust authority that SNAM is in an unacceptably dominant position in the industry, remains to be seen.[96]

Belgium and Austria: privatization without liberalization and competition

In both Belgium and Austria the sale of equity in transmission companies Distrigaz and OMV was carefully managed to exclude major European gas and energy companies. In Belgium an all-Belgian 'buy-out' was implemented, while in Austria a Middle East investor was finally allowed to purchase equity in OMV. Neither government has shown anything other than opposition to liberalization, despite the fact that the geographical position of both countries (but especially Belgium) would leave their companies ideally placed to take advantage of gas-to-gas competition.

Elsewhere in Europe

In much of former communist Europe, restructuring and privatization of energy and gas industries has been widespread.[97] In gas, the fastest change has been in *Hungary* where both MOL (production and transmission) and the gas distribution companies were privatized, the latter with substantial foreign shareholdings. These companies were regulated by the Hungarian Energy Office, the region's first specialized energy regulatory authority, established in 1994. A similar pattern of privatization has been seen in the *Estonian* and *Latvian* gas industries. Privatization has also taken place in the former Yugoslav republics of *Croatia* and *Slovenia*, but without substantial foreign ownership.

---

[96] 'Rome urges small firm links', *International Gas Report*, 9 January 1997, p. 18.
[97] For a general overview of change in these countries, see John Leslie, *Central European Energy: Markets in Transition* (London: Financial Times Energy Publishing, 1996).

Elsewhere, the pace of change has been slower. In the *Czech Republic* the privatization of gas distribution companies should be on the government's 1998 agenda, but plans to change the status of the immensely profitable (transmission company) Transgas continue to recede into the future. In *Romania*, the privatization of Romgaz is scheduled for 1998 and restructuring of the industry seems likely as part of that process. Romania is the only country in the region where liberalized access to gas networks is under way with Romgaz transporting gas for Wirom (the Romgaz/WIEH joint venture) among others. In *Poland*, privatization and restructuring of PGNiG has been on the agenda for some time, but progress has been painfully slow. In *Bulgaria*, the restructuring of the gas market has been immensely difficult and in early 1998 the outcome of disagreements over the future of (the Gazprom/Bulgarian joint venture) transmission company Topenergy were still not clear.[98]

In the emerging markets of southern Europe, gas industries in *Turkey*, *Greece* and *Portugal* are showing rapid growth, but with a traditional structure of dominant transmission and distribution companies. Understandably, the priority of these new industries is growth rather than liberalization.

The picture that emerges here is one of diversity and uncertainty, but in the context of rapid change. There is virtually no gas industry in a European country in which some major event is not occurring. However, this event is as likely to involve privatization and restructuring as it is liberalization, competition and regulation. This does not mean that the one may not lead to the other, it is only to point out that it is difficult to be certain as to the details and timing of such developments.

Conclusions

Most European gas industries, with the notable exception of Germany, have anti-competitive transmission structures featuring single transmission companies with de facto monopolies of transportation and imports. As far as distribution is concerned, the British structure was particularly anti-

---

[98] Reports in early 1998 suggested that Topenergy had broken up and would be replaced by a new joint venture. *Eastern Bloc Energy*, January 1998, pp. 25–26.

competitive in having a single monopoly of distribution as well as transmission. Most Continental European gas industries feature a number of gas distribution companies with monopoly franchises (often as part of a range of services provided by municipalities). In this respect, the development of competition may be encouraged by the existence of multiple players in distribution.

However, in Continental Europe there seems little keenness to introduce competition legislation and support this with an aggressive and proactive regulatory authority. Indeed there is significant opposition within many European countries to setting up the type of regulatory institutions which are required to implement and police competition, and great fear of the complexity which inevitably results when competition is introduced. A large part of this opposition includes the major gas transmission companies which show few signs of mirroring British Gas' indecisive defence of its interests. They have already mounted a ferocious defence of the status quo in their own countries and in Brussels. However, in the Netherlands where, after being one of its fiercest opponents, the government suddenly embraced liberalization at the beginning of 1996, and in Spain where the same process was repeated later that year, there are plans to open markets to competition faster than the demands of the EU Directive. Furthermore, in Continental Europe there is significantly greater government sensitivity towards public service obligations, and security of supply – neither of which has been satisfactorily resolved in Britain (at least thus far). On a macroeconomic level, the huge reduction in the labour force in both the British gas and electricity industries, resulting from privatization and liberalization, may be a greater cause for concern in Continental Europe than it appeared to be in Britain. For these reasons it seems highly unlikely that the driving forces for liberalization and competition in the British market – government and regulatory interventions into the business of a relatively compliant dominant player – will be repeated on the European Continent.

The other feature of the British experiment has been the determination to extend competition to the smallest, residential gas customers. Even in North America, where competition and liberalization commenced nearly a decade earlier than in Britain, competition experiments at the residential level only began to get underway in the mid-1990s, without the British determination to open the entire market within three years. With the exception of the Netherlands and Spain, there is as yet no sign in Continental Europe that liberalization of the residential market is even on the far horizons of government thinking.

In many countries the 1990s have seen a progressive breakdown in the power of the transmission companies and the institutional and policy assumptions which have underpinned their pre-eminence. In part their power is being broken by competition and attempted competition – either by new entrants (of which the clearest example is Wintershall in Germany) or by established energy companies in the same country (principally from the power sector), or by established gas companies from other countries (e.g. Ruhrgas in Austria). In terms of policy assumptions, widespread privatization of gas and other utility industries has, to some extent, removed from transmission companies the traditional protection which they enjoyed from their governments. While the clearest example of this was British Gas, companies such as Gazprom which were hitherto 'untouchable', as part of the government, are increasingly required to take the views of governments and (newly created) regulators into account. For dominant electricity companies this will increasingly mean investing in the least-cost form of power generation, in the face of competition from independent power projects. While in a former era this might have brought power companies into the gas industry as suitors, looking to woo suppliers and transmission companies, today it brings powerful new entrants with financial clout and market ambition looking to push aside traditional companies and break established rules. Power companies are of a size and influence that the resistance of traditional gas companies is unlikely to be successful.

Meanwhile, many of the transmission companies themselves are rapidly changing their behaviour, stemming from a combination of fear of competitive challenges in their own markets, and a recognition that they will need to expand beyond their national borders in order to compensate for, at least a degree of, market share which will inevitably be lost in the future. The activities of Ruhrgas and OMV in each other's markets are a good example of these trends, as are Gasunie's extension of contacts with traditional foreign customers and attempts to enter central/east European markets in compensation for losing domestic market share.

In summary, institutional change and institutional breakdown is being witnessed everywhere in European gas markets and the countries which supply them. Companies are changing their shape (due to privatization), and their commercial behaviour business relationships (due to the removal of monopoly protection and the appearance of new entrants). This raises the question of how such companies may change further in the future, in order to prepare for a more risky and competitive future. A large part of the early answer appears to be the development of vertical integration. Foreign purchases of (former East) German transmission and distribution companies were explained in terms of attempts, largely by producers, to gain access to markets.[99] Foreign purchases of Hungarian gas distribution companies were explained in a similar fashion.[100] In the vertical integration model, companies in different parts of the chain purchase equity in, or form alliances with, companies in other parts of the chain, in order to 'lock in' a market for their product, be it gas or transmission/distribution services. Thus Wintershall and Gazprom, Ruhrgas and German distribution companies are good examples of this trend. Such integration between producers, transmission and distribution companies or large consumers (such as power stations), may be considered a partial substitute for long-term take or pay contracts, or demarcation and concession agreements, which are likely to be more difficult or impossible to continue in their present form.

New joint ventures (or alliances) in the gas industry are being formed between companies which have something to offer each other by virtue of being in different parts of the business in different countries, with different skills – thus Wintershall/Gazprom, Sonatrach/BP. This is notably different from the old joint ventures such as Shell/Esso, where the withdrawal of Esso from the British marketing venture (Quadrant) may be a harbinger of divorces in other markets. Likewise the BP/Statoil alliance seemed to have been fashioned with the past, rather than the future, in mind; and the

---

[99] While this was a sound idea, it proved to be too much of a long-term prospect for some foreign investors which have already sold or are in the process of selling their original stakes, e.g. ELF to Preussenelectra in VNG, BG plc to VNG.
[100] 'European future to boost Hungarian prices', *Gas Matters*, September 1996, pp. 14–23.

break-up of their British marketing venture was not surprising.[101]

Another form of market restructuring as competition and liberalization get under way is horizontal integration. This is already seen in the distribution sector in countries such as the Netherlands, where gas is just one product of distribution companies selling electricity, water, telecoms and cable television. In Britain, the joint ventures between energy companies and a range of organizations with direct access to consumers, such as high street retailers, trades unions and local authorities, demonstrates another potential form of restructuring.

National and EU competition authorities will have something to say about the legality and the scope of activities of different types of corporate alliance in terms of what is held to constitute anti-competitive behaviour. Nationally, companies are likely to look for defensive alliances with companies which would otherwise be seeking to encroach on their markets. For gas companies this will overwhelmingly be electricity companies – both generators and distribution companies. Alliances both remove competitors and potentially guarantee markets. Internationally, at least two types of alliances appear visible at present: transmission and/or marketing company with a large producer (Wintershall/Gazprom, Sonatrach/BP, Ruhrgas/GFU); and large established company with aggressive foreign entrant, e.g. the ENI/Enron and Enel/Enron joint ventures in Italy.[102]

Institutional change towards competition and liberalization may, in a number of countries, take the form of large companies – integrated vertically or horizontally – which can square off against each other in terms of market power. This will result in a rather limited degree of competition. If this observation is valid, one might expect a number of European gas markets to move from single gatekeepers in each part of the chain, to large energy conglomerates, both for gas and electricity, integrated vertically or horizontally either as a single company, or in strategic alliances.

---

[101] However, the BP/Statoil alliance may have been more focused on oil, and particularly oil developments in the Caspian Sea region.

[102] The announcement of possible joint ventures between ENI and Enron, and Enel and Enron, to convert 5,000 Mw of plant to combined cycle gas-fired power generation has the appearance of two large national energy competitors seeking to put pressure on each other by threatening to introduce a powerful aggressive foreign company as an ally. 'Focus on Enron', *European Gas Markets*, 29 August 1997, pp. 3–4.

Chapter 6
Scenarios and Security

This chapter advances two scenarios for the development of European gas markets: 'evolution' and 'unravelling'. Clearly these are not the only possible outcomes for gas markets, but on the basis of previous chapters, they seem plausible and also assist the consideration of the consequences for liberalization and competition within a more specific market framework. All prices advanced in the scenarios are in 1997 dollars.

Market evolution scenario

In the evolution scenario, sellers offer modest volumes of short-term gas at European borders at prices somewhat below current long-term contracts.

Supply/demand circumstances

Britain Small volumes of gas (less than 20% of the pipeline's capacity) are traded through the Interconnector pipeline on a short-term basis. Prices are not sufficiently high for UKCS producers to bring forward substantial additional reserves to market, and the increase in British demand – largely in the power generation sector, plus an increase in deliveries to Ireland (north and south) – rapidly restricts Britain's exports to the long-term contracts which have been signed with Continental European customers. Shortly after 2000 Britain imports and exports to the Continent are roughly in balance on an annual basis.

Russia The first Belarus–Poland ('Yamal') line is delayed until after 2000. By the time it is finally completed, its capacity is fully contracted on long-term contracts with little spare capacity for short-term sales. The second line is delayed until the end of the first decade of the next century.

The Netherlands   Gasunie continues to be more active on the international market – both buying and selling – but operating on long-term contracts with little gas available for short-term trading.

Norway and Algeria   Although a short-term (spot) market does emerge the GFU and Sonatrach are unable to participate because their governments insist they limit their sales to traditional clients on long-term contracts.

Some major importers decline to purchase lower price gas offered on short-term contracts, preferring to include this in existing or new long-term contracts.

Price and contractual outcomes

Prices for short-term gas fall to around $2.00/mmbtu, but volumes traded at this price are relatively small. Although the phenomenon of a 'spot market' is announced and prices start to be quoted, the number and liquidity of trades fail to reach the level required to create a reliable index against which long-term gas contracts could be priced until after the year 2000. Little disturbance is caused to existing long-term contracts and take or pay commitments can be honoured with minimum inconvenience. Prices drift downwards, reaching a new equilibrium around $2.00–2.25/ mmbtu (around 20% below the average levels seen in the first half of 1997). By the time a spot market and spot price markers are established (after 2000), the terms of virtually all existing long-term contracts include automatic take or pay reductions and immediate spot price adjustments.

Market unravelling scenario

In the unravelling scenario, sellers with spare capacity in their transmission systems begin to offer volumes of gas at European borders in northwest Europe at prices significantly below those of long-term contract prices.

Supply/demand circumstances

Britain Long-term gas contracts account for around 60% of Interconnector pipeline capacity. The remaining 40% of capacity is fully utilized in short-term trading. UKCS producers continue to find and to bring forward gas at prices below $2.00/mmbtu.

Russia Gazprom pushes volumes through the first Belarus–Poland ('Yamal') pipeline to the limit of its capacity. Construction of the second pipeline commences, even though spare capacity remains in the first line.

Norway The GFU/FU system collapses under the joint weight of EU/EFTA pressures and claims from both Norwegian and foreign companies that such arrangements cannot be sustained in a competitive market. Individual producers begin to sell substantial volumes of incremental gas through a unitized and optimized transportation system.

The Netherlands The owners of low-calorific value Groningen gas start to find their customers being poached by high-calorific value competitive supplies. Since Groningen gas may only be sold to lo-cal customers through lo-cal networks – and a large part of the customer base will be lost if it shifts to hi-cal gas – a decision is taken to sell Groningen supplies on an accelerated basis at lower prices.

Algeria Finding that all other major suppliers are beginning to encroach into its markets offering low price gas, Sonatrach is forced to compete (at least in southern Europe) in order to maintain market share. Sonatrach also uses spare capacity in its pipeline and LNG systems to retaliate against competition from other suppliers.

The major merchant transmission companies have already over-contracted in an attempt to 'mop up' available gas. None can ignore the volumes on offer as they come under enormous pressure from (especially large industrial) customers to allow direct purchase and access through their pipeline systems.

Price and contractual outcomes

Prices for short-term gas fall below $1.50 mmbtu. The price collapse starts in northwest Europe and takes more time to reach the south of the Continent. 'Spot' prices become transparent and widely quoted using Bacton, Zeebrugge and somewhere in Germany as principal trading points. Pressure starts to mount on long-term contract prices. Within a year, spot prices become the determining form of indexation in long-term contract prices in northwest Europe (Germany, Belgium and the Netherlands). Prices stabilize at between $1.50 and $1.75 (40% below the average prices in the third quarter of 1997) for two to three years. All major European markets feel this impact within a year. Some producers adjust rapidly to these new conditions, recognizing that the consequences of not doing so will be loss of market share and an uncertain future. However, some insist on holding buyers strictly to the terms of long-term contracts. Buyers either enter litigation or, as their merchant margins become negative, engage in distress sales which exacerbate the price collapse.

Scenarios: timing, actions and reactions of individual players

There is a temptation with both scenarios to try to identify which parties are likely to be principally responsible for the move towards competitive markets in Europe. The more interesting and legitimate reason for doing so is to try to specify the timing of events. Less legitimate and useful is a desire to apportion 'blame' for potential disruptions to traditional market and pricing structures. If blame is to be apportioned, there is only one appropriate recipient and that is the British government which deliberately orchestrated – indeed ordered – UKCS producers to form a consortium to build a pipeline to export gas to the Continent. In so doing, it ensured that Britain would become a gas exporter, in a manner and on a scale which would never have occurred without government intervention. But, in fact, the question of 'who is responsible' for the coming of gas-to-gas competition fails to recognize that in mature gas markets, such developments are likely to take place as a natural evolution of the business. The short-term issue is whether a smooth transition to competition ('evolution') or a sudden and rapid shift in market fundamentals is the more likely scenario.

In terms of timing, the scenarios seem to indicate that one of the most important issues will be the timing of the completion of the first Belarus–Poland line and indications as to when (and whether) the second line will be built. Since it appears that, of the major pipeline systems currently under construction from Britain, Norway, Algeria and Russia, the Belarus–Poland line will be completed in late 2000, and Europipe II in early 2000, it seems likely that the buyers of gas from these two pipelines are intending to sell to many of the same markets, particularly in Germany. If gas from the Interconnector has not started a slide in northwest European gas prices by 1999, then the opening of these two pipelines could be the trigger. If the slide has already started, then these pipelines could conceivably move the market from evolution into unravelling.[1]

Faced with these scenarios, market players advance three different types of response:

(1) a (dwindling) number who believe that the present system can be maintained without significant changes;
(2) those who believe that 'evolution' is most likely, mainly because they believe that none of the major market actors has any incentive to trigger the unravelling scenario, and that most have a reason to prevent this happening;
(3) those who believe that 'evolution' is the most likely scenario for the beginning of gas-to-gas competition, but that it will inevitably lead to 'unravelling'.

The 'rational' approach to evolution

Particularly interesting is the notion that evolution is most likely because of the strong self-interest, on the part of producers and transmission companies, to prevent unravelling. As a rational approach to market behaviour it has some superficial appeal. However, as a guide to human and corporate behaviour in a competitive market it is unpersuasive for two

---

[1] For Norway's Europipe 2 volumes have been fully contracted. This is why the question of how much capacity will be signed up on long-term contracts, for which importers have assured (captive) markets, is so important for the other pipelines.

reasons: mutual suspicions arising from competitive behaviour and fear of risk exposure.

As far as the development of competitive behaviour is concerned, one of the principal problems in the type of European gas market which is evolving is widespread fear on the part of suppliers about losing market share to competitors. This is likely to increase, as suppliers see competitors building major pipelines which would give them huge increases in capacity and the ability to challenge for substantially larger market shares. This type of perception could encourage a 'pre-emptive strike' by a supplier attempting to establish a dominant position in a specific market place. It would be exactly this type of action which could trigger an 'unravelling' of the market.

Some have suggested that, in the face of such competitive dangers, the dominant actors in European gas markets will come together in an attempt to cartelize and control the business. Attractive as this course of action might be, it would probably have been possible only in a previous era. Not only would competition authorities both of national governments and of the European Commission take exception to such measures, but the increased size of the market and the growing number of players mean that such action could not succeed.

An example of the growing inability of dominant actors to control the market was demonstrated by their actions regarding the Interconnector pipeline between Britain and Belgium. Since Interconnector gas seems very likely to be a destabilizing force in Continental European gas markets there appeared to be two possible strategies for existing major players:

- to refuse to buy any volumes, and at the same time deny access to any buyer wishing to do so;
- to purchase the entire volume on traditional long-term contracts, thereby 'sterilizing' its effects on the market.

The first course of action was probably ruled out when major Continental European actors (Ruhrgas, Gazprom, Distrigaz) purchased equity in the Interconnector project, but the second option remained open and for a time seemed to be actively under discussion. The fact that this course of action was not fully adopted suggests either that the major players were not of the same opinion, or, more likely, that they considered the risk of being burdened with an additional large volume of gas in rapidly developing competitive conditions to be too great. However, it is arguable that certain companies have over-bought gas (relative to their likely market) on long-term contracts with the risk that the development of competition may require them to drop their prices very sharply in order to retain their customers.

The impact of falling crude oil prices

The problem of advancing scenarios based on absolute price levels is that these can be affected by factors other than gas-to-gas competition. It was noted in Chapter 3 that weakening crude oil prices would cause border gas prices to fall, irrespective of development in the gas market. To the extent that gas prices are forced down by falling oil prices, this may provide an even greater incentive for gas suppliers to sell more gas in order to maintain revenues, thereby hastening competition. However, a serious and sustained fall in crude oil prices below $12/barrel would make it very difficult for gas to win additional market share from customers using oil products. As such, it would leave the large available volumes of gas which have been foreseen here with much poorer market prospects unless they were able to compete with lower priced oil products.

The impact on different market players

By 1998, having apparently accepted that the development of competitive market conditions could not be stopped, most market players appeared to be trying to develop strategies to adapt their activities and reposition their companies accordingly.

Clearly an important question for both industry players and governments is which groups are likely to benefit from these competitive developments. For economists the simple answer tends to be that since competition increases efficiency, there are general societal benefits from this process. For our purposes the question is more complex because of the variety of countries involved and the different groups of players within these countries.

First to be affected by competition will be *producers and exporters*, as the border price of gas begins to fall with the onset of gas-to-gas competition. Upstream margins will be eroded as border prices move towards marginal costs – perhaps rapidly and dramatically if the unravelling scenario proves closer to reality. The financial pain of sharp downward movements in prices would be considerable. A fall of $1/mmbtu (for example from $3.00/mmbtu to $2.00/mmbtu) would give rise to a revenue loss of $35m for each billion cubic metres of gas sold. On the basis of 1996 figures for European gas sales, and assuming (over-simplistically) that such a reduction would take effect immediately for the entire European market, the drop in revenues would amount to more than $4.0bn per year for Gazprom, around $1.6bn for Dutch sellers, $1.3bn for Norwegian sellers and $1.4bn for Sonatrach. By the time of the price fall the volume sales, and hence the fall in revenues, of all exporters (with the exception of the Dutch) will be greater. While the revenue figures are necessarily approximate, the purpose of this example is to illustrate that under 'unravelling', the revenue consequences for all sellers – but especially Gazprom because it has no significant oil revenues to soften the impact – would be extremely significant.[2] The potential for destabilization arising from such a large fall in revenue should not be under-estimated.

The development of much more transparent reporting of short-term prices, evolving into a 'spot market' across Continental Europe, will begin to put pressure in two respects on *transmission companies* which are the major buyers (importers) of gas. First, offers of gas at lower prices will attract the attention of consumers and increase pressure for access to networks. Second, the difference between spot price offers and prices being paid by the customers of transmission companies will begin to make more transparent the margins earned by these companies. Merchant margins will immediately come under pressure, but eventually the question of transmission charges, and how these are calculated, will become subject

---

[2] Gazprom only produces around 9 mt of oil per year, but its liquid reserves are around 2 bn tonnes. The alliance which Gazprom formed with Shell in 1997 was aimed at developing those reserves and creating a major oil business for the company. However, it will require a few years to produce revenues. 'Gazprom shells out for oil', *Gas Matters*, November 1997, pp. 1–3.

to greater scrutiny, and provide a starting point for the regulation of transmission systems.

Under market evolution, negotiated access may be a way of 'buying off' customers with market power and resisting what is seen as the ultimate evil of regulated access. However, negotiated access is only a staging post – and in an unravelling market a very temporary one – in the transition to regulated transmission tariffs. If transmission companies are allowed by governments and regulators to restrict access to a few large companies with which they reach a 'common understanding', then they may be able to resist regulated tariffs (we return to this issue in Chapter 7). But this will not simply be an issue of resisting pressure from governments and regulatory authorities. Pressure for regulated access is likely to come from both ends of the chain: from consumers seeking well-defined tariffs and access rules which have been independently derived; while producers which, having seen their own margins severely eroded, see no reason why transmission companies should continue to retain their previous levels of profitability.

Transmission companies will need to concentrate on how best to respond to consumer pressures arising from lower priced gas which may be on offer, and how to narrow the differential between short- and long-term contract prices. A refusal on the part of transmission companies to buy this lower priced gas will simply increase the pressure for access to their networks. Yet the purchase of significant quantities of this gas will put pressure on the take or pay commitments of existing long-term contracts. Transmission companies will be compelled to buy lower priced gas and pass on the savings to their customers, while simultaneously trying to reopen the price clauses in existing contracts with producers, and create mechanisms to bring prices more into line with the short-term market. To the extent that transmission companies and producers are unsuccessful in restructuring long-term contracts, the resulting contractual breakdown will hasten the development of competition and liberalization. However, the nature of Continental European long-term contracts with 'reopener' clauses may allow an easier transition to new 'spot related' price indices than was seen in North America and Britain.

As transmission companies reach a new equilibrium, probably requiring some form of separation between merchant functions and transmission functions, with regulation of the latter, the activities of distribution companies are likely to come under greater scrutiny. As transmission company activities become more transparent, so the charges and margins of gas distributors will, in their turn, be the subject of consumer and regulatory interest. However, so many other issues of local government finance, and local and national politics, are involved in municipal utility distribution (of gas, electricity and water) in Continental European countries, that it becomes difficult to make any kind of generalization as to how these issues will be resolved.

Governments will have a considerable influence on the speed and content of the process. In particular, governments will have a choice between encouraging price reductions to be passed through to end-consumers – thereby increasing industrial competitiveness – and taxing away the value to provide themselves with additional revenues, perhaps under the heading of 'green taxation'. Assuming that governments do not appropriate for their treasuries all of the value resulting from a price fall, the principal positive impact will be on consumers. A particularly interesting aspect of this will be the impact on demand of these lower prices. In the case of unravelling, the impact on demand could potentially be dramatic. Traditional forecasts of demand have been based on price competition between gas and other fuels. As prices of gas fall, relative to other fuels and especially oil products, the potential for gas to increase market share will be considerable. As such it will not simply be in the power generation sector that gas would increase market share, but residential sectors where gasoil has a significant market share, and industrial sectors in countries where low sulphur fuel oil is widely used. However, movements in oil product prices will also have a major bearing on the competitiveness of gas. A downward shift in crude oil prices would leave gas prices needing to fall further in order to exploit any competitive advantage.

Regulatory scenarios

The evolution and unravelling scenarios outlined earlier are almost entirely market driven, with little suggestion that national and EU regulation and/or government policy will play a significant role in the development of a competitive market. This may seem particularly strange to British and North American readers whose regulatory authorities and governments had a significant, and in many respects decisive, role in determining how far and how fast competition unfolded in those gas markets. We saw (Chapter 5) in respect of the British experience how important the repeated and proactive government and regulatory interventions proved in terms of driving the development of competition which was very slow to start, despite the existence of a gas-specific regulatory body and a legal/regulatory framework.

Most Continental European countries have neither the legal/regulatory framework nor proactive regulatory institutions in place. Indeed, in early 1998 the prospect of developing proactive regulatory and government interventions in support of competition and liberalization was dubious in many countries, and completely out of the question in others. However, to say that regulation will not be a principal driver does not mean that it will be irrelevant to the European liberalization process. Indeed, the establishment of liberalization, particularly access to networks, in European gas industries will depend most importantly on the speed at which regulatory regimes develop.[3] To the extent that such regimes will not – at least at the outset – mirror the British and North American models of aggressive 'independent' regulatory bodies, they will need to have significant powers and expertise in order to have any effectiveness.[4] Aside from its role, allowed for in the Gas Directive, in examining and ruling on derogations (from take or pay contracts and for emerging regions), the European Commission will have little influence over (at least the initial development

---

[3] The standard text on the existing frameworks is Peter Cameron, *Gas Regulation in Europe: from Monopoly to Competition* (London: Financial Times Energy Publishing, 1995), 2 vols.
[4] On the question of the extent to which regulatory bodies can be considered independent, see Jonathan Stern, 'What makes an independent regulator independent?', *Business Strategy Review*, Volume 8, Issue 2, Summer 1997, pp. 67–74.

of) regulatory regimes. The principle of subsidiarity allows each member state to make its own decisions on the type of institution and the extent of powers. Arguably, the greatest victory of the gas companies, in the final form of the Directive, was to succeed in excluding the Commission from any regulatory role in the initial stage of liberalization.

This is the major reason why the popular weight of expectation attached to the European Commission's passing of the Gas Directive is misplaced. As has been shown in Chapter 4, the culmination of a 10-year EU process has been a relatively protracted timetable for opening up gas markets. But despite the slow speed and lack of dynamism in the EU process, it will perform an extremely important function in at least three respects:

- stimulating (both member and non-member) countries to make preparations for the implementation of the Directive;
- establishing the minimum level of progress that national governments and industries must continue to make towards liberalization and regulation;
- making judgments on 'derogations' from access provisions for companies and regions which are able to present a special case within the framework of the Directive.

In the longer term, probably around 2005, the EU will also provide a harmonization process to even out the different regimes which will have developed in different countries.

Stimulating preparations within countries

Much of the development in the Netherlands, Spain and Italy towards liberalization and regulation can be attributed (at least in part) to anticipation of a Directive. Denmark has also laid out a significant change in the financial and taxation arrangement for the industry.[5] Central and east European countries looking for accession to the Union – most immediately Hungary, the Czech Republic, Poland, Slovenia and Estonia – will also be careful to

---

[5] Komgas, *Annual Report 1996*.

ensure that their legal/regulatory frameworks comply with the Directive. But more generally, for all countries in Europe, the Directive is likely to provide a common reference point to which all must pay attention.

Reciprocity may become a significant issue, not merely within the Union, but for those who trade with it. The form of reciprocity included in the EU Electricity and Gas Directives is limited and vague, referring to the need for suppliers to treat customers in both systems:

- 'single buyer' and 'negotiated third party access' for electricity;
- 'negotiated access' and 'regulated access' for gas.

The treatment is to be applied irrespective of the system in which the supplier is operating.[6] However, it remains to be seen whether governments wish, or will be allowed to adopt an extreme form of reciprocity favoured by some gas companies, whereby no company would be allowed to participate in gas supply or investment opportunities in a liberalized market, unless foreign companies are allowed similar opportunities in its own gas market. While such sentiments would be contrary to European law, it is entirely possible that dominant players in gas markets that are clearly protected against foreign investment and foreign company activity will find their own overseas aspirations increasingly circumscribed.

Minimum levels of progress towards liberalization and regulation

Under the Gas Directive, even customers with an annual consumption of 5 million cubic metres per year will need to wait until around 2008 before they can choose their supplier. But the industry will be required to make at least this minimal progress towards liberalization. Once these foundations have been laid, some superstructure may follow at a faster pace as market pressures begin to mount. Thus, although the timetable for opening the

---

[6] For electricity this is contained in Article 19(5) of 'Directive 96/92EC of the European Parliament and of the Council of 19 December 1996 Concerning Common Rules for the Internal Market in Electricity', *Official Journal of the European Communities*, No. L 27/20, January 1997. The corresponding provision is in Article 19(1) of the Gas Directive, see Appendix 4.1.

market is likely to be largely irrelevant (except for determined opponents of the process), it is important as a means of putting member states on notice that indefinite procrastination has become an increasingly difficult option.

The extent to which industries and governments will choose to fall back on any emerging EU regulatory process will depend critically upon how their national regulatory arrangements evolve. To the extent that European companies and governments have acknowledged this issue, they have shown a bias in favour of 'light-handed' regulation which in the early stages is likely to mean a small number of people with limited experience attempting to introduce and police some very general rules. Likewise there is an in-built bias against what is seen in Continental Europe (usually without a great deal of clarity and understanding) as the North American model of a large professional, quasi-independent regulatory body enforcing highly complex methodologies and procedures. The British model has reinforced these in-built prejudices as highly intrusive, and increasingly complex measures have been used to create and enforce the processes of competition and liberalization. It has also shown the incompatibility of light-handed regulation with any serious attempt at liberalization.

As we have seen in Chapter 5, there have been only a few tentative moves in Continental European countries (Italy, Hungary, Spain) towards the creation of an identifiable gas regulatory body. Whether there is to be any serious intention to make such a body independent of government remains to be seen. This could be a crucial component in any Continental European model of liberalization.

European Commission: dispute resolution body and regulator of last resort

If national governments fail to make progress to the satisfaction of consumers and new entrants, the Commission will provide a regulatory appeal process by which individual cases can receive a hearing. It is uncertain (at least in the mind of this author) whether such cases would be heard in the European Court, or be submitted to the Competition Directorate (DGIV). The idea of an EU super-regulatory authority within the Energy or Competition Directorates has been frequently castigated by gas companies as unlawful, unnecessary and harmful to the industry.

Over a longer (probably 5–10-year) period, the Commission is likely to be extremely important, as the different and incompatible regimes which evolve in different countries within the Union begin to impact on international (intra-EU) trade. It is in this respect that the role of the EU may eventually be extended to encompass some part of the work of the US Federal Energy Regulatory Commission and the Canadian National Energy Board, neither of which has powers to intervene within the individual states or provinces, but which regulate interstate (and interprovincial) commerce. Whether elements of such a regime can be extended, via the Energy Charter Treaty, to include non-EU member countries will be an important issue for the future. The institutional dominance of the EU, combined with the inducement of future membership, will probably persuade most countries to adapt to EU procedures. But, as we saw in Chapter 4, only the Energy Charter Treaty has the potential geographical reach to cover dispute resolution and enforcement of decisions with the countries of the former Soviet Union.

Rethinking security in a post-Cold War context under changing market conditions

When faced with these types of scenarios, the standard answer from traditional European gas companies has been that such developments will have serious negative consequences for security of supply and the continued delivery of public service obligations. But one major problem of the issue of security of supply is that too often over the past 30 years it has been used by the major companies as an excuse for maintaining the status quo; and by governments and other energy (principally electricity and coal) companies as a reason for preventing the construction of gas-fired power stations (usually in favour of coal or nuclear power). The traditional security issues raised in relation to the gas market have been concerns regarding:

- the adequacy of gas reserves, usually expressed as 'running out of gas';
- the importance of maintaining an adequate and diverse group of supply sources which requires oversight by a national gatekeeper;

- the importance of safeguarding long-term take or pay contracts to ensure that new gas projects are developed.

We suggested in Chapter 3 that in terms of reserves and the adequacy of supply, even if such concerns were warranted in the early development of European gas markets, the argument that they constitute a general case for refusing to introduce competition and liberalization policies is much weaker today.[7]

International gas security concerns are a real and serious issue in their own right. Continental European countries are in a different position relative to those which have liberalized their gas industries thus far – the United States, Canada, Britain, Australia and New Zealand. These countries, which are largely or wholly self-sufficient in gas, have little or no experience of large-scale imports, and none from countries outside OECD commercial and legal frameworks, where shared rules and norms are weak or non-existent. German imports of Russian gas and French imports of Algerian gas cannot be compared with similar trade between the United States and Canada or Britain and Norway. Not only is the dependence of Continental European countries much greater, but the political risks of the trade are of an entirely different type and magnitude to those of intra-OECD commerce. In that context, it is perhaps not surprising that the Netherlands should be the first country on the Continent to embrace liberalization.

However, recalling what was said about security being used as a reason for maintaining the status quo, these differences are not an argument against competition and liberalization. They are the reason why security arguments need to be made much more carefully in Continental Europe and why the EU Directive allows for derogations from access provisions if there is a serious security crisis. Perhaps the most interesting judgment on security of supply is whether a serious crisis in Russian or Algerian supply would halt liberalization and competition, forcing the industry back into a traditional context of a 'managed market', controlled by gatekeepers.

---

[7] But this rationale still holds good in new markets such as Portugal and Greece.

Disruption scenarios

Both the International Energy Agency (IEA) and the European Commission (EC) have published studies on security which include disruption scenarios (principally) for west and south European countries.[8]

Table 6.1 shows two scenarios used by the IEA to examine the impact of a disruption on firm customers (i.e. those without an alternative source of fuel supply):

- *best case:* under which all non-disrupted supplies could be maximized and supplies to interruptible customers cut for the duration of the shortage;
- *worst case:* where non-disrupted sources were not increased, and interruptible supplies were only cut within existing contractual commitments.

As far as Russian supplies are concerned, the vulnerability of Turkey is obvious, with Austria (in the worst case) not far behind and Finland needing to avoid a worst case situation. If Algerian supplies are disrupted, no country is affected immediately but in the worst case Spain would be in trouble after two months, followed rapidly by Belgium/Luxembourg and (after six months) by Italy. In the best case, Spain would be the only country affected within a six-month period. In general, even in the worst case, firm customers in the major Continental European countries – Germany, France and Italy – should be safe from supply interruptions from these two major sources for at least a year (with the exception of Algerian supplies to Italy).

The EC carried out a study looking at the effect of crisis measures – interruptible customers and production flexibility – if implemented by the individual countries affected by a disruption, compared with what could be achieved by concerted EU-wide action. Table 6.2 shows the Commission's case for organizing Union-wide action. The figures show the effect of security measures in terms of the percentage reduction of EU

---

[8] International Energy Agency, *The IEA Natural Gas Security Study* (OECD, 1995); Commission of the European Communities, *European Community Gas Supply and Prospects*, Brussels, COM(95) 478 final, 18/10/1995.

Table 6.1: Security indicators for countries supplied by Russia or Algeria

Country	Gas share of TPES (%)	Number of significant[a] supplies	Russia's share of supplies (%)	Algeria's share of supplies (%)	Months prior to supply curtailments
Austria	20.8	2	74	–	
Belgium/Luxembourg	17.7	3	–	40	
Finland	8.8	1	100	–	
France	12.1	5	32	27	
Germany	16.7	4	31	–	
Italy	25.8	4	27	30	
Spain[b]	6.2	5	–	51	
Switzerland	7.6	3	17	–	
Turkey	6.9	2	95	–	

▓ Worst Case　　☐ Best Case　　　　　　　　0　10　20　30

[a]　Significant suppliers representing more than 5% of total (includes domestic production)
[b]　Refers to data for 1994.

Source: International Environment Agency, *The IEA Natural Gas Security Study* (Paris: OECD, 1995), Table 6.4, p.151.

imports from the different sources. Thus the Commission has a particularly strong argument in the case of an Algerian disruption where Community-wide security measures would have the effect of increasing the availability of gas from 25% to 56% of total EU Algerian imports.

Tables 6.3 and 6.4 show how the IEA projects likely consequences of Russian and Algerian disruptions in 2010, for individual importing countries. Perhaps surprisingly, the Agency finds that despite a major increase in imports, the vulnerability of most countries will be no worse in

Table 6.2: EU impact of security measures on disruptions from Russia and Algeria[a] (% reduction of EU imports from individual sources)

	Individual country measures	Community-wide action	Storage cover (import days)[b]
Russian disruption	29	36	283
Algerian disruption	26	56	625

[a] Based on supplies as of first quarter 1994.
[b] Estimated by dividing the strategic storage capacity by the volume of imports per day needed after applying the security measures.

Source: European Community Gas Supply and Prospects, Brussels, October 1995, p. 478.

2010 compared with 1992. The only exceptions would be Greece (where Russian supplies commenced in 1996) and Spanish reliance on Algerian supplies. A number of countries are projected to be in a significantly more advantageous position in 2010: Turkey and Austria with respect to Russian supplies; Belgium, Luxembourg and France with respect to Algerian supplies.

Security problems as a commercial opportunity

In the market conditions likely to obtain in Europe after 1998, a prolonged supply disruption from any of the major sources would give rise to political problems, but also to greatly increased commercial opportunities for other suppliers. Interesting scenarios can be sketched involving the disruption of Norwegian, Russian, Algerian and British supplies.[9] The essential features would be a significant short-term sale of gas from competing suppliers to countries with available transmission capacity to replace the disrupted supplies.

Norway In the event of a major Norwegian disruption, due, for example, to some major technical problem at an offshore field on in a pipeline

---

[9] Disruption of Dutch supplies, while always possible, is the most difficult scenario to draw, given the location of fields and infrastructure which is in place.

Table 6.3: Spare supply capacity: possible response to a Russian disruption (mtoe)

	1992 ('best' case)				2010				Missing supplies[a] and demand	
	Demand	Supplies lost	Increased production and imports	Missing supplies[a]	Demand	Supplies lost	Spare supply capacity[b]	Missing supplies[a]	1992 %	2010 %
Austria	5.2	4.1	0.2	3.9	8.3	5.3	0.3	5.0	75	60
Finland	2.4	2.4		2.4	4.3	4.3		4.3	100	100
France	27.9	9.5	2.9	6.6	39.5	10.0	4.4	5.6	24	14
Germany	56.8	18.2	13.5	4.7	79.5	17.0	11.2	5.8	8	7
Greece	0.1				3.2	2.7	0.1	2.6		81
Italy	41.0	11.5	1.7	9.8	69.6	23.9	6.6	17.3	24	25
Switzerland	1.9	0.3		0.3	3.2	0.3	0.2	0.1	17	4
Turkey[c]	3.8	3.6		3.6	25.1	12.0	2.3	9.7	96	39
Total (OECD)	241.8	49.6	18.3	31.3	395.9	75.5	25.2	50.4	13	13

[a] Required from storage, interruptibility and curtailments to firm customers.
[b] Potential supply capacity from increased production and imports from non-disrupted sources derived from load factors.
[c] Spare capacity for 2010 includes a contribution from Turkmenistan which may be dependent on transit through Russia.

Source: Intenational Environmental Agency, *The IEA Natural Gas Security Study* (Paris: OECD, 1995), Table 6.13, p. 173.

system, one could imagine a significant increase in Russian, British and Dutch supplies in northern Europe, and possibly Algerian supplies in southern Europe.

Russia   In the event of a major Russian disruption, due, for example, to technical problems in Siberia or political problems in the Russian–Ukrainian relationship, an increase in Norwegian, Dutch and British supplies to northern Europe would be likely, as would an increase in Algerian supplies to Italy.

Table 6.4: Spare supply capacity: possible response to an Algerian disruption (mtoe)

	1992 ('best' case)				2010				Missing supplies[a] and demand	
	Demand	Supplies lost	Increased production and imports	Missing supplies[a]	Demand	Supplies lost	Spare supply capacity[b]	Missing supplies[a]	1992 %	2010 %
Belgium and Luxembourg	9.5	3.9	2.0	1.9	14.7	3.6	2.4	1.2	20	8
France	27.9	8.1	1.6	6.5	39.5	9.3	4.5	4.7	23	12
Greece	0.1				3.2	0.5	0.5	0.0		1
Italy	41.9	12.6	2.9	9.7	69.6	25.8	6.3	19.5	24	28
Spain[c]	5.8	3.7	1.1	2.6	14.7	9.4	0.7	8.6	45	59
Turkey[d]	3.8				25.1	2.0	4.1			
Total (OECD)	241.8	28.4	7.6	20.8	395.9	53.6	18.5	37.1	9	9

[a] Required from storage, interruptibility and curtailments to firm customers.
[b] Potential supply capacity from increased production and imports from non-disrupted sources derived from load factors.
[c] Refers to 1994 data.
[d] Spare capacity for 2010 includes a contribution from Turkmenistan which may be dependent on transit through Russia.

Source: Intenational Environmental Agency, *The IEA Natural Gas Security Study* (Paris: OECD, 1995), Table 6.14, p. 174.

Algeria   In the event of a major Algerian disruption – as a result of political turbulence within the country – additional Russian, Norwegian and Dutch gas could be delivered to southern European markets. This would speed up the introduction of new supplies (e.g. from Libya).

Britain   In the event of a prolonged disruption of British supplies, due to terrorist action against the Interconnector pipeline, Dutch, Norwegian and Russian supplies would have little difficulty in covering any shortfall.

Disruption scenarios involving Britain and Norway would probably cause the least inconvenience to importers since this gas flows into countries best equipped to cope, either by substituting alternative supplies of gas, or by use of storage and interruptible customers. Scenarios involving Russian and Algerian disruptions could give rise to major problems in the central, eastern and southern part of the Continent particularly in countries such as Bulgaria, Turkey, Greece, Spain and Portugal.

A prolonged disruption from a non-EU source, such as Russian or Algeria, would attract the attention of both national governments and the European Union in terms of gas security arrangements. Disruption during a winter period would force European countries to test out how well their emergency provisions would work in practice. Such circumstances, particularly if the disruption were to persist over a period of weeks or months, might reduce the attention being given to liberalization and competition issues. Even if they could be relatively rapidly assured that no category of customers would be left without a fuel supply, the attention of governments would to some extent be diverted away from liberalization issues, at least until the supply situation had stabilized.

Yet in the market conditions which have been foreseen in this study, the supplier which had suffered the disruption might find itself in a very uncomfortable commercial position. Importers would be looking for additional supplies, possibly at higher prices, on a short-term basis in order to tide them over the period of disruption. The longer the disruption were to last, the more short-term gas would be likely to flow throughout the Continent and the more creative arrangements could become – involving displacement and swaps – to supply gas to those most in need, and therefore willing to pay the highest prices. It could be imagined that available spare capacity in all the major operating pipeline networks would be filled with suppliers able to take advantage of the opportunity to market short-term gas.

Following this line of thinking, it could be that a major supply disruption in the market conditions which have been anticipated in this study – while it could give rise to significant security (that is shortage) problems in central, eastern and southern Europe – could also be a major trigger for gas-to-gas competition and short-term trading throughout the Continent.

Security events as an obstacle to the development of competition and liberalization

It is argued here that, contrary to some expectations, a major supply disruption during the coming 5 years would not halt the march towards competition and liberalization advanced in this chapter and return the industry firmly to its traditional structures. Such is the surplus of supply which has been foreseen here that the principal short-term market consequence would be a shift in supplies away from the disrupted source to others. In the longer term, much would depend on the reason for, and the duration of, the disruption. Yet no cavalier generalizations can be made about single source markets. In multisource central/western Europe it can be said with some confidence that, barring security problems of huge proportions from multiple sources, the competition/liberalization process would not be derailed and under some conditions might even be speeded up.[10]

In competitive and liberalizing markets, the concept of security is to a much greater extent related to the potential to trade gas, both between countries and within countries. The likelihood of much larger volumes being used in power generation may improve security since combined cycle gas-fired plant can be adapted to use fuels other than gas (principally gasoil and coal). During a gas supply crisis (where the price of gas rises significantly above the prices of competing fuels), gas is switched out of power generation to more vulnerable end-users. In an environment which allows for significant short-term trading, the extent to which an annual net trade situation can be related to security of supply, traditionally defined as vulnerability to sudden interruptions of foreign (i.e. non-European) supply becomes much less obvious. This way of looking at security seriously undermines the traditional static 'reserve to production ratio' view of the supply adequacy which, as we saw in Chapter 3, has proved of very limited usefulness over the past 30 years as a guide to future development.

---

[10] A situation in which two out of four major sources of European supply were profoundly and simultaneously disrupted for a prolonged period of time could derail the competition/liberalization process.

Longer-term security

However, this perspective does not address the issue of longer-term security of supply, which traditionally requires all foreseen demand to be covered by long-term contracts, 5–10 years in advance. As noted in Chapter 3, this is one of the traditional objections of heavily import-dependent countries and companies to a short-term (up to 5-year) view of resource adequacy and contractual arrangements. No short answer is available to those who believe that the only way of ensuring adequate long-term security of supply for European gas markets is to sign long-term take or pay contracts for gas from multibillion dollar greenfield gas developments with development lead times of up to 10 years. This is another area where maturing markets of the late 1990s differ greatly from the early history of the business in Europe, where it could be convincingly argued that a 10-year perspective was necessary to finance and develop secure supplies for emerging markets. In most of the major European gas markets, however, this line of reasoning has lingered well beyond the circumstances which gave it credibility. Market players will learn to adapt to the risks inherent in shorter contractual time horizons. If they are unwilling or unable to do so, their task will be to persuade consumers that the difficulty of securing their future supplies 5 to 10 years hence is likely to be sufficiently acute that it requires them to forgo the immediate benefits of purchasing gas which is available at lower prices. This will not be easy.

Chapter 7
Competition and Liberalization: A Diversity of Models

The major purpose of this study is to shed light on how competition and liberalization may emerge in Continental European countries, and to investigate how these models may differ from those of Britain and North America. This concluding chapter attempts to disentangle the two different processes of competition and liberalization; identify the range of government intentions in respect of liberalization; and finally look at stages through which competition and liberalization may pass in different countries.

Competition and liberalization: disentangling the processes

One of the problems in the analysis of change in European gas markets is to disentangle the different processes of competition and liberalization, while simultaneously recognizing that there are strong linkages and reinforcing effects between them. Previous chapters have looked at the development of:

- competition: driven principally by changes in the supply/demand balance and by aspirations of new entrants to enter the gas business;
- liberalization initiatives: driven by national and European Union commitments towards open markets, greater efficiency and consumer choice.

Both processes (but particularly liberalization) will require regulation, carried out by a range of institutions to police and enforce abuses of dominant positions, and the rules by which parties are allowed access to gas pipelines and other facilities.

The fundamental difference between the much-cited British experiment and the likely development of most Continental European gas markets is the order of the two different processes. In Britain, legislation allowing the development of liberalization failed to create competition. Competition was eventually created and reinforced by draconian regulatory processes (involving a range of regulatory bodies – see Chapter 5). In the early years of the British experiment the market forces of 'supply push/demand pull' were almost entirely absent. Regulation was targeted specifically at breaking the gatekeeper functions of British Gas: management of upstream supply and near-total control of the downstream market. When that task had been achieved, self-sustaining competition was able to unfold in the non-residential market, driven by market affiliates of producing companies and powerful new entrants from the privatized electricity industry.

In Continental European gas markets, and particularly the northern and western part of the Continent, competition has been gradually increasing as a surplus of supply and transmission capacity has developed. New entrants from Britain and elsewhere with new and different agendas are struggling to break the hold of the transmission gatekeepers. As this process progresses, the larger customers, principally power generators and chemicals companies, are trying to obtain gas which they perceive to be available at much lower prices.

At the same time, some national governments, in anticipation of the European Union's Electricity and Gas Directives, are slowly moving to liberalize their gas and electricity markets (with the electricity industry often the driving force). In the late 1990s these two processes are becoming mutually reinforcing: as the dominant gas transmission companies start to lose their near-total control of the market, so the pressures for market liberalization, and especially access to networks, are growing. But up to the late 1990s Continental European gatekeepers have thus far had major advantages over (the former) British Gas (and its North American counterparts): the lack of any strong ideological commitment by their national governments to competition or liberalization, and the absence of regulatory authorities required to enforce these processes. The speed and intensity of gas market liberalization will depend critically on how those government intentions and regulatory institutions develop.

Liberalization: the range of government intentions

Box 7.1 lists various criteria that can be used to determine government commitment to its intentions for competition and liberalization.

In an attempt to separate the 'strategy and tactics' from the 'real intentions' of governments, Box 7.1 lists six different sets of criteria by which the seriousness of government intentions to introduce liberalization and competition can be judged.

Box 7.1: Criteria for judging government commitment to competition and liberalization

1. Devising a pro-liberalization policy:
   – timetable for access (eligibility) faster than that set by the EU Gas Directive
   – targets for competition
   – similar measures for electricity

2. Promoting transparency:
   – of accounts ('unbundling')
   – of prices
   – of tariffs, and methodology of tariff calculation

3. Abolishing *de facto* exclusive rights and barriers to entry:
   – to import/export
   – construct pipelines
   – transport
   – distribute

4. Structure of industry:
   – promotion of competitive restructuring
   – intention to promote unbundling

5. Attitude to status of dominant player(s):
   – tolerance of barriers to entry (*de facto* monopolies)
   – acceptance of dominant market share
   – encouraging new entrants

6. Regulatory/legal reforms:
   – creation of a separate regulatory/legal institution (as opposed to ministerial regulation or reliance on competition law)
   – 'independence' of institution
   – remit of institution to promote competition (proactive/responsive)
   – authority to set/monitor tariffs
   – remit to pursue discrimination/barriers to entry

Pro-liberalization policies

While governments may be required to make 'statements of principle' in favour of liberalization, the real test of intentions will be whether time-tables and targets are set which commit industries to significant change within a 5-year period, and more specifically whether any near-term action is planned, for example, within a year. An important indication will be whether a national government is prepared to advance liberalization on a timetable significantly faster than that dictated by the EU Gas Directive.[1]

Transparency

Availability of information is one of the principal requirements of a liberalized market. The determination, particularly of a government or regulatory authority, to ensure that such information is available in a form which is both easy to understand and easy to obtain, will be an important component of liberalization. The scope and complexity of this information are likely to exceed greatly the formal requirements of existing EU Directives.[2] Since most of the information will be supplied by the dominant player(s), the requirement that the scope of information be sufficient, and that the methodology used in calculations of tariffs and prices be adequately explained, will be extremely important.

Exclusive rights

The rights to carry out the various functions of the industry – including both construction of facilities and the commercial functions – will need to be opened to new entrants. Barriers to entry will also need to be addressed. The capital requirements for new facilities are a sufficiently high barrier for most companies. Allowing new entrants to intrude into the

---

[1] In this chapter, as elsewhere in the study, the term 'EU Gas Directive' refers to *European Parliament and Council Directive concerning Common Rules for the Internal Market in Natural Gas.*

[2] For example the Directive of 29 June 1990: 'Concerning a Community procedure to improve the transparency of gas and electricity prices charged to industrial end-users', *Official Journal of the European Communities*, No. L185/16, July 1990.

traditional relationships between the established companies and authorities which provide rights of way (across land), site approval (for installations) and operational safety, may require government and regulatory authorities to break through considerable institutional barriers.

Structure of industry

Where an industry has an anti-competitive structure with little opportunity for new entrants to break into the market and little requirement to unbundle services (which would give new entrants a foothold in the industry), then a government commitment to liberalize the industry will be judged by its continued tolerance of this structure.

Attitude to status of dominant player(s)

Given the likely inertia of industries dominated by a single player, the intentions of governments and regulatory authorities will be judged by the extent to which they concern themselves with the speed of change, particularly in terms of new players taking market share from current incumbents. Where a government sees the task as simply 'going through the motions' of passing legislation in order to comply with the EU Directive, without any commitment to liberalization and competition, then the most likely outcome will be little immediate change.

Regulatory institutions

The extent to which a government decides to create a new and industry-specific regulatory body to deal with gas industry liberalization, as opposed to relying on existing competition and legal processes, will be a significant pointer to its commitment in this area. In order to be convincing as a promoter of competition and liberalization, a regulatory body will require not only adequate staffing and expertise, but also a commitment to proactive investigation of problems, particularly relating to discrimination and barriers to entry.

With the exception of the Dutch and Spanish governments which have established liberalization programmes (see Chapter 5), in early 1998 it was difficult to identify a Continental European government which has any public commitment to move beyond what has been agreed at EU level. In the negotiations on the Gas Directive, many governments mounted campaigns at EU level to resist even the most minor reforms.

Government attitudes will be an extremely important determinant of the liberalization process. However, the number of countries involved, and the variety of government responses to early liberalization initiatives, suggest that attitudes may vary significantly across the Continent. The following classification of government attitudes appeared recognizable – during 1997 – in terms of the stances adopted by governments in EU discussions and actions in respect of their national gas industries.

Continental European governments: a classification of positions

Ideologically committed

Proactive government policy and regulation will pursue competition and liberalization down to the residential level on the fastest possible timetable. There are two principal differences between the ideologically committed and other positions:

- a refusal to accept the continued dominance of the market by a single player. The lack of development of competition, defined as bringing in new entrants and reducing the share of the dominant player, will be met by a determination to restructure the market in a way which forcibly reduces the dominant player's market share;
- a willingness to create regulatory institutions independent of government and with sufficient powers vigorously to promote competition and liberalization.

Convinced proponents

Affirmative government policy should contain commitments to open progressively larger sectors of the market to competition, on a timetable which might be faster than that dictated by the EU Gas Directive. At the same time, the options for market players in all segments of the gas chain will be broadened, with all destined to enjoy the benefits of greater choice. However, if competition does not evolve quickly, it is uncertain whether these governments will make any moves towards restructuring, although they will encourage new entrants. Small consumers served by distribution companies will have to wait a considerable time for a choice of supplier. The big uncertainty is whether convinced proponents will create a regulatory framework for implementing and policing competition.

Willing accepters

Affirmative government policy will be proposed with elements already in place. These governments accept that liberalization and competition will occur, but will not make any proactive moves to promote such developments and will not be especially concerned if there is no significant change. Whether they will be prepared to encourage new entrants remains uncertain. They are unlikely to set out any timetable for the opening of markets beyond the minimum required by the EU. These governments are also unlikely to press for significant transparency of tariffs or any unbundling of services.

Grudging accepters

Here, there is a lack of affirmative government policy with none of the elements of such a policy in place. If other countries move down the liberalization road, or if competitive market conditions are created, the government is likely to accept these developments grudgingly. No attempt will be made to promote competition or remove barriers to market entry. These governments will be prepared to see their industries be the subject of cases before the European Courts, where the legal requirements on some member states to compel the opening of gas markets may eventually be decided. New entrants from foreign countries, even other EU member states, will find it almost impossible to break down entry barriers. Any liberalization which does take place will involve only national companies in relatively non-transparent arrangements. All regulation will be carried out by government ministers with recourse to competition law only where necessary.

Table 7.1: Likely government positions on most important elements of liberalization

	IC	CP	WA	GA
Government policy:				
Affirmative policy with targets	Yes	Yes	Yes	No
Timetable faster than that of EU	Yes	Yes	No	No
Transparency:				
Of accounts	Yes	Yes	Yes	No
Of prices	Yes	Yes	Yes	Yes
Of tariffs	Yes	Yes	No	No
Abolition of exclusive rights and barriers to entry:				
Import and export	Yes	Yes	Yes	No
Construction of facilities	Yes	Yes	Yes	?
Transmission	Yes	Yes	Yes	?
Distribution	Yes	No	No	No
Structure of industry:				
Restructuring for competition	Yes	No	No	No
Unbundling of services	Yes	Yes	?	No
Attitude to status of dominant player:				
Tolerance of *de facto* monopoly	No	Yes	Yes	Yes
Acceptance of dominant market share	No	Yes	Yes	Yes
Encourage new entrants	Yes	Yes	?	No[a]
Regulatory rules and institutions:				
Creation of separate regulatory institution	Yes	?	?	No
Independence of regulatory institution	Yes	?	?	No
Remit to promote competition	Yes	No	No	No
Authority to set tariffs	Yes	?	?	No
Remit to pursue discrimination and barriers to entry	Yes	?	?	No

IC = ideologically committed; CP = convinced proponent; WA = willing accepter; GA = grudging accepter; ? Uncertain commitment; [a] Except from the same country.

Table 7.1 places these government attitudes against the criteria in Box 7.1. In this classification, only 'ideologically committed' governments are prepared to break the monopoly power of the dominant player and back this up with comprehensive regulatory rules and institutions. The table makes the judgment that 'grudging accepters' will fail to implement some of the provisions of the EU Directive such as transparency and abolishing exclusive rights. While their actions will eventually be challenged in the courts, they could be the subject of lengthy court processes.

In early 1998 a majority of Continental European governments could be located in the continuum between 'willing accepters' and 'grudging accepters'. Few governments would continue to claim that the current monopolistic system will remain intact over the next decade, even if this would be their preferred outcome. The principal differences are between:

- those which are relatively relaxed about the present system being replaced by a liberalized and increasingly competitive market and will not oppose this development – but neither will they make great efforts to give it their support. Their principal hope is that benefits will flow through to consumers without government needing to make a major institutional change which would incur the wrath of powerful vested interests, principally labour unions;
- those which are against any significant change in the present system, believing that a centralized utility sector over which government maintains significant control remains the best structure.

However, it should not be believed that governments will remain frozen in their 1997 positions. Changes in market conditions, circumstances and indeed governments themselves, mean that policy may change radically and rapidly. An example of this can be seen in the Netherlands, which moved very rapidly from a 'grudging accepter' to a position which could be characterized as close to a 'convinced proponent', as a result of a combination of circumstances:

- a change in government in 1995 which brought into power a Minister of Economics committed to liberalization policies;

- anticipation of its Presidency of the European Union during which there would be a significant opportunity to pass the Gas Directive;
- the clear indication that the Interconnector pipeline (between Britain and Belgium) would be built.

A similar change in position was taken by the Spanish government elected in mid-1996. Its commitment to reducing industrial energy prices produced a change of policy in favour of liberalization, entirely contrary to its predecessor.

But neither should it be expected that a majority of Continental European governments will suddenly undergo a 'conversion' to liberalization. There remains:

- insufficient conviction of the benefits in terms of lower prices, competitiveness and efficiency;
- considerable concern about the perceived disadvantages in terms of increased unemployment, potential threats to security of supply and the contractual problems arising from take or pay commitments.

In early 1998 the most telling criterion remained the apparent disinclination of the majority of Continental European governments to require a faster pace of liberalization than that foreseen by the EU Directive. The reason that government reluctance is so significant is that in Britain, the only European example of an 'ideologically committed' government, history shows that even with maximum government and regulatory effort, it required a decade of proactive policy and a compliant dominant player to achieve significant competition and liberalization.

The speed with which governments are prepared to move down the competition and liberalization path seems likely to be influenced by three issues in particular:

(1) the demonstration that industrial gas (and electricity) prices in European countries that have followed this path have fallen so significantly over a sustained period of time that the international competitiveness of industries in countries which have not followed these policies is endangered;

(2) the demonstration that, despite dire warnings from the gas industry about threats to security of supply, public service obligations and take or pay contracts, no significant problems have been encountered, or that these have been surmounted at minimal cost;

(3) the degree to which a concept of 'reciprocity' is introduced by national governments in respect of commercial opportunities for foreign companies. There is the possibility that governments which are liberalizing their utility markets may move to prevent companies from non-liberalizing markets from participating in major business opportunities. While reciprocity is a difficult concept to define in concrete terms, it should be easy to operate in the majority of countries, where it may require many years for enforceable transparency and non-discrimination measures to be implemented.

Stages of competition and liberalization

Having looked at the attitudes and intentions of governments, we now move to examine more concretely the content and timing of the stages through which competition and liberalization may move in Continental Europe.

Stage 1. Before 2000: competition and the start of a lower price era

The first stage of the process will be gas-to-gas competition at European borders driven by market surplus. As early as 1998, but certainly before 2000, strong competition will begin in northwest Europe for those first to be affected by a combination of the Interconnector, the Belarus–Poland line, and the Europipe/Norfrapipe lines. Somewhat later, but probably not more than 1–2 years, the same trends are likely to spread to southern Europe, with the GME expansion being an important development.

All multisource markets have already been to some degree affected by this process which will quicken from 1998 as these major new pipelines are completed. Markets in northwest Europe (Germany, Belgium, the Netherlands and France) are likely to be particularly strongly affected. Multisource markets in southern Europe (Spain, and particularly Italy), will also be affected, but more slowly.[3] These developments will give central and east European markets (especially the Czech and Slovak Republics, Poland and Hungary) major opportunities to diversify away from Russian gas, or to exert significant downward price pressure on Russian supplies. Unisource markets far from northwest Europe are likely to be less affected: Romania, Bulgaria, Greece, Portugal and Turkey.

During this first stage, the principal losers will be producers and exporters who will experience a very sharp downturn in their margins. Some will come under severe financial pressure.

Consequences for liberalization The degree to which the emergence of gas-to-gas competition and lower prices will accelerate liberalization in this first stage strongly depends on which of the 'evolution' or the 'unravelling' scenarios, set out in Chapter 6, turns out to be closest to reality. Under both scenarios, the consequences for market organization will be similar, with the emergence of spot pricing and market hubs; pressure on long-term contractual structures; pressure for access from suppliers and large customers. Border gas prices and transit tariffs will become much more transparent and uniform across Europe. The speed of this process will be much faster under 'unravelling'. However, the consequences for institutional change will be entirely different under the two scenarios, with relatively slow change under 'evolution', contrasting with rapid and potentially revolutionary industry restructuring which could be envisaged under 'unravelling'.

Evolution: gatekeepers retain overall control In the evolution scenario, the gatekeepers remain in overall control of the gas industry. They do this:

- either by purchasing lower priced gas available at their borders;
- or by compelling the suppliers, with which they hold long-term contracts, to reduce prices to competitive levels.

---

[3] But there exists the possibility that southwest Europe will be able to choose between a variety of suppliers through different pipelines. See Jerome Ferrier, 'Your Hub or Mine? The Southern Europe Case', European Autumn Gas Conference, Barcelona, 4 and 5 November 1997.

If they choose the first option (purchasing lower priced gas), the gatekeepers may place themselves in some difficulty with the take or pay clauses in their long-term contracts. However, there is evidence that many (if not most) contracts signed in the 1990s contain 'reopener' provisions in the event of gas-to-gas competition. All other contracts contain 'reopeners', but some may not be sufficiently flexible to cope with rapid and radical shifts in market conditions. Revision of these older contracts may be required if buyers are to avoid some degree of take or pay difficulty. However, in an evolution scenario, take or pay is not likely to be a serious problem.

The crucially important action for gatekeepers is that they *must* rapidly pass through the benefits of lower prices, particularly to larger customers seeking to purchase this gas. If larger customers decline the option, then they must engage in 'negotiated access' and ensure that it becomes a broadly acceptable and workable process. These actions will help to defuse the immediate pressure for regulated access, and also meet the principal concern of governments for price reductions to industrial customers. By this means, new entrants who would disturb the status quo further can be largely excluded (at least initially) and gatekeepers can claim that negotiated access is a 'success'.

Refusal, or failure to take advantage of lower priced gas which is being offered and/or failure to pass lower prices through to customers, will more rapidly usher in liberalization as customers demand direct access to lower priced gas. Governments will be in no position to defend gas companies as (initially) their large energy-intensive industries (quickly followed by smaller industrial customers) will demand access to a choice of supplier. Once gas transmission companies give customers reasons to investigate seriously the benefits offered by more competitive arrangements, their merchant portfolios will start to unravel very quickly.

Unravelling: gatekeepers lose control   If, in contrast to the 'evolution' scenario, market pressures become irresistible and prices fall rapidly to much lower levels, it will be much more difficult for gatekeepers to retain control of their merchant portfolios. Customers will be aware of such attractive purchasing opportunities at international borders that it will be increasingly difficult to deny them direct access to this gas. Gatekeepers will then be facing a series of dilemmas:

- changing their long-term contracts with suppliers (producers and exporters) sufficiently rapidly to avoid mounting take or pay liabilities;
- moving sufficiently rapidly to a new regime with their customers to maintain (at least a proportion of) their merchant business;
- managing a relatively rapid transition to some form of pipeline access for most of their large customers.

But the additional problem under 'unravelling' is the institutional break-down which will occur with organizations such as the GFU, likely to be swept away and replaced by many more producers all trying to sell their own gas – a phenomenon which will further accelerate market competition.

While the transmission companies will try to manage a transition to negotiated access, this will rapidly crumble. Fierce competition for market share will place consumers in an increasingly strong position to insist on regulated and non-discriminatory access, a demand which transmission companies, with rapidly diminishing merchant portfolios, will find very difficult to resist. This will send an urgent message to governments and emerging regulatory authorities that regulatory regimes need to be quickly established.

Stage 2. Up to 2010: access for larger customers

Stage 1 is mainly a phase of establishing gas-to-gas competition with the beginning of access for larger consumers of gas. In the evolution scenario, liberalization will move through the stage of negotiated access, but this will eventually give way to a greater degree of regulation as 'negotiators' increasingly fail to find common ground. Accelerated development of regulated access will also take place where gatekeepers fail to pass the benefits of competition on to consumers, or try to resist gas-to-gas competition entirely. In the unravelling scenario, regulated access arrives much more quickly, due to the immediate demands of the majority of industrial customers.

In Stage 1, the principal commercial pain will be experienced by producing and exporting companies. By Stage 2, gas-to-gas competition will expose, and begin to put pressure on, the merchant margins being earned by transmission companies. But, once access begins, not only merchant margins but also transmission charges will come under attack. For this reason, initial transmission tariff proposals are likely to be highly opaque and discouraging, since strong regulation will not exist to enforce transparency.

In countries where many new pipelines are being built, principally Germany, access is likely to develop more quickly as owners find they have significant unused capacity and will be prepared to make concessions in order to generate additional revenues. Increasingly transparent access arrangements will put pressure on those trying to make a case for maintaining tariff charges significantly higher than 'cost of service' levels.

First moves towards access are likely to be highly discriminatory, with concessions being made to those with market power, principally large customers (chemical companies and power generators). New entrants will try to use a combination of the Gas and Transit Directives, as transposed into national legislation, to move gas to end-users. If this proves unsuccessful, legislation may be re-examined with the possibility of being held to be anti-competitive against new entrants.

However, in the period up to 2005, gatekeepers and governments seeking to defend the status quo may procrastinate by forcing new entrants, particularly from outside the EU, through tortuous legal processes at both national and EU levels, in the hope of discouraging them. The evolution of legal/regulatory regimes, by means of landmark cases, will begin to eliminate discrimination and tariff anomalies. As legal/regulatory regimes evolve and tariff designs are required to become more sophisticated and non-discriminatory, regulatory bodies will emerge, although the extent to which they can be considered 'independent' from government will vary from country to country. Market developments will maintain and probably increase the pressure on merchant transmission companies.

Assuming an evolutionary scenario, by 2005 Continental European industries will be divided into at least two categories:

(1) *'convinced proponents'* and *'willing accepters'* where major steps towards access to networks have taken place and the opening of markets has moved much faster than anticipated by governments or by the EU Gas Directive. In these industries, new entrants have begun to challenge the positions of dominant players;

(2) *'grudging accepters'* where the industry is still operating in a largely traditional mode. The government and the gatekeeper(s) have been successful in fighting off, or buying off, any significant change. The only successful new entrants will have been large national companies, either energy competitors (oil and electricity), or large customers, which may have resorted to building their own facilities.

By 2005 'convinced proponents' and 'willing accepters' will largely have completed Stage 2, and unbundling (separate charging for services) will begin to enter the picture in the majority of these countries. However, 'grudging accepters' will require up to a decade to complete Stage 2 and may continue to resist throughout that period. The EU Directive is likely to guarantee access within a decade, for entities with an annual demand of more than 5 million cubic metres per year. But an entity with an annual demand of 5 million cubic metres is a relatively large gas user. For 'grudging accepters', it could be as late as 2005 before even the principle, let alone the reality, of pipeline access for industrial users with an annual consumption below 5 million cubic metres is established.

But in an unravelling scenario, governments will have to fight extremely hard to protect national companies. Their own industrial sectors will be crying out for the cheaper gas on offer, and political support for the status quo is likely to evaporate rapidly if the only arguments against change are dire warnings about potential longer-term security problems. Events under unravelling are in general harder to foresee because of their potentially revolutionary nature, but all developments are accelerated in the majority of countries, with only those on the geographical periphery of Europe able to remain in relatively traditional mode over an extended period.

Stage 3: 2005 onwards: access for smaller customers

For gas users with an annual demand greater than 5 million cubic metres, connected to low-pressure distribution systems, liberalized access will arrive in Stage 2 via the EU Directive. However, for the majority of smaller consumers, for example those with an annual consumption of less than 10,000 cubic metres, and particularly for residential customers liberalization is well out of sight beyond Stage 2.

'Convinced proponents' and 'willing accepters' will begin to consider opening up these markets by 2005. The principal driver could be the building of (what the Gas Directive calls) 'direct lines' to customers; in North American parlance this is known as 'bypass'. However, this could be an even more hard-fought battle than Stage 2, with local politicians putting great pressure on national governments to resist such developments. In countries where cross-subsidy at local government level is significant, with concession payments from distribution companies and/or direct profits from gas and electricity prices accounting for a considerable amount of the municipal budget, resistance to liberalization will be considerable and protracted. When change does occur, the principal gain will be for gas and electricity customers who are not major users of municipal services. Residential consumers may find themselves spending the savings from their utility bills on increased charges for public transportation and other local services (such as leisure and child care), or doing without those amenities.

Because of the institutional changes required, even 'convinced proponents' and 'willing accepters' may continue to resist liberalization of municipal and local distribution systems until at least 2010. For 'grudging accepters', Stage 3 is probably too far off to make any meaningful projection. Even market unravelling may fail to accelerate this process significantly in countries where national governments are unable or unwilling to oppose the wishes of strong regional and local political forces.

Different scenarios for different countries

One of the most difficult aspects of a Continent comprising more than 30 countries is the strong likelihood of diversity in the development of the gas industry. Chain reactions and domino theories are only partly persuasive. The likelihood is not great that the development of gas industries in Ireland, Finland, Romania and Germany (to take four countries at random) will be comparable. This is not so much a factor of size or the stage of development of the industry – important as both those criteria undoubtedly are. The key issue is likely to be the location of markets and their access to a choice of gas suppliers.

What has been identified in this study is that the closer a market is to the northwest of the Continent, the greater the likelihood of swift evolution or possible unravelling of current market arrangements. The closer to the south and east, the less the likelihood of rapid change. Indeed the southeast of the Continent could be fertile territory for grudging accepters.

Continental European compared with British and North American models

The three-stage Continental European model set out earlier could simply be considered similar to the British and North American models but requiring another two decades to complete. This would be to misunderstand the process and content of the different models.

In Continental Europe, competition will arrive first and drive liberalization. This will be more akin to the North American situation, where a surplus of gas drove competition, but could only do so when wellhead prices and access to pipeline networks were liberalized (in the very special circumstances of North American 'deregulation').[4] It will be completely different to Britain where competition only arrived after almost a decade of increasingly desperate legislative and regulatory efforts to kick-start the process. The principal similarity, if the unravelling scenario takes place, will be that radical institutional change will resemble what occurred in Britain. Whether this process will go so far as to see the complete break-up of the major gatekeeper's market and the eventual disappearance of the

---

[4] Deregulation is a term which is only applicable to North America, because only in the United States and Canada did a body of regulation exist which needed to be abolished in order to liberalize the market. In Europe, as we have seen in Chapters 5 and 6, a very important element of liberalization will be the creation of a body of regulation.

company itself, as in Britain, will depend both on specific circumstances and on the behaviour of specific companies.

Ideology In terms of ideology, the conviction of British and North American governments regarding the desirability of the maximum possible introduction of competition, consumer choice, unbundled services and non-discrimination, is almost entirely absent in Continental Europe. But in respect of competitiveness and lower energy prices for industrial customers, Continental Europeans are likely to take on some of the British and North American missionary zeal. Moreover, in the British and North American models the principle of consumer choice is to the fore, requiring the emergence of a range of suppliers offering a range of (unbundled) services, while no such elevation of consumer sovereignty has yet been seen on the Continent.

Partly for this reason, the extent to which Continental European governments will be concerned to move up to Stage 3 remains uncertain. Concern about security of supply and public service obligations may outweigh promised reductions in residential gas prices. Moreover, in a range of countries, particularly in central and eastern Europe, the next decade will be concerned principally with completing the task of raising prices to residential customers which were kept artificially low during the communist era. This has proved to be extremely difficult politically even in countries such as Hungary and the Czech Republic, which have otherwise been in the vanguard of economic development and market reforms.[5]

Regulation The central role of regulatory authorities in the British and North American model was a feature that accorded with the traditional administrative culture of US and Canadian gas industries. By contrast, Britain created specialized regulatory institutions, although its initial conception of 'light-handed regulation' was rapidly shown to be naive. Over the past decade, complex regulation has become part of British utility culture with no pressure to dismantle the structure and reabsorb these functions into government departments. Both of these examples

---

[5] 'European future to boost Hungarian prices', *Gas Matters*, September 1996, pp. 14–23.

stand in marked contrast to Continental European countries where the antipathy of gas industries towards regulation is based on a negotiating position which advances the spectre of massive regulatory bureaucracies 'taking over' the industry. By contrast, the antipathy of Continental European governments is more focused on giving unelected bodies, particularly if they are not under direct government control (following the Anglo-North American dictum of 'independent regulation'), the power to make important strategic decisions. However these problems are resolved, the absence of detailed and specialized regulation will be a significant difference between Continental European, and the British and North American models. Regulatory uncertainty and the lack of an institutional framework will greatly assist the procrastination of governments and companies opposing the process of liberalization.

Timing   In terms of timing, Stages 1 and 2 required a combined period of more than 10 years in the Anglo-North American models; that is from first legislation and regulation to a situation of self-sustaining competition with access to pipeline networks for all large consumers. However, this time period is misleading because once competition and liberalization truly took hold, markets changed radically within a few years. This is why in Continental Europe, 'convinced proponents' and 'willing accepters' may reach the end of Stages 1 and 2 by 2005 – conceivably earlier, if the market unravels, and/or their governments become 'ideologically committed' along the way. However, in countries in which governments remain unconvinced of the merits of liberalization (grudging accepters), a decade may remain a more realistic time frame for these developments.

The impact on industry structures

As liberalization is introduced into Continental European gas markets and competitive pressures become increasingly strong, the structure of the industries is likely to change. The most likely change will be the development of marketing companies, vertically or horizontally integrated, either formally incorporated or unincorporated joint ventures. At the outset, these new entrants will be buying gas principally for their own use and arranging access through high-pressure pipelines. Over time, they will become marketing companies for a range of customers, in direct competition with established merchant transmission companies. The important characteristic of these new marketing companies is that they will be sufficiently powerful commercially to be able to negotiate favourable access terms with the gas transmission company. If they are unable to negotiate favourable terms, they will be sufficiently powerful politically to force the government and the regulatory authority to pressurize the transmission company into offering acceptable tariff and access (use of system) terms.

Initially, these new marketing companies are likely to be formed by large gas users (particularly power companies). Distribution companies may choose to combine their purchasing functions in order to strengthen their commercial positions, and mergers are likely, particularly in countries with a multitude of small distribution companies. When these have blazed a trail, gas producing companies, trying to recapture lost upstream margins, may follow. The degree and speed with which these marketing companies appear will depend on the behaviour of the major transmission companies. The greater the resistance to change on the part of the transmission company, the faster and more widespread will be the appearance of marketing companies.

Yet gas marketing in Continental Europe will be a game for large players. This is, in large part, because of the weakness of regulatory institutions and their likely unwillingness and/or inability to break down barriers to entry in the industry. As such, it would be surprising if, at least in Stages 1 and 2, more than three or four such companies were established in each Continental European gas market. Industrial customers are likely to become clustered around these conglomerates and competition for customers is likely to be limited to this relatively small number of companies.

Competing visions of the future

Continental European government resistance towards liberalization and competition is founded on a reluctance to change the institutional and regulatory basis of the industry. This should not be taken to indicate an indifference towards prices charged to industrial consumers. Indeed concerns regarding the competitiveness of industry are high on the agenda of all European governments. The ultimate test of the British and North American models will be whether they deliver gas to industrial customers at prices which are significantly lower than those of Continental European competitors over a long time. A significant price differential over a protracted period will go a long way towards providing a conclusive demonstration of competitive advantage conferred upon economies with liberalized gas markets. In such circumstances there is a possibility that 'grudging accepters' may be forced by their industrial sectors to capitulate and move radically in the direction of liberalization.

However, the competition which has been anticipated in Continental European gas markets may achieve significant price reductions with only minimal liberalization. If supplier competition at the border delivers price reductions which are passed through by transmission companies, then insistence on access to a wide choice of suppliers may prove to be less important.

Such arguments will not be persuasive to those convinced that creating 'contestable markets', in which free market entry and consumer choice need to be pursued to the maximum possible extent, is the only way to maintain downward pressure on prices. It is not impossible that the priority of industrial competitiveness will compete increasingly with other concerns on national and international political agendas such as environment and sustainability issues. It is also possible that Continental European governments will choose to negate the price advantages of liberalization by taxing away the rent in the chain squeezed out by competition, and representing this as environmental taxation.

The next decade of European gas commerce will demonstrate whether the British and North American vision of competitive and liberalized gas markets will make an eventual appearance in Continental Europe gas markets. The evidence assembled in this study suggests that while competition will be strongly in evidence throughout the Continent, liberalization outcomes are likely to be very different in different countries. But even where liberalization is embraced, it is likely to require a longer time frame and take forms different from those its British and North American disciples would recognize. The principal reasons for this are:

- concern about unemployment and the political power of labour unions;
- too many institutional/political/cultural obstacles, in particular, an aversion to complex and 'independent' regulation;
- too many unanswered concerns about security of supply and public service obligations.

In summary, the claim made by a former UK Energy Minister to have 'won the intellectual argument' about liberalization rings hollow in this author's perception of the attitudes and beliefs of Continental European governments and their gas industries in early 1998.[6] The argument which the British and North Americans *have* won is to demonstrate that by creating a competitive and liberalized gas market in the circumstances of their own industries:

- prices to all classes of consumer have been reduced (but some groups have benefited more than others);
- none of the dire warnings of the traditionalists on security and public service obligations has yet been borne out.

The problems of settling take or pay contracts imposed a huge financial burden on the entire gas industry, principally transmission companies but also producers, in North America, and on the former British Gas and its marketing successor, Centrica. Continental European gas companies have, or should have, recognized this danger and taken appropriate avoiding action in their contractual relationships.

What the Anglo-North American models have not demonstrated is whether:

- this could have been achieved in their own countries (and can be achieved elsewhere) without strong and proactive regulation;
- markets with growing dependence on imported gas, as opposed to the self-sufficiency of Britain and North America, will have particular security problems under competition and liberalization;

---

[6] Former UK Energy Minister, Tim Eggar, commenting on the Brussels negotiations on the EU Gas Directive.

- as liberalization moves to include smaller (especially residential) customers, the elimination of cross-subsidy will create serious problems of public service obligations.

Of these caveats, the regulatory issue is likely to be tested earliest, but security concerns could suddenly overtake all other issues. The two events most likely to trigger a European gas security crisis would be serious political instability within Algeria, and a determination by a future Russian government to break up Gazprom. However, neither of these events is likely to halt the march of competition in European gas markets. Indeed there are strong possibilities that either could hasten it.

Whatever the destiny of liberalization, gas-to-gas competition will be the dominant feature of European gas markets in the period up to 2000, as supply surplus upsets the contractual and market management which gatekeepers (with the approval of their governments) have carefully organized over the past three decades. This competition will arrive earliest and become fiercest in northwest Europe where a surplus of gas from a variety of different sources will compete for large industrial customers, principally power generators and chemicals companies, in the early years. Price reductions are likely to gain the attention of an increasingly wide range of customers.

Whether border prices in northwest Europe drift down to a new equilibrium, or collapse to substantially lower levels, can only be guessed. Price evolution could allow for a relatively gentle process of adjustment to the introduction of liberalization. Price collapse would cause much greater problems for the traditional organization of markets. It would hasten liberalization for those countries where governments proved willing to accept the problems of institutional disruption, and a brutal adjustment for dominant producers and transmission companies, in return for the economic benefits to their industrial sectors.

The end and the means: a diversity of models

Which vision proves to be closest to reality will be one of the most interesting features of the next decade in European gas markets. But despite the fact that the anticipation of both competition and liberalization has given rise to major debates within the European gas business over the past decade, in an important respect these issues are of limited relevance because they are both a means to achieve an end, rather than the end in itself. The end which all governments will be trying to achieve is lower prices for (particularly) industrial gas customers. The means by which this end will be achieved, and the extent to which it will be pursued, will be different in different countries.

One possible outcome in many Continental European countries would be a situation in which consumers were able to reap most of the benefits of substantially lower prices through gas-to-gas competition at the borders of their countries, without the contractual upheaval and regulatory complexity of the British and North American liberalization experiences. Many Continental European governments and gas companies, determined to maintain large parts of the status quo, believe this type of evolution to be a realistic prospect over the next decade. By contrast, the British and the North Americans, unable to conceive of any developments radically different to those which have taken place in their own countries, believe that only through liberalization can efficiency be maximized and costs and price minimized.

Both perspectives are almost certainly wrong. The next decade will see both continuity and change in European gas markets. The challenge will be to identify the speed and content of this process in *individual countries and regions* as a series of diverse models unfolds throughout the European geographical space.

Index

Figures in **bold** refer to tables, figures, maps and boxes.